Michelin Travel Partner

Société par actions simplifiées au capital de 11 288 880 EUR
27 Cours de l'Ile Seguin - 92100 Boulogne Billancourt (France)
R.C.S. Nanterre 433 677 721

© Michelin, Propriétaires-Éditeurs

Dépôt légal octobre 2015

Printed in Canada - septembre 2015
Printed on paper from sustainably managed forests

Compogravure : Nord Compo à Villeneuve d'Ascq (France)
Impression et Finition : Transcontinental (Canada)

Dear Reader

I t's been an exciting and formative year for the entire team at the MICHELIN guides in North America, and it is with great pride that we present you with our 2016 edition to Chicago. Over the past year our dynamic inspectors have extended their reach to include a variety of establishments and multiplied their anonymous visits to restaurants in our selection in order to accurately reflect the rich culinary diversity this great city has to offer.

The Michelin Red Guides are an annual publication that recommends an assortment of delicious destinations and awards stars for excellence to a select few restaurants. Our company's founders, Édouard and André Michelin, published the first MICHELIN guide in 1900, to provide motorists with useful information about where they could service and repair their cars as well as find a good quality meal. Later in 1926, the star-rating system was introduced, whereby outstanding establishments are awarded for excellence in cuisine. Over the decades we have made many new enhancements to the Guide, and the local team here in Chicago eagerly carries on these traditions. As part of the Guide's historic, highly confidential, and meticulous evaluation process, our inspectors have anonymously and methodically eaten their way through the entire city with a mission to marshal the finest in each category for your enjoyment. While they are expertly trained professionals in the food industry, the Guides remain consumer-driven and provide comprehensive choices to accommodate your every comfort, taste, and budget. By dining and drinking as "everyday" customers, our inspectors are able to experience and evaluate the same level of service and cuisine as any other guest. This past year has seen some unique advancements in Chicago's dining scene. Some of these can be found in each neighborhood introduction, complete with photography depicting our favored choices.

For more information and to get our inside scoop, you may follow the Inspectors on Twitter (@MichelinGuideCH) and Instagram (@michelininspectors) as they chow their way around town and talk about unusual dining experiences, tell entertaining food stories, and detail other personal encounters. We thank you for your patronage and truly hope that the MICHELIN guide will remain your preferred reference to Chicago's restaurants.

Contents

The MICHELIN Guide

"This volume was created at the turn of the century and will last at least as long".

This foreword to the very first edition of the MICHELIN guide, written in 1900, has become famous over the years and the Guide has lived up to the prediction. It is read across the world and the key to its popularity is the consistency in its commitment to its readers, which is based on the following assurances.

→ Anonymous Inspections

Our inspectors make anonymous visits to restaurants to gauge the quality of cuisine offered to the everyday customer. They pay their own bill and make no indication of their presence. These visits are supplemented by comprehensive monitoring of information—our readers' comments are one valuable source, and are always taken into consideration.

→ Independence

Our choice of establishments is a completely independent one, made for the benefit of our readers alone. Decisions are discussed by the inspectors and editor, with the most important considered at the global level. Inclusion in the Guide is always free of charge.

→ The Selection

The Guide offers a selection of the best restaurants in each category of comfort and price. A recommendation in the Guides is an honor in itself, and defines the establishment among the "best of the best."

How the MICHELIN Guide Works

→ Annual Updates

All practical information, the classifications, and awards, are revised and updated every year to ensure the most reliable information possible.

→ Consistency & Classifications

The standards and criteria for the classifications are the same in all countries covered by the Michelin Guides. Our system is used worldwide and easy to apply when selecting a restaurant.

→ The Classifications

We classify our restaurants using XxXxX-X to indicate the level of comfort. A symbol in red suggests a particularly charming spot with unique décor or ambience. The ✿✿✿-✿ specifically designates an award for cuisine. They do not relate to a chef or establishment and are unique from the classification.

→ Our Aim

As part of Michelin's ongoing commitment to improving travel and mobility, we do everything possible to make vacations and eating out a pleasure.

How to Use This Guide

The Michelin Distinctions for Good Cuisine

Stars for good cuisine

❀❀❀ Exceptional cuisine, worth a special journey
❀❀ Excellent cuisine, worth a detour
❀ A very good restaurant in its category

❀ Bib Gourmand
Inspectors' favorites for good value

Areas or neighborhoods
Each area is color coded...

🚉 El station

Average Prices

⊜	Under $25
$$	$25 to $50
$$$	$50 to $75
$$$$	Over $75

Symbols

💵	Cash only
♿	Wheelchair accessible
☂	Outdoor dining
🍳	Breakfast
🥂	Brunch
✗	Dim sum
⌘	Notable wine list
⌘	Notable sake list
♕	Notable cocktail list
⌑	Notable beer list
BYO	Bring your own
🚗	Valet parking
⟳	Private dining room

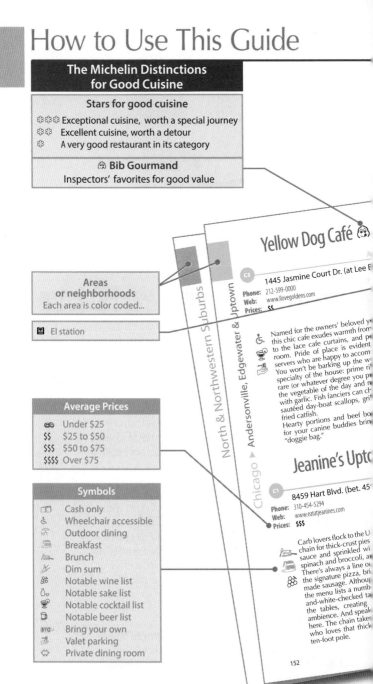

North & Northwestern Suburbs

Chicago ▶ Andersonville, Edgewater & Uptown

Yellow Dog Café ❀

C3   1445 Jasmine Court Dr. (at Lee B...

Phone: 212-599-0000
Web: www.Ilovegoldens.com
Prices: $$

Named for the owners' beloved ye...
this chic cafe exudes warmth from...
to the lace cafe curtains, and pe...
room. Pride of place is evident...
servers who are happy to accom...
You won't be barking up the wr...
specialty of the house: prime ri...
rare (or whatever degree you pr...
the vegetable of the day and n...
with garlic. Fish fanciers can ch...
sautéed day-boat scallops, gri...
fried catfish.
Hearty portions and beef bo...
for your canine buddies brin...
"doggie bag."

Jeanine's Upto...

C1   8459 Hart Blvd. (bet. 45...

Phone: 310-454-5294
Web: www.eatatjeanines.com
Prices: $$$

Carb lovers flock to the U...
chain for thick-crust pies...
sauce and sprinkled wi...
spinach and broccoli, a...
There's always a line ou...
the signature pizza, bri...
made sausage. Althou...
the menu lists a numb...
and-white-checked ta...
the tables, creating...
ambience. And speak...
here. The chain takes...
who loves that thick...
ten-foot pole.

152

8

Restaurant Classifications by Comfort

	More pleasant if in red
X	Comfortable
XX	Quite comfortable
XxX	Very comfortable
XxxX	Top class comfortable
XxxxX	Luxury in the traditional style
📖	Small plates

Map Coordinates

Sonya's Palace ✿ ✿

Italian XxxX

B5 100 Reuther Pl. (at 30th Street)

Dinner daily
LaSalle/Van Buren

Phone: 415-867-5309
Subway: 14th St - 8 Av
Web: www.sonyasfabulouspalace.com
Prices: $$$

Chicago ▶ Andersonville, Edgewater & Uptown

Home cooked Italian never tasted so good than at this unpretentious little place. The simple décor claims no big-name designers, and while the Murano glass light fixtures are chic and the velveteen-covered chairs are comfortable, this isn't a restaurant where millions of dollars were spent on the interior.

Instead, food is the focus here. The restaurant's name may not be Italian, but it nonetheless serves some of the best pasta in the city, made fresh in-house. Dishes follow the seasons, thus ravioli may be stuffed with fresh ricotta and herbs in summer, and pumpkin in fall. Most everything is liberally dusted with Parmigiano Reggiano, a favorite ingredient of the chef.

For dessert, you'll have to deliberate between the likes of creamy tiramisu, ricotta cheesecake, and homemade gelato. One thing's for sure: you'll never miss your nonna's cooking when you eat at Sonya's.

153

(partial text from adjacent page, left margin)

XX

Lunch daily
Addison

retriever,
g waitstaff
the dining
of friendly
requests.
u order the
to medium
mpanied by
golds tinged
ishes such as
on, and pan-

to take home
g to the term

pizza X

es.)
Tues-Sat dinner only
Washington

f this local pizzeria
the house marinara
gs such as organic
and pancetta.
patrons rave about
pperoni and house-
main attraction here,
pastas as well. Red-
Chianti bottles adorn
ed Italian restaurant
t's the wine of choice
the owner's daughter,
n't touch meat with a

9

Where to Eat

Chicago

A walk through Chicago's North side, rich with culinary traditions from centuries of immigrant settlers, is like globe-trotting. A number of local businesses, specialty stores, row houses, and hotels populate the quaint streets of Andersonville, and architecture buffs never grow weary of the numerous art deco buildings set along Bryn Mawr Avenue and Lake Michigan's beaches.

HOW SWEDE IT IS

A water tower emblazoned with the blue-and-yellow Swedish flag rises above Clark Street, proudly representing Andersonville's Nordic roots. Step inside the Swedish-American Museum for a history lesson. Then head to one of the last extant Swedish emporiums in the area—**Wikstrom's Gourmet Foods'** online-only gift shop—to take home a bag of red fish or even meatballs and herring among other packaged goods. While some early birds line up for cinnamon-streusel coffeecake at the **Swedish Bakery**, others may be found perched at their counter for an individually sized treat and complimentary cup of coffee. For the heartiest appetites, a Viking breakfast at **Svea Restaurant** complete with Swedish-style pancakes, sausages, and toasted limpa

bread fits the bill. Beyond the well-represented Scandinavian community, Andersonville brings the world to its doorstep thanks to those amply stocked shelves at **Middle East Bakery & Grocery**. Their deli selection features a spectrum of spreads, breads, olives, and hummus making it entirely feasible to throw a meze feast in minutes. But, if your tastes run further south (of the border), then **Isabella Bakery** is gem for all things Guatemalan—and turns out a host of tamales to die for. Adventurous foodies depend on the grocery section to keep their pantries stocked with fresh spices, dried fruits, rosewater, nuts, teas, and more.

AN ASIAN AFFAIR

A cross town, the pagoda-style roof of the Argyle El stop on the Red Line serves as another visual clue to the plethora of eats available here. Imagine an East Asian lineup of Chinese, Thai, and Vietnamese restaurants, noodle shops, delis, bakeries, and herbalists. Platters of lacquered, bronzed duck and pork make **Sun Wah BBQ** an inviting and popular spot for Cantonese cuisine, while **dak Korean** is always a fave for spicy chicken wings and rice bowls served from a counter. Andersonville's charming and family-run **Sunshine Café** specializes in Japanese noodles and potato croquettes, but sushi lovers will need to content themselves with just one, very delicious maki. For those less inclined to cook for themselves, a new genesis of casual eateries is prospering along these streets. **BopNgrill** for instance specializes in fusion food like *loco moco* or fantastically messy burgers including the "Umami" packed with truffled mushrooms; and **Little Vietnam** is quite divine for a steaming bowl of *pho*.

MEAT, POTATOES —AND MORE

Chicagoans can't resist a good sausage, so find them giving thanks regularly to the German immigrants who helped develop Lincoln Square and whose appreciation for fine meats still resonates in this neighborhood. Old World-inspired butchers ply their trade, stuffing wursts and offering specialty meats and deli items at **Gene's Sausage Shop**. For a more refined selection of chops, steaks and free-range poultry,

market hours every Thursday evening. Also in Lincoln Square, **HarvesTime Foods** wears its sustainability on its sleeve, with a solar-paneled roof and impressive array of regionally sourced produce. A collaboration between beloved artisans Co-op Sauce and Crumb Chicago, Edgewater's **Sauce and Bread Kitchen** brings two of the city's favorite local products together at one café. Made-to-order breakfast and lunch sandwiches filled with delectable maple sausage or applewood-smoked turkey are lavished with house-made condiments like tomato sauce (a fan favorite for fitting reason), while other party treats like hot sauce and pickled vegetables have a cult-ish following.

head to **Lincoln Quality Meat Market**. And speaking of meat treats, **Wolfy's** serves one of the best red-hots in Uptown, piling its dogs with piccalilli, pickles, peppers, and other impossibly colored condiments. Its iconic neon sign (a crimson frankfurter jauntily pierced by a pitchfork) only intensifies the urge to stop here.

For dinner party essentials like fresh vegetables, fruits, flowers, and baked goods, the Windy City boasts a farmer's market in most neighborhoods, most days of the week. The **Andersonville Farmer's Market** (held on Wednesdays) hosts a number of bakeries and an orchard's worth of Asian fruit. Then there's the **Lincoln Square Farmer's Market**, which throws its doors open on Tuesdays and hosts live music during

RAISE A GLASS

Critically acclaimed as one of the country's best boutique coffee shops, **The Coffee Studio** pours a mean cup of joe. Their locally roasted brews pair exceedingly well with a box of the "glazed & infused" doughnuts, which may need to be ordered in advance but are known to bring about interminable pleasure. In Edgewater, the creative community convenes at **The Metropolis Café**, an offshoot of Chicago's own **Metropolis Coffee Company**. Searching for something stronger than caffeine to bring to your next reservation? As the name suggests, family-owned producers and small-batch offerings are the focus at **Independent Spirits Inc.**, a wine and liquor shop replete with global selections.

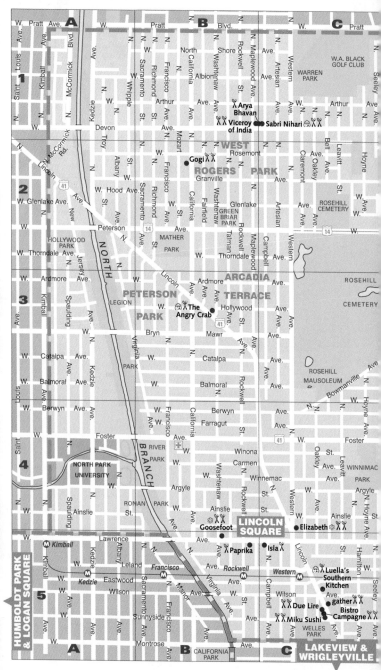

Andersonville, Edgewater & Uptown

Blvd. **D** W. Pratt **E** Blvd. **F** 1

W. Columbia Ave.

N. Damen Ave. Ridge Ave. Blvd. Ravenswood Clark St. Ashland Ave. W. North Shore Ave. Glenwood W. Shore Ave. Sheridan Ave. Loyola Ave. *Loyola* LOYOLA UNIVERSITY CHICAGO

Ⅹ Taste of Peru W. Albion W. Arthur Ave. Loyola Rd. LAKE

SCHREIBER PARK W. Devon Ave. W. Sheridan Rd. LOYOLA UNIVERSITY CHICAGO MICHIGAN

W. Highland Ave. Lakewood N. Ave. Rosemont Ave.

EMMERSON PARK Paulina W. Greenview W. Granville Ave. *Granville* Ave. Broadway Sheridan Ave. ✚ 2

N. Damen Ave. Hood Ave. Norwood St. W. Hermitage Ave. W. Hood Ave. W. Glenlake Ave. Glenwood Ave. W. Glenlake Ave. Winthrop

Peterson Ave. St. W. Elmdale Ave. EDGEWATER

SENN PARK W. Thorndale Ave. *Thorndale* Ave. Kenmore Sheridan LANE PARK

Ⅹ Ras Dashen ● W. Ardmore Ave. W. Ardmore Ave. KATHY OSTERMAN BEACH

Clark Ridge Ave. W. Early Ave. Ave.

Hollywood Ave. W. Hollywood Ave. N. Lake 3

W. Ave. Olive St. W. Ave. N. Ave. FOSTER AVE. BEACH

W. Bryn Mawr N. Ave. *Bryn Mawr* ● Ave.

ANDERSONVILLE W. Catalpa St. ⊕ Ⅹ Jin Thai

W. LAKEWOOD-BALMORAL Lakewood ● Herb ⊕ ⅩⅩ

Summerdale Damen Ave. ⅩⅩ Big Jones ● Vincent ⅩⅩ W. Balmoral Ave. Pearl's ● Southern Comfort ⅩⅩ

Ⅹ Anteprima ● W. Ⅹ Ombra Glenwood Ave. *Berwyn* Ave.

Wolcott Ave. Ravenswood Ave. W. Farragut Ave. Jin Ju Ⅹ W. Berwyn Ave. Taketei Ⅹ

⊕ Ⅹ Hopleaf ● W. Foster Ave. Winona Broadway Ave. St. LINCOLN PARK 4

N. Winchester Ave. W. Winnemac Ave. ✚ W. Ainslie St. St.

ⅩⅩ ampersand ● wine bar Ashland Ave. Clark St. ST. AUGUSTINE COLL. Pho Xe Tang - Tank Noodle ● *Argyle* W. Argyle St. Pho 777 Ⅹ MARGATE

RAVENSWOOD ST. BONIFACE CEMETERY W. Ainslie St. Sheridan Rd. PARK UPTOWN

CHASE PARK Ⅹ Demera ● *Lawrence* W. Lawrence Ave. LINCOLN PARK

N. Wolcott Damen Leland W. Ave. Hermitage Paulina SHERIDAN Magnolia W. Leland Ave.

Ⓜ *Damen* W. ⅩⅩ Magnolia Cafe ● 42 Grams ✱✱ ⅩⅩ 5

Damen Ave. W. Ave. Greenview St. PARK Beacon Wilson *Wilson* W. Wilson Ave. Halsted

W. Sunnyside Ave. TRUMAN COLLEGE Marine Dr. Sunnyside Ave. CLARENDON PARK

Spacca Napoli ● ⊕ Ⅹ

Ave. Ⓜ *Montrose* **D** W. St. **E** Montrose Ave. Hazel **F**

GRACELAND CEMETERY

19

ampersand wine bar

D4

American ✗✗

4845 N. Damen Ave. (bet. Ainslie St. & Lawrence Ave.)

Phone: 773-728-0031
Web: www.ampersandchicago.com
Prices: $$

Lunch Sat – Sun
Dinner Tue – Sun
🚇 Damen (Brown)

This cool wine bar cuts a stylish figure with its pale walls, gorgeous blonde wood, and sun-flooded dining room. Combine that urbane setting with polished service and a simple, but perfectly executed menu and you have one of the best new spots in town. Grab a seat at the long, L-shaped bar, the best perch in the house to ask a zillion questions—or just dig in as the small plates begin their march from behind the counter.

The menu, at the moment anyway, is small but packs a big punch—what's available is seasonal, diverse, and extremely fresh. A cold and creamy gold tomato gazpacho features tart strips of roasted eggplant and cool cucumber; while a deconstructed strawberry shortcake arrives in layers of luscious basil caramel and sweet berries.

The Angry Crab 😊

B3

Seafood ✗

5665 N. Lincoln Ave. (bet. Fairfield & Washtenaw Aves.)

Phone: 773-784-6848
Web: N/A
Prices: $$

Lunch Sat – Sun
Dinner nightly

Don't be shellfish—bring friends, beer, and wine to dinner at The Angry Crab for a messy, more-the-merrier experience. Lines form nightly for the chance to fill up on a Cajun-style **BYO** spread shot through with Vietnamese flavors that reflect the owners' heritage.

Order from the laminated menus or the large overhead chalkboard for a seafood feast with options like whole head-on shrimp or enormous snow crab legs. Choose from a choice of lemon, garlic, or spicy sauces, stake your claim on a roll of paper towels and a seat at the communal tables, and then rip open the plastic bags in which the seafood arrives and dig in with your claws. Still hungry? Make it a true crab boil and add sausage, corn on the cob, and red bliss potatoes to round out the meal.

Anteprima

D4

5316 N. Clark St. (bet. Berwyn & Summerdale Aves.)

Phone: 773-506-9990
Web: www.anteprimachicago.net
Prices: $$

Dinner nightly

🚇 Berwyn

♿ 🌂

Nestled into a vibrant strip of shops and eateries, this family-friendly gem is set apart by smart plate-glass windows and olive green-tinted woodwork. Inside, rusticity rules the roost with pressed-tin ceilings and intricate wood paneling. It's the kind of place where even solo patrons feel welcome, especially when perched on a window seat overlooking the bustling street.

Following its moniker, diners should "preview" the wide-ranging menu before opting for such delights as grilled sardines with sweet fennel, fragrant herbs, and fine olive oil. Delicious pastas include homemade ravioli—filled with a blend of crushed peas and mint—finished with a light, parmesan-flecked sauce. For dessert, a rich, well-made panna cotta wobbles with lemon syrup and zest.

Arya Bhavan

B1

2508 W. Devon Ave. (bet. Campbell & Maplewood Aves.)

Phone: 773-274-5800
Web: www.aryabhavan.com
Prices: 😊😊

Lunch Sat – Sun
Dinner Wed – Mon

BYO

Devon Avenue is rife with spots to sate Indo-Pakistani cravings, including dozens of longtime restaurants, catering halls, and markets serving curry, kebabs, and tandoori chicken. But Arya Bhavan stands out with personal, family-friendly service and fresh, carefully prepared Indian cuisine that also just happens to boast a few buzzwords (namely, vegan, organic, and gluten-free),

Even omnivores won't be able to resist the mixed basket appetizer, a substantial platter of tasty street snacks like tamarind-stuffed *mirch pakora* and spicy lemon-kissed potato *vada*. A classic rendition of garlicky, gingery *palak dal* blends hearty yellow lentils and fresh spinach. To finish the meal, take the plunge and reward your palate with outstanding avocado ice cream.

Big Jones

Southern ✕✕

E3

5347 N. Clark St. (bet. Balmoral & Summerdale Aves.)

Phone: 773-275-5725
Web: www.bigjoneschicago.com
Prices: $$

Lunch & dinner daily

🔲 Berwyn

Big Jones has all the genteel charm you'd expect from a restaurant specializing in Southern cuisine. Green brocade wallpaper surrounds large framed prints of haunting low-country landscapes. Guests are greeted with a "Guide to Good Drinking" upon arrival, featuring barrel-aged punch selections and a lengthy roster of Bourbon and whiskey.

Start with whole kernel-studded cornbread and honey butter, a fitting salvo for a meal steeped in Southern tradition. Sweet potato bisque is poured tableside over cornbread croutons, spicy apple chutney, and fried sage. Pickled pork shank and smoked jowl beef up red beans, braised voodoo greens, and aromatic Arkansas rice. An elderberry jelly roll sprinkled with Benne seeds finishes the meal on a classic note.

Bistro Campagne

French ✕✕

C5

4518 N. Lincoln Ave. (bet. Sunnyside & Wilson Aves.)

Phone: 773-271-6100
Web: www.bistrocampagne.com
Prices: $$

Lunch Sun
Dinner nightly
🔲 Western (Brown)

The romantic ideal of a French bistro is alive and well at Bistro Campagne. Light slants gently through wooden Venetian blinds, bouncing off cream-and-brick walls in the welcoming dining room. Choose a white cloth-covered table inside, under the red-golden soffit ceiling or outside under twinkling lights and green tree branches in the garden.

Inspired accompaniments make for memorable versions of rustic French standards. Meltingly tender *foie de veau* sparks happy sighs from calves' liver lovers, complemented by crisp bacon and Dijon mustard cream. House-made pappardelle and maitake mushrooms soak up the lavender-infused jus that finishes white wine-braised rabbit. Black figs are tucked into a moist brown butter *pain perdu* drizzled with caramel.

Demera

Ethiopian X

E5

4801 N. Broadway (at Lawrence Ave.)

Phone: 773-334-8787
Web: www.demeraethiopian.com
Prices: $$

Lunch & dinner daily

 Lawrence

Demera's well-lit corner location welcomes hungry Uptown residents looking to immerse themselves in Ethiopian cuisine. Colorful wicker seating at the dining room's communal table gives groups an authentic dining experience, while picture windows offer plenty of people-watching for everyone.

Vegetarian and omnivorous offerings abound on the menu, which features a small glossary of terms to help newcomers. Pleasantly spicy *ye-siga wot* combines tender chunks of beef with onions and ginger in a rich *berbere* sauce. Served with turmeric-infused split peas and jalapeño-laced collard greens, this stew is a hearty pleasure. Sop up extra sauce with piles of tangy and soft *injera*, presented in the traditional Ethiopian manner in lieu of silverware.

Due Lire

Italian XX

C5

4520 N. Lincoln Ave. (bet. Sunnyside & Wilson Aves.)

Phone: 773-275-7878
Web: www.due-lire.com
Prices: $$

Dinner Tue – Sun

 Western (Brown)

Naples native and gentleman's gentleman Massimo Di Vuolo welcomes guests from near and far to charming Due Lire. Smartly situated near the Old Town School of Folk Music, the dining room is often dotted with locals enjoying a pre-show dinner or lingering on the back patio with a glass of Falanghina. Abstract art brings bright color and energy to the otherwise understated décor.

Comforting but refined modern Italian dishes offer hearty satisfaction: creamy polenta sops up the slow-simmered stew ladled over braised lamb shank and tender root vegetables, and strands of freshly made spaghetti are bathed in rich, porky *amatriciana*-style ragù. For a refreshing finish, bite-sized ricotta *ciambelle* doughnuts—topped with *limoncello*-orange *crema*—keep things light.

Elizabeth ❀

Contemporary **✗✗**

C4

4835 N. Western, Unit D (bet. Ainslie St. & Lawrence Ave.)

Phone: 773-681-0651
Web: www.elizabeth-restaurant.com
Prices: **$$$$**

Dinner Tue – Sat

🚇 Western (Brown)

Find an owl, a deer, and a diamond over an unremarkable door on this rather commercial street—these are foodie hieroglyphs for homey yet conceptual Chicago dining.

The diminutive interior has only a handful of tables, all surrounding the brightly lit kitchen spectacle. The whitewashed tin ceiling and shelves stocked with everything from Dutch ovens to jars of pickles make it seem like we're all dining in Chef Iliana Regan's cottage-chic underground restaurant. You might even see her refilling your water glass; this is a humble place where dedication trumps attitude.

The nightly 17-course menu is a clear treatise on local, organic, and foraged cuisine. Don't be surprised to find bear jerky showcased in the deliciously inventive "rock course" that is literally served on a jet-black rock, along with a sticky bite of wild puffed rice mixed with mushroom marshmallow, and topped with Wisconsin cheddar as well as a vibrant pink peppercorn. When the glazed bowl containing a perfectly cooked duck egg and shaved truffles arrives at the table, expect a bit of theatrics as the server explains that the "twigs" decorating the table all along are actually fried breadsticks to enjoy with the dish.

42 Grams ❀ ❀

Contemporary ✗✗

E5

4662 N. Broadway (bet. Clifton & Leland Aves.)

Phone: N/A Dinner Wed – Sun
Web: www.42gramschicago.com
Prices: $$$$ 🖳 Wilson

♿

BYO

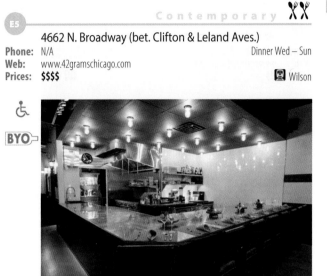

To know the name refers to the supposed weight of two souls is to also know that this is not your usual restaurant. In fact, it's hardly a restaurant at all and more like a dinner party with strangers—you even need to arrive with a bottle or two of wine under your arms. There are two sittings: the first is at the counter where you watch Chef/owner Jake Bickelhaupt and his two colleagues in action; for 8.30 P.M. arrivals, it's the large communal table. For both, you'll be sharing your dinner with people you don't know, but the ice is usually broken by someone asking where their fellow diners have eaten recently.

The set menu offers no choice but any allergies are discussed during the bothersome flurry of e-mails that follow the initial impersonal booking process. Then it's over to Jake's smiling wife, Alexa, to guide diners through the parade of dishes. The cooking is clever and contemporary and the ingredients superlative, whether that's the peekytoe crab "dumpling" or *mojama de atún* (air-dried, salt-cured tuna) plated on black slate and perched above a light green pea gelato. Dishes are wonderfully well-balanced and modern techniques are used to great effect to deliver superb flavors.

A coffee "spuma" flavored with cardamom and whipped cream is an ideal way to cap off this exceptional meal.

gather

C5

American ❌❌

4539 N. Lincoln Ave. (bet. Sunnyside & Wilson Aves.)

Phone: 773-506-9300
Web: www.gatherchicago.com
Prices: $$

Lunch Sun
Dinner nightly
Western (Brown)

A chic, cozy space lets guests get up close and personal at gather. Diners seeking dinner and a show take front row seats at barstools lining the open kitchen's polished granite counter, while tall communal tables fill with patrons enjoying bites from the menu's "gather and share" section. A rear dining room offers more solitude and romance.

Family-style Sunday dinners are a local draw, but the à la carte menu showcases flavorful options nightly. Slice into a single large *uovo raviolo* to mingle poached egg and ricotta with white truffle butter, jalapeño slivers, and chopped chives, or share a crock of Pernod-splashed mussels. Fragrant and garlicky, they're served with sourdough toast points for soaking up every last drop of the white wine-cream sauce.

Gogi

B2

Korean ❌❌

6240 N.California Ave. (bet. Granville & Rosemont Aves.)

Phone: 773-274-6669
Web: www.gogichicago.com
Prices: $$

Lunch Sun
Dinner nightly

The surging popularity of Korean food continues to flourish along these shores of Lake Michigan; and as foodies would have you know, Gogi is one of the best places in the city to experience it. With its hip, industrial décor, imposing exhaust fans over each table (a clear sign that there's a ton of grilling going on), and lively palate of sweet, spicy, and sour, dinner here promises to be a sensory explosion like no other.

One could feast on the abundant pre-meal *banchan* alone—a stunning selection of kimchi, mirin-soaked fish cakes, sake-steamed black beans, and more. But, that would mean missing out on delicate slices of sirloin *bulgogi* smothered in a sweet, gingery marinade; or restorative, spicy *sundubu jjigae* bubbling away in an iron pot.

Goosefoot ✤

B5

2656 W. Lawrence Ave. (bet. Talman & Washtenaw Aves.)

Phone: 773-942-7547
Dinner Wed – Sun

Web: www.goosefoot.net

Prices: $$$$

🖳 Rockwell

♿
BYO

This understated plate-glass façade may seem lost in a sea of mediocrity, but the restaurant it houses is truly distinct. The soothing décor appears minimal, with splashes of orange banquettes, bare tables, and Rodin replicas to fashion a space that is instantly likeable. Menus are made of planting seed paper that guests are encouraged to take home, soak, and use to grow their own wildflowers. Dishes are intricate and take time for the well-versed staff to describe, which may explain the relatively slow pace of dining here.

The nine-course menu showcases noteworthy Chef Chris Nugent's classical edge and contemporary artistry. Start with a plump, butter-poached scallop seared until golden, set in a lobster-rich and coconutty sauce with maitake mushrooms and curry spices, surrounded by edible flower petals placed in gels redolent of lemongrass. This may be followed by a unique egg and shell presentation of black garlic custard dotted with shrimp, tucked with an enticingly sharp sprout purée. Superb cheese and dessert courses are a consistent highlight.

Goosefoot is still BYO, but an attached wine shop ensures that no one is caught empty-handed. Pay attention to the chocolate lab and market, too.

Chicago Andersonville, Edgewater & Uptown

27

Herb

E3

5424 N. Broadway (bet. Balmoral & Catalpa Aves.)

Phone: 773-944-9050
Web: www.herbrestaurant.com
Prices: $$

Dinner Wed – Sun

🚇 Bryn Mawr

BYO

In the sea of Thai restaurants that flank this area, elegant Herb stands out for its lovely wood and stone décor; and service staff friendly enough to use your name. This is killer Thai, elevated and prepared with care.

Herb offers both a three- and six-course prix-fixe dinner at tremendous value, but Chef/owner Patty Neumson's cooking is light (and delicious) enough to go the distance. A sample menu might begin with a cool pile of crunchy green papaya, carrot, and cucumber, laced in a beautifully balanced lime dressing with crispy vermicelli noodles and peanuts. Then move on to tofu and kabocha in a deliciously complex coconut curry full of wilted basil and heat. Soft glass noodles find their match in sautéed onions, fresh crab, and crunchy shrimp.

Hopleaf 😊

Gastropub X

D4

5148 N. Clark St. (bet. Foster Ave. & Winona St.)

Phone: 773-334-9851
Web: www.hopleaf.com
Prices: $$

Lunch & dinner daily

🚇 Berwyn

Perfectly ordinary from the outside, Hopleaf thrives as a labor of love for owners, Michael and Louise. Named after a pale ale brewed in Malta, this serious tavern has beer and food fans in raptures over their stirring selection of sips, snacks, and serious eats. Dine comfortably amid exposed brick walls, steelwork, and shabby-chic furnishings whether seated at the traditional front bar, in the rear, or by the glassed-in kitchen.

A great collection of enamel beer signs will put you in the mood for a brew with your Belgian or Thai-style mussels, followed by hearty shavings of porcetta folded into crusty ciabatta with tangy giardinera and creamy mayo. Dinner may flaunt extra variety—but for dessert, fix upon lavender-buttermilk panna cotta crowned with blackberry compote.

Isla

Filipino ✗

C5

2501 W. Lawrence Ave., Unit D (bet. Campbell & Maplewood Aves.)

Phone: 773-271-2988   Lunch & dinner Tue – Sun
Web: www.islapilipina.com
Prices: ⌘   🖿 Western (Brown)

BYO
Don't let Isla's plain-Jane décor dissuade you—despite the flimsy curtains and bare-bones dining room, the space is practically bursting with Filipino pride. From the convivial owners and servers, to the bantering patrons getting their fix of Filipino cable TV as they eat, the warmth and love for this Southeast Asian country is clear here.

Traditional dishes populate a menu that offers a whirlwind tour of the islands' bold flavors. *Tinolang manok*, a refreshing take on chicken soup, is redolent with ginger and punctuated by green papaya. Dried taro leaves in *laing sa gata* lend smokiness to tender, coconut milk-simmered pork and shrimp, and a side of Isla's famous adobo rice, spooned with the classic tart and garlicky pork stew, goes with everything.

Jin Ju

Korean ✗

E4

5203 N. Clark St. (at Foster Ave.)

Phone: 773-334-6377   Dinner Tue – Sun
Web: www.jinjurestaurant.com
Prices: $$

A sexy spot on a bustling stretch of North Clark, Jin Ju spins out luscious Korean classics with aplomb. Inside, dim lighting, dark wood furnishings, and luxuriant fuchsia-red walls create a sophisticated coziness, while servers are gracious and attentive.

A simply-named house salad showcases the restaurant's modern, accessible Korean ethos, combining meaty pan-seared portobello strips atop delicately bitter green leaf lettuce, torn sesame leaves, cucumbers, and scallions in a funky garlic-soy sauce. Without tableside barbecue grills, fatty pork slabs are sautéed in the kitchen for sweetly caramelized s*am gyup sal*. Wrapped in sesame leaves with Brussels sprouts, beets, crispy leeks, and a smear of kicky miso paste, the package provides instant gratification.

Jin Thai 🎈

Thai 🍴

E3

5458 N. Broadway (at Catalpa Ave.)

Phone: 773-681-0555
Web: www.jinthaicuisine.com
Prices: 💰💰

Lunch & dinner daily

🚆 Bryn Mawr

BYO

In-the-know locals fill up on tasty Thai at this sleek corner hot spot, whose curving glass windows beckon many a passerby with views of and aromas from vibrant curries and spicy *laab*. Inside, a row of splashy pillows lends color and comfort to a wooden banquette, and woven placemats dress up dark wood tables.

Start a meal with zingy *miang kum*, a chopped mix of dried shrimp, fresh ginger and lime, peanuts, and coconut, all wrapped in a betel leaf. From there, move on to hot curry catfish or *Sukothai* noodle soup teeming with minced pork and steaming broth (add pinches of warm spices from the accompanying condiment tray for an even more soul-satisfying slurp). For dessert, pick from either roti ice cream, wonton bananas, or warm Thai custard.

Luella's Southern Kitchen 🎈🎈

Southern 🍴

C5

4609 N. Lincoln Ave. (bet. Eastwood & Wilson Aves.)

Phone: 773-961-8196
Web: www.luellassouthernkitchen.com
Prices: $$

Lunch Sat – Sun
Dinner nightly
🚆 Western (Brown)

BYO

Luella's is named for Chef Darnell Reed's Southern-born great-grandmother, and for good reason: one bite of its soul-infused fare will transport you to her hometown of Morgan City, Mississippi, a place she left behind for Chicago many years ago—and one that lives on in her grandson's cooking. The no-frills, order-at-the-counter spot is simply adorned, with genuinely welcoming service that only adds to the charm.

Every spoonful of Luella's andouille and chicken gumbo is one to remember, thanks to a roux that's been cooked for five (count 'em) hours. The hot, sugary beignets are a pastry wonder, and chicken and waffles drizzled with Bourbon syrup are Southern by way of Brussels, featuring thick, eggy Liège waffles standing in for the usual rounds.

Magnolia Cafe

American

E5

1224 W. Wilson Ave. (at Magnolia Ave.)

Phone: 773-728-8785
Web: www.magnoliacafeuptown.com
Prices: $$

Lunch Sun
Dinner Tue – Sun
Wilson

Uptown residents turn to Magnolia Cafe for chic comfort in a homey neighborhood standby. Close-knit tables covered in kraft paper and tasseled lampshades hanging from exposed wood beams create a warm atmosphere for dining, while a small bar near the entry stands at the ready for creative pre-dinner cocktails and brunch mimosas.

Chef/owner Kasra Medhat's menu incorporates a melting pot's worth of ingredients into American bistro standards. *Huevos rancheros* are filling enough to soak up the excesses of Saturday night, with two sunny side-up eggs layered with homemade salsa and guacamole over a mix of black beans, sweet corn kernels, and crumbled chorizo. Composed salads and dishes like applewood-smoked chicken pappardelle round out a roster of dinner options.

Miku Sushi

Japanese XX

C5

4514 N. Lincoln Ave. (bet. Sunnyside & Wilson Aves.)

Phone: 773-654-1277
Web: www.mikuchicago.com
Prices: $$

Lunch & dinner daily

Western (Brown)

Miku Sushi piles on the style in a spacious location with a polished, airy room featuring a 12-seat counter plus a full bar for cocktail hounds. More than a simple sushi spot, the menu boasts artfully presented and inventive maki, ramen, *yakitori*, and small plates that make for a festive night of sharing with fellow food lovers.

Snack on the *robusuta* roll, surely to become a "Lincoln Square classic" pairing lobster and fried banana; or for a more traditionally savory but still modern option, the Miya maki combines white tuna, snow crab, and avocado with grilled asparagus. Warm up with a bowl of springy, correctly spicy ramen teeming with fresh mushrooms, soft-boiled egg, and tender pork belly in a cloudy, miso-rich broth spiked with garlic and sesame oil.

Ombra

Italian ✗✗

D4

5310 N. Clark St. (bet. Berwyn & Summerdale Aves.)

Phone: 773-506-8600   Dinner nightly
Web: www.barombra.com
Prices: $$ 🚇 Berwyn

Though it shares a kitchen with next-door gastropub Acre, Ombra is a destination in its own right. Booths patched with recycled leather jackets and "wallpaper" of vintage Italian newspapers give the cozy dining room a unique sense of place, and the Italian-inspired cuisine is just as interesting.
Diners make quick work of dishes like toothsome farro and mushroom "arancini," deviled eggs kissed with lemon aïoli, or parmesan-dusted meatballs in a chunky tomato sauce. Crispy skin-on whitefish is paired with buttery potatoes and takes a heavenly swim in caper-lemon sauce. Pizzas arrive charred from the wood oven, their dough flavorful and chewy, and creative cocktails like the Chicagroni—modernized with IPA and tea—keep the bar hopping.

Paprika

Indian ✗

B5

2547 W. Lawrence Ave. (bet. Maplewood Ave. & Rockwell St.)

Phone: 773-338-4906   Dinner Tue – Sun
Web: www.paprikachicago.com
Prices: $$ 🚇 Rockwell

Chef Shah Kabir and his family know hospitality. Prepare to be swept up in their warmth and care (with maybe a splash of kitsch) the minute you enter this richly colored space, adorned with artifacts. Even the chef himself is at the door welcoming guests to sit and sip a cool, refreshing *lassi*.
From aromatic, homemade curries to tasty twists on *dahls* (*turka dahl ki shabzi* is a revelation), everything is fresh and fragrant. Bengali fish curry is a notable attraction—its flavors mild yet lively with mustard seeds, firm and fresh green beans, and silky-sweet onions. A very nice selection of vegetarian dishes might include the veggie samosa: its soft, light shell is stuffed with spiced potatoes, peas, cauliflower, and served with a trio of tangy chutneys.

Pearl's Southern Comfort

Southern ✕✕

E3

5352 N. Broadway (bet. Balmoral & Berwyn Aves.)

Phone: 773-754-7419
Web: www.pearlschicago.com
Prices: $$

Lunch Sat – Sun
Dinner Mon – Sat
🚇 Berwyn

Chicago's been on a Southern food kick of late, and this sparkling Andersonville charmer is a straight up hep cat—its enormous arched windows opening up to a completely revamped 100 year-old room featuring long exposed ceiling beams; whitewashed brick; dark slate walls; and soft leather chairs.

But even with all that design swag, the main draw at Pearl's Southern Comfort is still the food. For starters, there's their ace barbecue, but guests should hardly stop there. Try the enormous double cut pork chop, grilled to supple perfection and paired with "dirty" farro salad, Cajun slaw, and pork jus. Another staple, the Louisiana jambalaya, is served decadently dark and spicy, bobbing with tender chicken, Andouille sausage, and Crystal hot sauce.

Pho 777

Vietnamese ✕

E4

1063-65 W. Argyle St. (bet. Kenmore & Winthrop Aves.)

Phone: 773-561-9909
Web: N/A
Prices: ⊜⊜

Lunch & dinner Tue – Sun
🚇 Argyle

A market's worth of fresh ingredients allows Pho 777 to stand out in a neighborhood where Vietnamese restaurants—and their signature soup—seem to populate every storefront. Bottles of hot sauce, jars of fiery condiments, and canisters of spoons and chopsticks clustered on each table make it easy for regulars to sit down and start slurping.

Add choices like meatballs, tendon, flank steak, and even tofu to the cardamom- ginger- and clove-spiced beef broth, which fills a bowl the size of a bathroom sink. Then throw in jalapeños, Thai basil, and mint to your liking. If you're not feeling like *pho* this time around, snack on spring rolls with house-made roasted peanut sauce; or a plate of lacy *banh xeo* stuffed with shrimp, sprouts, and herbs.

Pho Xe Tang - Tank Noodle

Vietnamese ✗

E4

4953-55 N. Broadway (at Argyle St.)

Phone: 773-878-2253   Lunch & dinner Thu – Tue
Web: www.tank-noodle.com
Prices: ⊜⊝   🚇 Argyle

BYO

A stone's throw from the Little Saigon EL, this simple corner spot keeps *pho* enthusiasts coming back for more. Communal cafeteria-style tables, crowded during prime meal times, are stocked with all the necessary funky and spicy condiments. Efficient service keeps the joint humming and lets the patrons focus on slurping.

Pho is the definitive draw here, and this fragrant, five-spiced, rice noodle- and beef-filled broth is accompanied by sprouts, lime wedges, and plenty of basil. Other delights on the massive menu include shrimp- and pork-stuffed rice flour rolls with addictive sweet and sour *nuoc cham*; followed by spicy catfish soup simmered with an intriguing combination of okra, pineapple, and bamboo shoots drizzled with garlic oil.

Ras Dashen

Ethiopian ✗

E2

5846 N. Broadway (bet. Ardmore & Thorndale Aves.)

Phone: 773-506-9601   Lunch & dinner daily
Web: www.rasdashenchicago.com
Prices: $$ 🚇 Thorndale

Take the hostess up on her offer to sit at a traditional table and enjoy Ras Dashen's Ethiopian items in a truly authentic environment. Cushioned rattan chairs surrounding low *mossab* tables with conical domed lids await communal trays arriving from the kitchen. The bar serves Ethiopian honey wine, African beers, and cocktails like the rosy champagne *qay arafa* for those who want to fully immerse themselves in the culinary culture.

Delicately crisp, lentil-stuffed *sambusas* whet the appetite for *doro wat*, the national dish of Ethopia, which does its country proud with aromatic and tender braised chicken in a sumptuous *berbere* sauce. Sides of warm *ib* cheese, freshly made from buttermilk, and spongy *injera* cool the palate from the creeping heat.

Sabri Nihari 😊

Indian
Indian ✗✗

C1

2500-2502 W. Devon Ave. (at Campbell Ave.)

Phone: 773-465-3272
Web: www.sabrinihari.com
Prices: 💰

Lunch & dinner daily

Sabri Nihari outshines the restaurant competition on this crowded stretch of West Devon Avenue. A recent expansion has doubled the size of the posh Indo-Pakistani spot, where crystal chandeliers make gold-hued walls gleam more brightly.

As with many Southeast Asian restaurants, vegetarian dishes abound—but that's only the beginning of the expansive menu. Whole okra pods add grassy, peppery bite to beefy *bhindi gosht*, and delightful chicken *charga*, an entire spatchcocked bird marinated in yogurt and lime, is rubbed generously with spices before crisping up in the deep fryer. No alcohol is served in deference to many of the abstaining clientele, but you won't miss it; buttery naan and creamy lassi with homemade yogurt help to balance out the spice-fest.

Spacca Napoli 😊

Pizza ✗

D5

1769 W. Sunnyside Ave. (bet. Hermitage & Ravenswood Aves.)

Phone: 773-878-2420
Web: www.spaccanapolipizzeria.com
Prices: $$

Lunch & dinner Tue – Sun

🚇 Montrose (Brown)

Long before Chicago deep-dish, Italy was famous for its Neapolitan pies. The "Vera Pizza Napoletana" sign at Spacca Napoli's door proclaims that this is the real deal, Naples-certified pizza, thanks to its authentic *pizzaiolo*, Jonathan Goldsmith. That glass-tiled custom Bisazza wood-burning oven in the center of the open kitchen is a tip-off, too.

The casual menu features a dozen varieties of red or white pizzas, along with antipasti and desserts for those who need more than a pie. Juice glasses filled with wine and served alongside crispy squash blossoms stuffed with ricotta and sweet peppers whet appetites. Pizzas arrive uncut, blistered, and charred, with just enough chewy bite to let the fresh mozzarella—cow's milk or *bufala*—and toppings shine.

35

Taketei

E4

1111 W. Berwyn Ave. (bet. Broadway & Winthrop Ave.)

Phone: 773-769-9292   Dinner Mon – Sat
Web: N/A
Prices: ⬤⬤   🚇 Berwyn

BYO

Though it's a mere sliver of a space, Taketei's Japanese temple to fresh piscine makes a bold statement in this neighborhood, noted for its Vietnamese joints. The wee room, so small there's not even a true sushi counter, remains serenely bright but minimal, filled with a handful of white tables and chairs. A limited menu makes the most of shiny pieces of fish. With the majority of nigiri available for less than $3 each, regulars know to load up or go all out with a sashimi platter featuring a wide selection of generously sliced seafood like mackerel, octopus, and *maguro* with a bowl of rice. Manageably sized, non-gimmicky rolls along with appetizers like pert, crunchy *hiyashi wakame* salad or spinach with sweet sesame sauce supplement this appealing array.

Taste of Peru

D1

6545 N. Clark St. (bet. Albion & Arthur Aves.)

Phone: 773-381-4540   Lunch & dinner daily
Web: www.tasteofperu.com
Prices: ⬤⬤

BYO

Tucked inside a strip-mall and entirely plain-Jane in appearance, foodies trek to this *caliente* fave for a formidable meal of authentic dishes. The owner is chatty and tunes groovy, all of which make for a wonderful precursor to such peppery items as *aji de gallina* (shredded chicken in a walnut sauce, enriched with parmesan) or *chupe de camarones* (a hot, spicy, bright bowl of shrimp and rice). This is clearly not the place for a pisco sour, but feels like Sundays *con la familia* where *papa a la huancaina* doused in *amarillo chile*, and *arroz chaufa* with veggies and beef jerky-like strips are merely some of the items on offer.

It's worth noting though that while the food is decidedly traditional, mysteriously there's no pork to be found anywhere on the menu.

Viceroy of India

B1

Indian ✗✗

2520 W. Devon Ave. (bet. Campbell & Maplewood Aves.)

Phone: 773-743-4100   Lunch & dinner daily
Web: www.viceroyofindia.com
Prices: ⬤⬤

The periwinkle and lavender walls, sky-blue ceiling painted with clouds, and steely booths lining the spacious dining room at Viceroy of India keep things cool, letting the spice-inflected cuisine churned out by the kitchen provide the heat. White linen-draped tables as well as a full bar and wine list make this West Rogers Park retreat a regal choice.

Though an à la carte menu is available for those who've got to get their fill of tandoori chicken, longtime patrons and lunch regulars make a beeline for the popular lunch buffet, stocked with North Indian standards like *pakoras*, samosas, *saag paneer*, chicken *makhani*, and goat curry. Complimentary naan is available by the basketful.

The grab-and-go café next door lets passersby get their sweet fix.

Vincent

E3

Belgian ✗✗

1475 W. Balmoral Ave. (bet. Clark St. & Glenwood Ave.)

Phone: 773-334-7168   Lunch Sun
Web: www.vincentchicago.com   Dinner Tue – Sun
Prices: $$ 🚇 Berwyn

Go Dutch at Vincent, where innovative yet approachable cooking meets a tried-and-true European bistro menu boasting enough cheese to satisfy even the pickiest turophile. Adding to the romance, high-top marble tables and brocade-papered walls make for a warm, intimate ambience that's accented by tall votive candles.

Got an appetite? An overflowing pot of P.E.I. mussels is a decadent meal on its own, brimming with bits of pork belly, chilies, scallions, and cilantro and accompanied by a big bowl of traditional frites with mayonnaise. Basil and lemon balsam perk up risotto with charred purple cauliflower and braised fennel. Also, you'll want to hold on to your fork for slices of lemon butter cake with Chantilly cream and blueberry compote.

Bucktown & Wicker Park

Like many of the Windy City's neighborhoods, Bucktown and Wicker Park have seen their residents shift from waves of Polish immigrants and wealthy businessmen who've erected stately mansions on Hoyne and Pierce avenues, to those young, hip crowds introducing modern taquerias and craft breweries to these streets. Still, the neighborhood knows how to retain its trendsetting rep, and continues to draw those who crave to be on the cutting edge of all things creative, contemporary, and culinary. Far from the internationally known boutiques along Magnificent Mile, indie shops and artisan producers of Milwaukee and Damen avenues offer one-of-a-kind treasures for all the five senses. Get a taste of Wicker Park's vast underground music scene at Reckless Records or at some of the city's largest music events, including the Wicker Park Fest, which is held each July and features no less than 28 bands. Likewise, the annual Green Music Fest draws every eco-minded resident around. Snap up funky home accessories and original works

at flea market-chic Penguin Foot Pottery, or wear art on your sleeve by designing your own Tee at the appropriately named T-shirt Deli.

HOT DOGS AND HAUTE TREATS

It's a well-known saying that you don't want to know how the sausage is made, but the person who coined this phrase clearly never tasted the bounty from **Vienna Beef Factory**. Their popular workshop tour leaves visitors yearning for a 1/3-pound Mike Ditka Polish sausage at the café, or even a make-your-own-Chicago-dog kit with celery salt, sport peppers, and electric-green pickle relish from the gift shop. For more Eastern European fun, **Rich's Deli** is Ukrainian Village's go-to market for copious cuts of smoked pork as well as *kabanosy, pasztet*, Polish vodka, and Slavic mustard among other terrific stuff. Unlike many local markets, the staff here is fluent in English, so don't be afraid to make your inquiries. All other lingering questions on meat may be answered after talking with husband-and-wife team, Rob and Allie Levitt, the brains (and stomachs) behind Noble Square's **The Butcher & Larder**. Combining the growing interest in whole animal butchery and a desire to support local farmers, the Levitt's showcase sausages, terrines, and house-cured bacon; while also conducting demos on how to break down a side of beef. If God is indeed in the details, then marketplace extraordinaire, **Goddess & Grocer**, brings to life this turn of phrase. While its vast selection of items may be the stuff of dreams among

snooty gourmands and top chefs, even novices can be found here, stocking up on soups, salads, and chili—better than what Mom used to make back in the day. They also cater, so go ahead and pretend like you crafted those delicate dinner party hors d'oeuvres all on your own!

SUGAR RUSH

A world of hand-crafted goodies make this neighborhood a rewarding destination for anyone addicted to sweet. For nearly a century, family-run **Margie's Candies** has been hand-dipping its chocolate bonbons and serving towering scoops of homemade ice cream to those Logan Square denizens and dons (including Al Capone, that old softy). Equally retro in attitude, the lip-smacking seasonal slices and small-town vibe of **Hoosier Mama Pie Company** brings old-timey charm to this stretch of Ashland Avenue. From tiered wedding cakes to replicas of Wrigley Field recreated in batter and frosting, a tempting selection of desserts is displayed in the window at **Alliance Bakery** and

W. Diversey Pkwy.   A   B   W.   Diversey   C   Pk

Owen & Engine ХХ

Elston

HUMBOLDT PARK
& LOGAN SQUARE

WRIGHTWOOD
PARK

Wrightwood   Ave.

N. Paulina St.

Clybourn

GreenView

Altgeld   St.

Racine   Ave.

I-90
I-94   W.   Fullerton   Ave.   Fullerton

Ashland   Ave.   Southport   Belden   DEP.

UNIVERS

Lyndale   St.   Webster   Southport

W.   Shakespeare   Ave.   ХХ The Bristol   W.   Webster
Charleston St.   🍴 Red Door   W.   Dickens

Western   Oakley   Leavitt   Dickens   BUCKTOWN   Ave.
Damen   Clybourn
Wilmot   Armitage   Coast Sushi Bar ХХ   Cortlandt   St.

Hoyne   Izakaya Mita Х   Wood   St.
Western Ⓜ   Le Bouchon Х
Belly Shack 😊Х   Ave.   Cortland   St.   Kennedy

Churchill   St.   En Hakkore Х
W. Bloomingdale Ave.   BLOOMINGDALE   TRAIL   Elston
Mindy's   Paulina   BRANCH
Hot Chocolate ХХ   Х Ada St.   N. Ada St.   Throop

Wabansia   Ave.   Bosworth   St.

ХХ Trenchermen   ХХ Enso   Lillie's Q ХХ   Ada   North   Ave.
W.   North   Damen   Ave.   Las Palmas ХХ   W.
Х Birchwood   😊 Dove's   Ⓜ Taxim ХХ   😊 Schwa
Kitchen   Luncheonette   Х Big Star   Cumin 😊Х   Mott St. 😊Х
WICKER   Oiistar Х   Blackhawk   St.
WICKER   PARK   PARK   Antique Taco Х
Hirsch   St.   Kokopelli Х
W.   Evergreen   Ave.   Smoke 😊   Carriage   I-94
Potomac   Ave.   Daddy ХХ   House   tocco 😊Ⓜ   Division
CLEMENTE   ХХ Nando   ХХ Mirai   ХХ Taus   Noble   St.
PARK   Milano   Division   Authentic   Х Bangers   Elston
Trattoria   ХХ Takito   Ⓜ Mana   Black   & Lace   Х Frontier
Kitchen   Х Food Bar   Bull 🍴   Division   Milwaukee
WEST   Blvd.   Walton   St.
TOWN   Leavitt   Hoyne   Augusta
Thomas   Damen   St.   Wood   St.   Ave.
Campbell   Oakley   Briciola ХХ
Iowa   St.   ХХ Ruxbin   ECKHART
W.   Chicago   Ave.   Green 😊ХХ   PARK   Chi
Х Arami   Zebra ●● Flo 🍴
W.   Superior   Wolcott   Yuzu Х   Mexique ХХ   Charlatan ХХ
UKRAINIAN   St.   Huron   Noble   Erie   St.
Erie   St.   Paulina   Racine
VILLAGE   Ohio   Armour   Ohio   St.
W.   Grand   Ave.   Х Coalfire   Х Tv
Pizza
Ⓜ Western   A   B   WEST LOOP   C

N

would make even Willy Wonka green with envy. But, if you're looking for something a little less traditional, unusual combinations are the norm at **Black Dog Gelato**, where goat cheese, cashew, and caramel come together for a uniquely satisfying scoop.

SUDS AND SPUDS

The craft beer movement has been brewing in Chicagoland for some time now, where lovers of quality suds and superlative bar snacks find an impressive listing of both in Bucktown and Wicker Park. Regulars at Logan Square's **Revolution Brewing** snack on bacon-fat popcorn and sweet potato cakes while sipping on the in-house Double Fist Pale Ale or Anti-Hero IPA. This holy union between food and beer

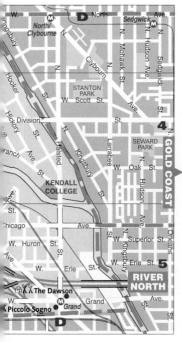

is always reaching epic heights at **Piece**, which not only serves up one of Chicagoland's most popular hand-tossed pizzas but also produces a roster of award-winning beers to accompany its crusty New Haven-style pies. And, for a master class on the wide and wonderful world of craft brews, the noted beer school at Wicker Park's **Map Room** gives students a greater appreciation for the art—though a self-taught tour of the bar's worldwide selection is quite educational and perhaps more enjoyable?

THE LUSH LIFE

Considering its dramatic role in the era of Prohibition, it's no surprise that speakeasy-inspired spots go over like gangbusters in Chicago. **The Violet Hour**, one of the pioneers of the bespoke cocktail trend, still shakes things up late into the night at its no-reservations temple—pair your updated Old Fashioned with frites and aïoli for a truly appetizing experience. The subterranean vaults of a former bank are now home to **The Bedford** whose heavy steel doors, walls of shining safe deposit boxes, and marble-limestone accents lead the way to a warren of lounge-y areas and dining dens. But, if that's not your speed and spicy, south-of-the-border flavor is what you really need? Then make a beeline for **Taco Burrito Express #3** on North Ashland. This fast, family-run, and cash-only favorite doles out *al pastor* and chorizo tacos until the party winds up—at 11:00 P.M. For those who prefer their Mexican food brought to them by *luchadores* donning wrestling masks, cool and quirky

Tamale Spaceship truck has touched down in these parts in the form of a brick and mortar storefront. Sports of another sort grab the spotlight at **Emporium Arcade Bar** where rows of video games and pinball machines from the 1980s bring back memories for those who grew up hitting the arcade. And this of course becomes even more fun when paired with a craft beer or whiskey shot.

KITCHEN SKILLS

Meals at **Kendall College Dining Room** let you brag about knowing future Michelin-starred chefs before they've hit it big. As one of Chicago's premier culinary institutions, this college gives its chef trainee's real-world guidance by way of elegant lunch and dinner service. Floor-to-ceiling windows overlook the fully functioning professional kitchen, where instructors can be seen helping students fine-tune their fine-dining skills. Reservations are required, but the experience is a must for home cooks looking to be inspired. For a more hands-on affair, classes at **Cooking Fools** lets aspiring Food Network stars hone their knife skills or prepare a batch of tamales from scratch. Feeling the need to flaunt your culinary credentials over a dinner party at home? Simply swing by the **Wicker Park & Bucktown Farmer's Market** (open on Sundays) and stock up your pantry with an impressive fleet of fresh produce, artisanal cheeses, and much, much more. Then, peruse the shelves of **Olivia's Market** for painstakingly sourced specialty items and a vast wine and beer selection. **LocalFolksFood** is a family-run enterprise whose chief mission is to develop natural gourmet condiments (mustard and hot sauce anyone?) for slathering over burgers or dogs. You may also purchase these same delightful treats from the lauded **Green Grocer** and make your next cookout the envy of everyone on the block. Finally, feel ready to grow your own vegetables? Sign up for a plot at **Frankie Machine Community Garden** and see if you've got a green thumb!

Ada St.

C3

1664 N. Ada St. (bet. Concord Pl. & Wabansia Ave.)

Phone: 773-697-7069   Dinner Tue – Sun
Web: www.adastreetchicago.com
Prices: $$

Despite its obscure location among the industrial warehouses of far-east Wicker Park, adventurous diners have no trouble seeking out Ada St. Reservations aren't accepted after 6:30 P.M., so the cozy, brick-walled lounge quickly becomes a party space where patrons peruse the wooden cubbies of vinyl to create their own soundtrack.

The menu of small plates is influenced by both hearty gastropub dishes and lighter Mediterranean bites. Tabasco mash ketchup heats up a plate of charred, tender octopus, while a poached egg gilds rich duck confit tossed with *cavatelli*. Even the snappy green beans need nothing more than Dijon butter to shine. Before you take off, show your appreciation by choosing the last item on the menu: a six-pack of beer for the kitchen staff.

Antique Taco

Mexican

B4

1360 N. Milwaukee Ave. (at Wood St.)

Phone: 773-687-8697   Lunch & dinner Tue – Sun
Web: www.antiquetaco.com
Prices: ☜☜   🚇 Damen (Blue)

No reservations and walk-up counter service lead to an inevitable wait at Antique Taco (wear comfortable shoes). Ease the pain by browsing well-curated racks of knickknacks while awaiting market-fresh Mexican food, which arrives on *abuela*-worthy china plates. Place your order and score a wooden stool at a boxy plank table.

Antique Taco piles its corn tortillas with substantial and delicious fillings. Crispy battered fish is spiced up with *sriracha*-tartar sauce and chilled smoked cabbage slaw. Shredded roast pork is rubbed with adobo, glazed in tamarind, and joined with creamy avocado and *queso fresco* for tasty carnitas. Pickled red onions add punch to chunky guacamole. Vodka-spiked *agua frescas* are nice, but the *horchata* milkshake is unmissable.

Arami 🏠

B5

Japanese ✗

1829 W. Chicago Ave. (bet. Wolcott Ave & Wood St.)

Phone: 312-243-1535   Dinner nightly
Web: www.aramichicago.com
Prices: $$ 🚇 Division

Come to this bamboo-clad *izakaya*, with its comfortable sushi bar and soaring skylights, for impressively rendered small plates and specialty cocktails featuring Japanese spirits. The night's *tsukemono* can reveal spicy okra, crisp hearts of palm, and sweet burdock root, and the nigiri selection has showcased New Zealand King salmon topped with pickled wasabi root. The *robata* produces grilled maitakes with Japanese sea salt and black garlic purée; and *gani korroke*, a crunchy-creamy crab croquette, is plated with *togarashi*-spiked mayonnaise.

Don't turn down the all-ice cream dessert menu, which includes enticing flavors like coconut-cinnamon-banana. It comes nestled in granola-like bits of miso-graham cracker crumble for a finish as sweet as it is unique.

Bangers & Lace

B4

Gastropub ✗

1670 W. Division St. (at Paulina St.)

Phone: 773-252-6499   Lunch & dinner daily
Web: www.bangersandlacechicago.com
Prices: $$ 🚇 Damen (Blue)

Despite the frilly connotations, this sausage-and-beer mecca's name refers not to doilies, but to the delicate layers of foam that remain in the glass after your craft brew has been quaffed. You'll also have lots of opportunity to study the lace curtains as you plow through their extensive draft beer menu, noted on blackboards in the comfortably worn-in front bar room.

Decadent foie gras corn dogs (actually French garlic sausage wrapped with soft-sweet brioche cornbread) and veal brats with melted Gouda elevate the humble sausage; while a slew of sandwiches suit simpler tastes. Grilled cheese gilds the lily with taleggio, raclette, and Irish cheddar; and dreamy house-made chips drizzled with truffle oil and malt vinegar are more than a bar snack.

Belly Shack 🐸

Fusion ✗

A2

1912 N. Western Ave. (at Milwaukee Ave.)

Phone: 773-252-1414
Web: www.bellyshack.com
Prices: 💷

Lunch & dinner Tue – Sun

Western (Blue)

Belly Shack's concise menu is an eclectic Asian-Latin mash-up that reflects the Korean and Puerto Rican backgrounds of Chef Bill Kim and his wife, Yvonne Cadiz-Kim. Place your order and take a number—a metal stand that looks like it was made by a high school shop class—then wait for your dishes to arrive.

Korean barbecued beef is a favorite, but regulars enjoy new tastes from the roster of daily specials that can include the *lechon tostada*. This treat is comprised of thinly sliced, slow-roasted pork loin piled high onto a fried corn tortilla with grated sharp cheddar, mashed smoky black beans, and pineapple-cilantro salsa. For dessert, lick up peaks of creamy vanilla soft-serve with topping combos such as caramel and freshly grated Vietnamese cinnamon.

Big Star

Mexican ✗

B3

1531 N. Damen Ave. (bet. Milwaukee & Wicker Park Aves.)

Phone: 773-235-4039
Web: www.bigstarchicago.com
Prices: 💷

Lunch & dinner daily

Damen (Blue)

Bucktown's favorite taqueria has all the fixings for a fiesta. Craft beers, custom-bottled Bourbons, and pitchers of margaritas wash down the affordable abundance. And, despite the grungy décor, the vibe is as intoxicating as the aroma of the *taco de chorizo verde*. The patio is even more of a party, and sun-starved Chicagoans can be spotted out there soon after the groundhog has (or hasn't) seen his shadow.

Tacos are served individually, thus allowing ample opportunity to graze on the likes of the *pollo pibil*—achiote- and citrus-marinated chicken thighs steamed in banana leaves, topped with pickled onion slices and cilantro. Save room for the s*alsa de frijole con queso*, a crock of pinto bean dip accompanied by lime salt-sprinkled tortilla chips.

Birchwood Kitchen

American ✗

A3

2211 W. North Ave. (bet. Bell Ave. & Leavitt St.)

Phone: 773-276-2100

Web: www.birchwoodkitchen.com

Prices: 🫘

Lunch Tue – Sun
Dinner Tue – Fri
🚇 Damen (Blue)

Every neighborhood needs a spot like this, where one can order a bowl of turkey chili followed by sourdough waffles simply because the mood strikes. (Speaking of the chili, it's perfectly spicy and studded with white beans, and those waffles arrive with vanilla bean butter and warm maple syrup.) The vibe here is enhanced by service that charms, and the team goes beyond mere smiles to engage with diners, even offering a cup of coffee for the road to help defend against winter's icy blast.

This "Kitchen's" periwinkle façade stands out like a gem. Inside, a refrigerated glass case displays lemon bars, chocolate chip-banana bread, and other goodies to-go. And, the low-key crowd seated along old church pews lining exposed brick walls, are loyal for good reason.

Black Bull

Spanish 〽

B4

1721 W. Division St. (bet. Hermitage Ave. & Paulina St.)

Phone: 773-227-8600

Web: www.blackbullchicago.com

Prices: 🫘

Lunch & dinner daily

🚇 Division

Like bulls, hungry foodies are drawn to the color red—at least that's what the thinking must be at this chic tapas spot dominated by a neon bull and candy-apple exterior. Inside, glasses of crimson and rosé sangria are in everyone's hands, helping the noise skyrocket as the night wears on.

Look at the colorful chalk-drawn mural above the kitchen, depicting Spanish scenes, products, and food terms, to get a sense of what's on offer. Shareable plates mix tradition with contemporary twists, like crispy hollowed-out *patatas bravas* filled with ketchup and aïoli. A half-dozen pickled mussels arrive in a tin beneath a layer of creamy potato foam; while an excellent consommé poured over a farm egg yolk and truffles is brightened by a dash of manzanilla sherry.

Briciola

B4

937 N. Damen Ave. (bet. Augusta Blvd. & Iowa St.)

Phone: 773-772-0889   Dinner Tue – Sun
Web: www.briciolachicago.com
Prices: $$ 🚇 Division

BYO

After decades of cooking and traveling, Chef/owner Mario Maggi was ready to open a small place—just a crumb, or "una briciola," of a restaurant. This tiny trattoria nestled between Ukrainian Village's brick buildings is indeed a speck of warmth and charm, festooned with party lights on the patio and mustard-toned walls inside.

Traditional Italian cuisine gets personalized tweaks from the chef. *Carpacci* may include paper-thin octopus, beets, or beef; *macaroncini alla Briciola* folds diced Tuscan sausage into a spicy garlic-sage sauce; and a hefty bone-in pork chop, pounded thin, breaded, and pan-fried until golden, is a house classic dressed with arugula and shaved parmesan.

A bottle from the wine shop down the block makes the meal even more convivial.

The Bristol

B2

2152 N. Damen Ave. (bet. Shakespeare & Webster Aves.)

Phone: 773-862-5555   Lunch Sat – Sun
Web: www.thebristolchicago.com   Dinner nightly
Prices: $$

Get to know your neighbors a little better at this dim, bustling haunt boasting a lineup of seasonal American treats with a Mediterranean twist. Regulars sit shoulder-to-shoulder at thick butcher block communal tables or at the concrete bar, squinting under filament bulbs to see the constantly changing menu's latest additions on chalkboards throughout the room. After sharing a Moscow Mule in a frosty copper mug, duck fat fries, or monkey bread with dill butter, it might be time for messy *elotes* tossed with sweet chili jam to be licked off each finger; or an heirloom tomato tart with a SarVecchio cheese crust and shaved onions. Do the right thing and save room for homemade Nutter Butter cookies with dark chocolate sabayon for dipping.

Carriage House

B4

Southern ✗✗

1700 W. Division St. (at Paulina St.)

Phone: 773-384-9700
Web: www.carriagehousechicago.com
Prices: $$

Lunch Sat – Sun
Dinner nightly
 Division

Carriage House brings South Carolina hospitality to the heart of Wicker Park. Gauzy shades cover large windows in the understated dining room. Wire cage light fixtures lend farmhouse flair; while bentwood bistro chairs and tufted leather ottomans add a contemporary touch.

The menu mixes traditional dishes with modern interpretations for a North-South blend of flavor and technique. Velvety Charleston she-crab soup is poured tableside over bright orange roe that bursts in the mouth. A scrumptious house-made garlic bologna- and pimento cheese-sandwich on brioche bridges the worlds of fine dining and country charm. Family-style suppers like a low-country boil with shrimp, clams, and rabbit *chaurice* sausage are meant to be shared around a table of friends.

Charlatan

C5

Mediterranean ✗✗

1329 W. Chicago Ave. (at Throop St.)

Phone: 312-818-2073
Web: www.charlatanchicago.com
Prices: $$

Lunch Sun
Dinner nightly
Chicago (Blue)

Despite what its moniker might suggest, Charlatan is in fact a genuine and authentic show of talent. Hip and comfortable, this gastropub boasts whimsical toile and velvet details, a trio of mounted animal heads, and quality fare that puts the average pub grub to shame.

The menu is anchored by a number of inventive pastas prepared in-house, like charred fennel-stuffed tortellini bobbing in a boldly seasoned porchetta *brodo* hit with fennel pollen and garlic-mustard oil. Unbelievably tender grilled octopus is plated with beef-braised carrots and fried bone marrow-enriched romesco; and the honeycomb-topped chocolate tart tastes as silky as a bowl of pudding. To make the most of your meal, wash it all down with a local brew or wine from a small producer.

49

Coalfire Pizza

Pizza ✗

C5

1321 W. Grand Ave. (bet. Ada & Elizabeth Sts.)

Phone: 312-226-2625
Web: www.coalfirechicago.com
Prices: 💰💰

Lunch Wed – Sun
Dinner Tue – Sun
🚇 Chicago (Blue)

Sure, you could come for a salad, but the focus here is on pizza—and yours should be, too. The cozy room features an open kitchen where pie production is on display for all to see. And in a playful bit of recycling, empty tomato sauce cans on each table become stands for sizzling pizzas churned straight from the 800-degree F coal oven.

This hot spot has its ratio down to a fine art and knows not to burden its thin, crispy crust that's blackened and blistered in all the right places. The mortadella is a delight, with chopped garlic and gossamer slices of peppercorn-flecked sausage. Care to go your own way? Build the perfect pie with toppings that run the gamut from Gorgonzola to goat cheese.

A second location in Lakeview continues to thrive.

Coast Sushi Bar

Japanese ✗✗

B2

2045 N. Damen Ave. (bet. Dickens & McLean Aves.)

Phone: 773-235-5775
Web: www.coastsushibar.com
Prices: $$

Lunch Sat – Sun
Dinner nightly

♿

BYO

Dimly lit but lively, this high-volume sushi bar cranks out a remarkable variety of rolls to keep up with demand especially on weekends from noon till night. Two spacious dining rooms and a narrow sushi counter armed with wood-framed chairs accommodate the chatty crowds. Bring your own sake, wine, and bottle opener to make the wait more tolerable.

The broad selection of Japanese dishes ranges from signature maki and nigiri to innovative appetizers like fried soft-shell crab with mango-shallot salsa. Miso soup spiked with jalapeño is served in a coffee cup for easy sipping. A deep bowl of boatman *chirashi* is laden with orange *tobiko*, pickled veggies, shiso leaves, and an array of sashimi. Dig right in or grab a sheet of toasted nori for a custom-wrapped hand roll.

Cumin 🐸

B3

Indian ✗

1414 N. Milwaukee Ave. (bet. Evergreen & Wolcott Aves.)

Phone: 773-342-1414
Web: www.cumin-chicago.com
Prices: 😊😊

Lunch Tue – Sun
Dinner nightly
🚇 Damen (Blue)

This proudly-run blend of Nepalese and Indian eats sits among a plethora of bars, coffee shops, and vintage stores in boho-centric Bucktown. While fans of the sub-continent love Cumin for its clean and modern surrounds, linen-lined tables struggle to contain the myriad plates that pile up during its ubiquitous lunch buffet.

Paintings of mountain scenes decorate crimson-red walls and prep diners for an authentic range of flavorful food hailing from the Northeast. Nibble on crispy samosas or onion *bhajis* (finely shredded onion fritters) teamed with mint chutney. Then soak pieces of buttery naan in rich and vibrant *saag* bobbing with soft chunks of chicken. For a sweet finale, dig into a creamy pistachio *kulfi* or opt for a light and fruity mango *lassi*.

The Dawson 🐸

D5

Gastropub ✗✗

730 W. Grand Ave. (at Halsted St.)

Phone: 312-243-8955
Web: www.the-dawson.com
Prices: $$

Lunch Sat – Sun
Dinner nightly
🚇 Chicago (Blue)

"See and be seen" should be the motto of this hip spot, where globe lights shine like beacons through the façade's towering windows. Inside, a wraparound bar attracts spirited guests like moths to a flame. A lengthy communal table and open kitchen with a chef's counter offer multiple opportunities for meeting, greeting, and eating.

Cocktails like the Surfer Rosa, which balances tequila and mezcal with blood orange and chilies, loosen-up diners jonesing for big flavors. When hunger strikes, caramelized onion sabayon, potato confit, and garlicky pea shoots add depth to an Arctic char fillet. And lest you forget dessert, Bourbon-pecan bread pudding set upon flash-frozen vanilla cream and drizzled with sea salt-butterscotch sauce, is meant for sharing—or not.

Dove's Luncheonette

American ✗

B3

1545 N. Damen Ave. (bet. Milwaukee & Pierce Aves.)

Phone: 773-645-4060   Lunch & dinner daily
Web: www.doveschicago.com
Prices: $$ 🚇 Damen (Blue)

With a chill, throwback vibe, all-day breakfast, and a drink list with more than 70 labels of agave spirits, this One Off Hospitality roadhouse is a Wicker Park hipster's dream come true. To drive the point home, the diner features wood-paneled walls, counter seating, a record player spinning the blues, and of course, Tex-Mex fare listed on a wall-mounted letter board. The daily special may be a blueberry quinoa pancake, while savory favorites include crunchy buttermilk fried chicken with chorizo verde gravy or the farmer's cheese-stuffed Anaheim *chile relleno*, served in a pool of tomato-serrano sauce with pasilla chiles and pickled chayote slices. Pies from Hoosier Mama Pie Co. are a grand finale; try the lemony Atlantic Beach with a saltine crust.

En Hakkore

Korean ✗

B3

1840 N. Damen Ave. (bet. Churchill & Moffat Sts.)

Phone: 773-772-9880   Lunch & dinner Mon – Sat
Web: N/A
Prices: 🍜   🚇 Damen (Blue)

Healthy doesn't have to be humdrum. This simple little Korean eatery, run by a husband-and-wife team and decorated with more than a hint of whimsy, specializes in big bowls of *bibimbap*. You choose your rice and protein, be it pork or barbecue beef, decide on the heat level and then dive straight in—up to 16 different vegetables are used and they're as tasty as they are colorful. Also worth trying are the steamed *mandoo* (pork dumplings) and the curiously addictive tacos made with *paratha*.
Simply place your order at the counter, grab a plastic fork and, if you're with friends, commandeer the large communal table. There's no alcohol (and it's not BYOB) so instead take advantage of an invigorating soft drink from the fridge. You'll feel so virtuous.

Enso

Japanese ✗✗

B3

1613 N. Damen Ave. (bet. North & Wabansia Aves.)

Phone: 773-878-8998   Lunch & dinner daily
Web: www.ensochicago.com
Prices: $$ 🚇 Damen (Blue)

All bases are covered at Enso, from tempura to ramen and *chirashi* to teriyaki, but it's mostly about maki. There are fairly classic combinations of ingredients on offer, but also more challenging blends of flavor. If you can't decide then you can always "make your own maki"—but you'll only have yourself to blame should the memory of your chosen flavors return to haunt you at a later date. The homemade steamed buns are also worthy; a filling of roasted pork belly with pickled vegetables inside one of these little pillows of delight is hard to beat.

The vaulted room looks like a Goth's cellar, all black and moody, with the open kitchen at the far end shining like a beacon of hope. Larger parties should try to snare one of the low-slung booths.

Flo

Southwestern ✗

C5

1434 W. Chicago Ave. (bet. Bishop St. & Greenview Ave.)

Phone: 312-243-0477   Lunch Tue – Sun
Web: www.flochicago.com   Dinner Tue – Sat
Prices: ⊜⊜   🚇 Chicago (Blue)

It's not Santa Fe, but the Southwest is well represented in West Town through the chili-packed flavors at Flo. This early meals joint cranks out a variety of spicy and tasty Tex-Mex dishes for diners crowded into the sunlight-dappled dining room. Pressed-tin ceilings, mirrors mounted on exposed brick, and narrow plank floors add quaint appeal.

Made-to-order breakfast and brunch is served until 2:30 P.M., allowing ample time for Fruity Pebbles French toast or breakfast burritos. *Pollo picante* quesadillas get a kick from pickled jalapeños and Jack cheese. *Sopapillas* come in sweet as well as savory varieties like house-made chorizo with scrambled eggs and cheddar. As in the Southwest, fresh red or green chili is always offered as an option.

Frontier

C4

American ✗

1072 N. Milwaukee Ave. (bet. Noble & Thomas Sts.)

Phone: 773-772-4322
Web: www.thefrontierchicago.com
Prices: $$

Lunch Sat – Sun
Dinner nightly
🚇 Division

If Davy Crockett is king of the wild frontier, then chances are he'd be smitten by this stylish, modern-day saloon. To start, a taxidermied grizzly bear, wolf, and bison head hang among football-flaunting flat-screens behind the 40 foot-long bar. And even Frontier's menu drives home the hunt-and-gather theme, with dishes divided into three sections: "Fried," "Foraged," and "Whole Animal Service."

Carnivores revel in the chef's signature duck tacos juiced with salsa verde, while pescetarians beg for crab Benedict—a superb staple of toasted muffins with sweet crabmeat, soft poached eggs, and spicy Hollandaise. Calorie-counters love the well-dressed house salad, but for dessert, there is no passing up on crispy sugar doughnuts—gently caressed with a rum-apple sauce in true Crockett fashion.

Green Zebra 🐲

C5

Vegetarian ✗✗

1460 W. Chicago Ave. (at Greenview Ave.)

Phone: 312-243-7100
Web: www.greenzebrachicago.com
Prices: $$

Dinner Tue – Sun

🚇 Chicago (Blue)

Named after a popular heirloom tomato variety, Chef/owner Shawn McClain's vegetarian standby is beloved among Chicagoans looking for an upscale meat-free experience. Japanese minimalism inspires the small space's décor, with palms and bamboo lining the entry and earthy tones throughout the room.

Diners graze on shared small plates paired with organic and biodynamic wines. Creamy hen of the woods mushroom pâté, served with caramelized Vidalia onion marmalade and toasted bread, ensures that no one misses the meat. Peppery arugula purée and a dollop of crème fraîche balance silky celery root soup. Thin shards of dark chocolate and dense peanut mousse with currant coulis are a match made in vegan heaven; a crushed pretzel garnish gilds the lily.

Izakaya Mita

B2

Japanese ✗

1960 N. Damen Ave. (at Armitage Ave.)

Phone: 773-799-8677   Dinner Wed – Mon
Web: www.izakayamita.com
Prices: 😊   🚇 Western (Blue)

This Bucktown addition is a family-run tavern worth seeking out for its homespun take on *izakaya* eats and gracious hospitality.

Start with single-serve sake in a jar so cute you'll want to smuggle it home, or a cocktail inspired by Japanese literature (the Norwegian Wood, a delicious interpretation of the Haruki Murakami novel "*Noruwei no Mori*," blends whiskey, Luxurdo, sweet vermouth, and orange bitters). The array of small plates brims with creativity and flavor: *tsukune* are coarse-ground, delightfully chewy, and achieve a mouthwateringly charred exterior from having been grilled over *bincho-tan*; while *tako-yaki* are as delicious as any found on a Tokyo sidewalk. *Korroke*, a panko-crusted potato croquette, comes with *tonkatsu* sauce for delicious dunking.

Kokopelli

B4

Mexican ✗

1324 N. Milwaukee Ave. (bet. Hermitage Ave. & Paulina St.)

Phone: 773-698-7670   Lunch Sat – Sun
Web: www.kokopellichicago.com   Dinner nightly
Prices: 😊   🚇 Division

This Wicker Park taqueria is the next best thing to a getaway from the shores of Lake Michigan to the Pacific Coast of Mexico. Sure, it's north of the border, but the cooking is as authentic as it gets. Inside, the space is warm and comfortable with bar seating aplenty, bright green banquettes, and an accent wall painted a shade that can only be described as Baja blue.

Seafood is the focus of the unique menu, and octopus reigns supreme. The eight-armed delicacy works its way into a number of items including *pulpo* ceviche and the Kraken taco, which features a grilled, pesto-marinated version. Equally excellent are the poblano tacos stuffed with smoked rainbow trout, charred corn, and a creamy salsa made from roasted pumpkin seeds and Serrano chiles.

Las Palmas

B3

1835 W. North Ave. (at Honore St.)

Phone: 773-289-4991
Web: www.laspalmaschicago.com
Prices: $$

Lunch Sat – Sun
Dinner nightly
Damen (Blue)

Vivid décor complements the spirited flavors on the menu at Las Palmas, from the colorful Mexican artwork on adobe-style walls to exposed ductwork welded to resemble a scaly dragon winding through the deceptively large space. If the weather suits, the outdoor garden or glassed-in atrium beckon; if not, a cozy fireplace in the front room keeps things intimate.

The cocktail menu draws inspiration from both South and Central America, featuring a variety of capirinhas and mojitos alongside inventive cucumber-lime and pineapple margaritas. Vibrant and modern Mexican dishes like crispy *taquitos* with chicken *barbacoa*, pickled red onion, and tangy salsa *cruda*; as well as seafood-filled cornmeal empanadas with peanut-jalapeño relish showcase the kitchen's flair.

Le Bouchon

B2

1958 N. Damen Ave. (at Armitage Ave.)

Phone: 773-862-6600
Web: www.lebouchonofchicago.com
Prices: $$

Lunch & dinner Mon – Sat

Damen (Blue)

Pressed-tin ceiling? Check. Brick-and-Dijon color scheme? Check. Close-knit tables in a snug space? Check. A warm welcome from an actual Frenchman? Check. Owner Jean-Claude Poilevey has fashioned the quintessential bistro experience at Le Bouchon, where straightforward French food never goes out of style. The informal atmosphere gets convivially raucous as the night goes on with regulars lining the bar and petite dining room.

Familiar, approachable favorites rule the menu: *soupe à l'oignon*, wearing its traditional topper of broiled Gruyère on a moist crouton, oozes and bubbles over the sides of a ramekin; and an ample fillet of *saumon poché* napped in beurre blanc is the essence of simplicity. A lunch prix-fixe keeps the wallet light but belly full.

Lillie's Q

B3

Barbecue ✗✗

1856 W. North Ave. (at Wolcott Ave.)

Phone: 773-772-5500
Web: www.lilliesq.com
Prices: $$

Lunch & dinner daily

🚇 Damen (Blue)

Bucktown's urban barbecue shack takes a scholarly approach to 'cue, as each table bears a caddy stocked with six regionally specific sauces for embellishing the slow-smoked meats to come. Cocktails served in Mason jars are a specialty made from "moonshine" offered at three proof levels, and servers in modern mechanic's shirts tend to the crowds clamoring for heaps of smoked meats rubbed in "Carolina dirt." Tri-tip is tender and pink-tinged after its time in the smoker with the joint's signature dry rub; while the succulent smoked hot link rests in a butter-griddled, top-sliced brioche bun served with Southern-style coleslaw.

And if at-home grilling is your thing, you'll be pleased to know that the mouthwatering sauces are available by mail order.

Mana Food Bar 😀

B4

Vegetarian ✗

1742 W. Division St. (bet. Paulina & Wood Sts.)

Phone: 773-342-1742
Web: www.manafoodbar.com
Prices: 💰💰

Lunch Sat
Dinner nightly
🚇 Division

Feeling like your body needs a jump-start? Mana, whose name translates to "the life force coursing through nature," is a good place to get your mojo back. Though welcoming to vegans, vegetarians, gluten-free diners, and anyone who's looking for a nutrient boost, it's not just health food: the small space also offers a full bar with sake cocktails, smoothies, and freshly squeezed juices.

Mana may be a tiny spot, but its diverse menu of vegetarian dishes is big on taste—and spice. Korean *bibimbap* mixes a roster of vegetables like pea pods, roasted carrots, and pickled daikon with a fresh sunny side-up egg; while horseradish and cracked black pepper sneak into macaroni and cheese.

House-made hot sauce with serranos and jalapeños adds extra pep to any dish.

Mexique

Mexican ✕✕

C5

1529 W. Chicago Ave. (bet. Armour St. & Ashland Ave.)

Phone: 312-850-0288   Lunch & dinner Tue – Sun
Web: www.jbandala.mx/mexique
Prices: $$ 🚇 Chicago (Blue)

Large groups fill most of the banquettes in this slender space, but a bar stretching half the length of the room makes it easy for smaller parties to stop in for a glass of sangria. A large rear window offers a glimpse of Chef Carlos Gaytan at work in the kitchen, and congratulatory graffiti from visiting chefs provides a fun distraction on the way to the restroom.

Many of Mexique's contemporary Mexican dishes are inspired by classical French techniques. From the *platos fuertes*, the *mar y tierra* is a delightful composition of Michoacán-style braised pork belly over silken sweet potato purée dressed with a complex dark *mole* prepared from over 20 ingredients; sea scallop with bacon-apple jam and pickled onions complete this intoxicating one plate feast.

Mindy's Hot Chocolate

Contemporary ✕✕

B3

1747 N. Damen Ave. (bet. St. Paul Ave. & Willow St.)

Phone: 773-489-1747   Lunch Wed – Sun
Web: www.hotchocolatechicago.com   Dinner Tue – Sun
Prices: $$ 🚇 Damen (Blue)

Bucktown wouldn't be the same without this sweet spot run by pastry chef extraordinaire, Mindy Segal. Diners walk past decadent hot chocolate mix and cookies on display before hitting an industrial-chic space fitted out with sleek dark wood, caramel-brown walls, and chocolate-toned leather banquettes.

Get the point yet? Decadent chocolate is the name of the game here, though guests will be delighted to discover savory items beyond their expectations. Try the roasted tomato soup, garnished with bright green onion slivers; or the BLT with pesto aïoli, heirloom tomato, avocado, and thick, crispy maple-cayenne bacon. An affogato—a scoop of coffee-cocoa nib ice cream paired with the chef's namesake hot chocolate—makes for the perfect finale.

Mirai

B4

Japanese ✕✕

2020 W. Division St. (bet. Damen & Hoyne Aves.)

Phone: 773-862-8500
Web: www.miraisushi.com
Prices: $$

Dinner Tue – Sun

📺 Damen (Blue)

Mirai is a bit like Disney World. You know it's not real, but who cares? The Japanese food is westernized and by no means traditional, but unless you're dining out with Mr. Shinzo Abe, rest assured that nobody will cry foul.

Bold and appetizing flavors beg to take center stage. It's really all about the fish at this spot—just look around and you'll find most devotees feasting on sashimi, *unagi*, and maki. If raw fish doesn't float your boat, take a shot at one of the house specialties like *kani nigiri*, a baked king crab concoction. There is also a surfeit of hot dishes—think chicken *togarashi* with spicy, sweet, and tangy flavors. Affable and alert service combined with a relaxed atmosphere make this a hit among area residents.

Mott St. 😊

B3

Fusion ✕

1401 N. Ashland Ave. (at Blackhawk St.)

Phone: 773-687-9977
Web: www.mottstreetchicago.com
Prices: $$

Dinner Tue – Sat

📺 Division

New Yorkers know Mott St. as the bustling artery in the heart of Chinatown, but to Chicagoans the name connotes something off the beaten path. Inside the low-slung, standalone red structure, a chicken wire-caged pantry is stocked with jars of red pepper, black vinegar, and other pungent edibles—all of which appear again in the food on your plate.

Offerings at this hip haven crisscross the globe, melding diverse ingredients for an utterly unique dining experience. Shredded kohlrabi substitutes green papaya for a Thai-inspired salad tossed with candied shrimp, poached chicken, and plenty of fresh herbs. Stuffed cabbage bears a Korean accent with tender chunks of slow-braised pork, tangy Napa cabbage kimchi, and crunchy sticky rice.

Nando Milano Trattoria

Italian Italian 🍴🍴

A4

2114 W. Division St. (bet. Hoyne Ave. & Leavitt St.)

Phone: 773-486-2636   Dinner nightly
Web: www.nandomilano.com
Prices: $$ 🚇 Division

A corner bar television constantly tuned to (European) football, vintage *aperitivo* posters, and a welcoming patio tailor-made for afternoon glasses of prosecco: charismatic host Dario Vullo has installed his own little slice of Milan in Wicker Park. The chic trattoria offers an intensely Italian menu and wine list to match the authentic accents of Vullo and family.

A trio of *arancini* are playfully prepared, with each rice ball sporting a unique shape—sphere, triangle, and cube—to denote a special filling like Bolognese ragù and smoked mozzarella; or mascarpone and spinach. House-made pastas like beet gnocchi in saffron sauce steal the show from equally flavorful and fresh focaccia sandwiches layered with creamy burrata and Prosciutto di Parma.

Oiistar

Asian 🍴

B3

1385 N. Milwaukee Ave. (bet. Paulina & Wood Sts.)

Phone: 773-360-8791   Lunch & dinner Tue – Sun
Web: www.oiistar.com
Prices: 🍜🍜   🚇 Damen (Blue)

It's easy to mistake Oiistar for yet another trendy ramen joint—but don't. Sure, it's got all the design hallmarks—from a minimalist wood-planked dining room and industrial open kitchen, to a turned-up soundtrack. But, the internationally influenced menu makes it much more than your average slurp shop.

In fact, "It's A Small World" could be the unofficial theme song for their lineup of steamed buns and comforting ramen bowls showcasing noodles hand-pulled in-house each day: fiery *kochujang* complements barbecue chicken on the *pollo* bun, while the saltimbocca bun goes Italian with sage, prosciutto, and mozzarella. Extra special is the *chadolmen*, which blends a tangle of delicate wheat noodles with brisket and ground pork in a spicy miso and kimchi broth.

Owen & Engine

A1

Gastropub ✗✗

2700 N. Western Ave. (at Schubert Ave.)

Phone: 773-235-2930
Web: www.owenengine.com
Prices: $$

Lunch Sat – Sun
Dinner nightly

Owen & Engine's charm extends from its glossy black façade into its warm polished wood interior and all the way to the second-floor dining room that sees action into the wee hours. Brocade wallpaper, gas lights, and studded leather club chairs lend a Victorian feel. A frequently changing draft list always features a few selections pulled from a beer cask (or "engine").

British-inspired gastropub grub matches the impressive roster of brews and Pimm's cups. Bar nibbles like mustard-glazed soft pretzels with Welsh rarebit for dipping; or peanuts tossed in *sriracha*, Worcestershire, and brown sugar cater to the snacking sort. Hearty entrées like bangers and mash feature house-made Slagel Family Farm's pork sausage and potatoes smothered in onion gravy.

Piccolo Sogno

D5

Italian ✗✗

464 N. Halsted St. (at Milwaukee Ave.)

Phone: 312-421-0077
Web: www.piccolosognorestaurant.com
Prices: $$

Lunch Mon – Fri
Dinner nightly
Grand (Blue)

In-the-know locals craving mouthwatering Italian fare head to this swanky spot, usually packed with a dressy crowd. Inside, they are welcomed by a palette of rich, cool hues, crystal-beaded light fixtures that hang overhead, and an open kitchen boasting a wood-burning oven.

Piccolo Sogno's rustic, yet refined menu offers traditional dishes with a twist. A version of the ubiquitous beet salad (both red and golden) is elevated here by shaved fennel, a drizzle of bright citrus oil, and a dollop of creamy, lush buffalo milk ricotta. If you need further encouragement, let us recommend the rabbit. Braised in a white wine sauce redolent of rosemary and lemon, the tender meat is served with wilted escarole and porridge-like semolina pudding.

Red Door

International 〣

B2

2118 N. Damen Ave. (at Charleston St.)

Phone: 773-697-7221
Web: www.reddoorchicago.com
Prices: $$

Lunch Sat – Sun
Dinner Tue – Sun

Even with no sign, it's easy to find this funky Bucktown bar: that red door is impossible to miss. Grab a metal barstool or a raised wooden banquette for an evening of seasonal cocktails, craft beers, and internationally inspired pub fare. On warm evenings, the backyard patio becomes romantic with candlelit communal tables and a canopy of twinkling lights overhead.

Gastropub classics take a spin around the globe, while often featuring local ingredients (sometimes right from the patio). *Bulgogi*-style hanger steak and eggs is a weekend brunch favorite, layering tender chunks of meat over scrambled eggs with a pile of spicy, hangover-busting kimchi on the side. Poutine boasts Wisconsin's Brunkow cheese curds and spicy curry gravy.

Ruxbin

American XX

B4

851 N. Ashland Ave. (at Pearson St.)

Phone: 312-624-8509
Web: www.ruxbinchicago.com
Prices: $$

Dinner Tue – Sun

🚇 Division

BYO

Refurbished and repurposed is the rationale behind Ruxbin's funky décor. In the tiny first-floor space, salvaged apple juice crates form wall panels and seat belts become chair backs. Up a few stairs, a stainless steel communal table offers a view into the semi-open kitchen.

Meals usually start with popcorn seasoned with changing flavors like sesame and seaweed—a preview of the menu's mix of American and international ingredients. A fresh oyster trio gets three distinct garnishes: *sambal*-pickled ginger, tangy apple mignonette, and pork belly with a smoked aroma revealed by lifting a glass cloche. Seared scallops and pork carnitas meld with black raisin emulsion. Rest easy that you won't miss the booze here after trying a house-made basil-hibiscus soda.

Schwa ఢ

Contemporary ✗

1466 N. Ashland Ave. (at Le Moyne St.)

Phone:	773-252-1466	Dinner Tue – Sat
Web:	www.schwarestaurant.com	
Prices:	$$$$	🚇 Division

BYO

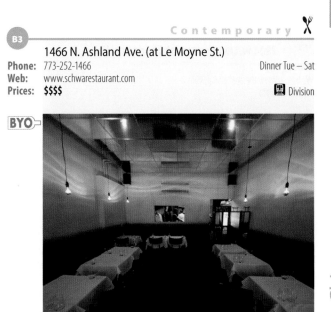

There comes a point when pared-down style jumps from being easy-to-miss and becomes hard-to-forget (think security grills on the façade). When a utilitarian and self-consciously bare interior seems modern and industrial. When temporarily disconnected phone lines and full mailboxes make every hipster in the room feel like he hit the jackpot to score this reservation. The booming hip-hop peppered with expletives reflects the deeply talented chefs' ethos, going well beyond laissez-faire to reach the point of "we don't give a damn." That said, you probably won't either. The food really is that good.

The 14-course nightly tasting has no menu really to speak of, but there are plenty of tattooed servers ready to describe each dish with details that come at you rapid fire.

While some courses may seem way out of balance in terms of flavor and textural complexity, others have been known to show nuance and delicacy—as evident in the smooth and fine Osetra caviar sitting in a mélange of cashew nut purée, tender hearts of palm, and fried plantain chips; or a single quail egg *raviolo* with its glossy and unctuous brown butter sauce. Desserts can be pure genius, beginning with watermelon ice and unagi ice cream—a sprinkle of *togarashi* perfectly foils the intensity of this treat.

Smoke Daddy

American ✗

B4

1804 W. Division St. (at Wood St.)

Phone: 773-772-6656

Web: www.thesmokedaddy.com

Prices: ⊝⊝

Lunch & dinner daily

🚇 Division

After a renovation doubled the size of this barbecue joint and live music venue, it's become easier to grab a bite of burnt ends and a touch of the blues. The original room still oozes soul and smoke from its brick walls and vinyl floor, while the new space is bright and airy with a retractable glass door leading to an umbrella-shaded patio.

No matter which barbecue style you pledge allegiance to—Kansas City, Memphis, or Carolina—you'll find something worth gnawing on, from moist pulled pork and chicken to spare and baby back ribs. Order any sandwich "Daddy Style" to get a few slices of brisket slapped on top, or fill up on jalapeño cornbread. Fans of the in-house Bloody Mary mix should grab a bottle to-go, along with smoked pig ears in a true doggy bag.

Takito Kitchen

Mexican ✗✗

B4

2013 W. Division St. (bet. Damen & Hoyne Aves.)

Phone: 773-687-9620

Web: www.takitokitchen.com

Prices: $$

Lunch Fri – Sun

Dinner Tue – Sun

🚇 Division

Chicago's upscale taco circuit gets a new contender with Takito, where fresh ingredients make Latin-inspired food sing. Tequila takes pride of place in a chile-salted margarita, while skylights and mirrors make the narrow, mod-industrial space seem even brighter and larger. Sure, you can get a corn tortilla here, but sesame and hibiscus options let the kitchen get creative as evident in tacos filled with cornmeal-crusted redfish, beef *barbacoa*, or tamarind-chayote *pequin*. Shared plates like *sope de carne asada* blur culinary boundaries with the addition of Brunkow cheddar and green onion kimchi. It's an across-the-board mishmash of colorful flavors, but certainly a good way to go over the top.

Sister spot Bar Takito also boasts a notably concise menu.

Taus Authentic

International ✗✗

B4

1846 W. Division St. (bet. Marion Ct. & Wolcott Ave.)

Phone: 312-561-4500
Web: www.tausauthentic.com
Prices: $$

Lunch Sun
Dinner Tue – Sun
🚇 Division

You'll want to make an evening of it at this Wicker Park newcomer, where a stylish front lounge—complete with a working fireplace—makes for a cozy spot to enjoy a beer or cocktail. Then you may proceed to linger over a meal in the beautiful dining room, a modern vision of wood, powder blue velvet, and plate glass windows.

Chef Michael Taus has designed a menu made for grazing: think charcuterie, cheese, and starters including a sunchoke dosa. Made from lentils and basmati rice, this lacy crêpe is topped with chunks of tender sunchokes in a spicy red curry sauce sweetened by golden raisins and candied pumpkin seeds. A tasting portion of pan-seared fluke, plated with sweet chili vinaigrette and a Korean-style pancake studded with dried shrimp, is equally delicious.

Taxim

Greek ✗✗

B3

1558 N. Milwaukee Ave. (bet. Damen & North Aves.)

Phone: 773-252-1558
Web: www.taximchicago.com
Prices: $$

Dinner nightly

🚇 Damen (Blue)

Though Taxim channels the spirit of Greece in its food, the Moroccan-esque décor takes inspiration from Turkey and other Mediterranean coastal neighbors. The large room glints with light from hanging Moorish lanterns and copper-topped tables. Share small plates on the sidewalk patio to take full advantage of Wicker Park people-watching.

Many of Taxim's dishes get a modern twist while remaining respectful to the islands' traditional cuisine. Wild Greek oregano and ouzo-preserved lemon offer a perfect balance to roasted Amish Miller Farms chicken; while *loukoumades* prove that no one can resist fried dough, especially when tossed in wildflower honey and topped with rosewater-infused pastry cream. The all-Greek wine list is an adventure for oenophiles.

tocco

Italian Italian XX

B4

1266 N. Milwaukee Ave. (bet. Ashland Ave. & Paulina St.)

Phone: 773-687-8895   Dinner Tue – Sun
Web: www.toccochicago.com
Prices: $$ 🚇 Division

Are we in Milan or Wicker Park? Tocco brings haute design and fashion to the table with such upscale textural touches as polished resin, faux ostrich skin, and bubblegum-pink accents in this sleek black-and-white space. Don your catwalk best before visiting: a fashion-centric display near a long communal table hints at the chichi theme present throughout.

The décor is cutting-edge, but the menu respects and returns to Italian standbys. *Gnocco fritto*, a dough pillow served with charcuterie, is irresistible to even the most willowy fashionistas; while cracker-crisp artisan pizzas from wood-burning ovens are equally pleasing. Traditional *involtini di pollo*, pounded thin and rolled around prosciutto, gets a hit of brightness from lemon and white wine sauce.

Trenchermen

Contemporary XX

A3

2039 W. North Ave. (bet. Hoyne & Milwaukee Aves.)

Phone: 773-661-1540   Lunch Sat – Sun
Web: www.trenchermen.com   Dinner nightly
Prices: $$ 🚇 Damen (Blue)

In old-timey slang, a trencherman is a hearty eater and drinker, a definition that lets you know what you're in for at this glossy but comforting Wicker Park gastropub. Housed in a former Russian bathhouse, the black-and-white tiles and notched brick walls dividing the eclectic warren of rooms give a nod to the former tenant of this 1920s building.

Bar snacks and weekend brunch are taken just as seriously as full-on lunch and dinner here. Corned beef adds a manly touch to eggs Benedict, especially when drizzled with piquant *choron* sauce. Dense pretzel cinnamon rolls straddle the salty-sweet line. A menu favorite at any time of day, fried pickle tots are served with kicky beet-tinged red onion yogurt and thinly sliced chicken breast *bresaola*.

TWO 😋

American ✗

C5

1132 W. Grand Ave. (at May St.)

Phone: 312-624-8363   Dinner Tue – Sun
Web: www.113two.com
Prices: $$ 🚇 Chicago (Blue)

This urban interpretation of a Midwest tavern was set up by two owners, features two chefs, second-hand furnishings, and an address whose last digit is—you guessed it—the number two. Step past the vintage Toledo scales to arrive at this reclaimed wood-paneled space dressed with antique meat cleavers, quaint ceiling fans, and large barn doors.

If that doesn't scream farm-to-fork cuisine, consider what's being whipped up in the open kitchen (the banquette across from it affords the best view): a ramp *raviolo* filled with ricotta, a perfectly cooked hen's egg, and enhanced by brown butter and shiitakes; or a halibut fillet with cherry tomatoes and asparagus. On the sweet front, homemade puppy chow is chilled, crisp, and delicious with a uniform sugar dusting.

Yuzu

Japanese ✗

B5

1715 W. Chicago Ave. (bet. Hermitage & Paulina Sts.)

Phone: 312-666-4100   Lunch & dinner daily
Web: www.yuzuchicago.com   🚇 Chicago (Blue)
Prices: ⊜⊜

Ancient and modern accents work in harmony at Yuzu, where hand-painted anime murals catch the eye above weathered plank wainscoting. A century-old wooden slab finds new life as a sushi counter, where diners sip sodas from Ball jars and groove to hip tunes.

Whole ginger- and garlic-glazed grilled squid is sliced into rings, then sprinkled with scallions and creamy jalapeño sauce. Succulent *robata*-grilled skewers, purchased by the piece, arrive with specialized accompaniments like marinated pork shoulder with sweet chili sauce or *kalbi*-glazed short rib. The *tobiko*-topped Black Sea roll is one of a roster of quirky but manageably sized maki, all of which arrive with an artistic flourish—think intricate, paisley-patterned sauces painted onto plates.

Chinatown & South

For years, the Red Line was the only true link between Chinatown and the South Loop. They may be neighbors geographically, but continue to remain distinct opposites in the culinary, architectural, and demographic spheres. Recent development on both sides of the line has brought the two worlds closer together, combining old and new flavors that make them irresistible to Chicago food lovers. The Great Chicago Fire spared many of the South Loop's buildings, making this architecture some of the oldest in the city. Residential palaces like the Glessner House and Clark House are now open for tours, but a quick walk along Prairie Avenue gives a self-guided view of marvelous mansions. Further north, those massive former lofts along Printers Row have been converted into condos, hotels, bookstores, and restaurants, as has the landmark Dearborn Station—the oldest train depot in Chicago.

SUN-UP TO SUNDOWN

The South Loop has the breakfast scene covered—quite literally—with dishes piled-high at casual neighborhood spots. Sop up an Irish Bennie adorned with corned beef hash or any number of egg favorites from frittata to French toast at **Yolk**, located on the southern end of Grant Park. The aptly named **Waffles** smothers its signature squares with both sweet and savory flavors. Varieties like cheddar cheese are topped with coffee-braised short ribs, while red velvet waffles come with strawberry compote and whipped cream cheese. As long as you're adding to your cholesterol count, stop at one of the many locations of **Ricobene's** for a breaded steak sandwich or big slab of juicy barbecue ribs.

If you're strolling through the Museum Campus for lunch, grab cash for a bite at **Kim & Carlo's Hot Dog Stand** between the Field Museum and Shedd

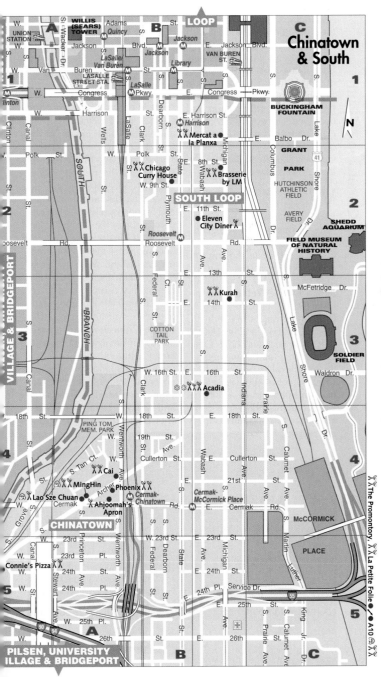

A

WILLIS
(SEARS)
TOWER

UNION
STATION

W. Wacker Dr.

Adams

St.

Quincy

B

St.

Jackson

Jackson
Blvd.

LaSalle/
Van Buren

LaSalle
St.

Jackson

Library

E. Jackson Blvd.

VAN BUREN
ST.

C

Chinatown
& South

W. Van Buren

LASALLE
STREET STA.

W. Congress

Pkwy.

E. Congress — Pkwy.

N

1

linton

Canal

St.

Clinton

St.

W. Harrison

Wells St.

St.

Harrison

LaSalle St.

Clark St.

E. Harrison St.

Harrison

BUCKINGHAM
FOUNTAIN

GRANT

PARK

HUTCHINSON
ATHLETIC
FIELD

Lake Shore

Balbo Dr.

41

2

Polk St.

Canal St.

S. Clinton St.

W. Polk St.

Dearborn St.

Mercat a
la Planxa

State St.

Chicago
Curry House

W. 9th St.

8th St.

Michigan

Wabash

Brasserie
by LM

SOUTH LOOP

AVERY
FIELD

SHEDD
AQUARIUM

oosevelt Rd.

Plymouth St.

E. 11th St.

Eleven
City Diner

Roosevelt

Roosevelt

Rd.

Ave.

FIELD MUSEUM
OF NATURAL
HISTORY

2

S. Canal St.

BRANCH

S. Federal St.

Ct.

E. 13th St.

14th

Kurah

S.

St.

McFetridge Dr.

COTTON
TAIL
PARK

SOLDIER
FIELD

3

Lake Shore

Waldron Dr.

18th St.

S. Canal St.

W. 16th St. E.

Clark St.

16th

St.

Indiana

Acadia

18th St.

E. 18th St.

Prairie

3

PING TOM
MEM. PARK

Wentworth

19th
St.

St.

Tan Ct.

Cullerton St.

Wabash

Cullerton

Calumet Ave.

4

4

Cai

MingHin

Lao Sze Chuan

Cermak

Archer

Ahjoomah's
Apron

Phoenix

Cermak-
Chinatown

E.

21st

St.

Cermak-
McCormick Place

Cermak

Rd.

McCORMICK

CHINATOWN

Princeton Ave.

23rd

Wentworth

W. 23rd St.

Dearborn St.

E. 23rd

State

St.

Michigan

PLACE

Martin Luther King Jr. Dr.

5

W.

Stewart Ave.

23rd
Pl.

24th
St.

S. Canal St.

W. 24th St.

Connie's Pizza

Federal St.

E. 24th St.

Calumet Ave.

Prairie Ave.

5

W. 25th Pl.

90
94

W. 26th

A

St.

24th Pl. Service Dr.

24th Pl.

E. 25th St.

Service Dr.

55

B

26th St.

King Jr. Dr.

C

PILSEN, UNIVERSITY
VILLAGE & BRIDGEPORT

PILSEN, UNIVERSITY VILLAGE & BRIDGEPORT

The Promontory, La Petite Folie, A10

Aquarium. Vegetarians applaud their special veggie dog with all the Chicago toppings, while everyone gets a great skyline view from Grant Park. For a glimpse of real Windy City politics in action, grab a seat at **Manny's**, the venerable coffee shop and deli; then sink your teeth into a giant pastrami on rye or a plate of crispy potato pancakes, while watching the city's wheelers and dealers do business.

When night falls, the South Loop really gets rocking. Buddy Guy himself often hits the stage at **Buddy Guy's Legends**, where live blues ring out nightly. Catch a set while digging into classic Southern soul food like fried okra, gumbo, or jambalaya. Similarly **The Velvet Lounge**, founded by late jazz legend Fred Anderson, moved from its original location in 2006, but still puts on a heckuva show. Other cutting edge and contemporary musicians also perform here several times a week. For a blast from the past but of a different sort, comedy and history come together at **Tommy Gun's Garage**.

This dolled-up speakeasy hosts a riotous nightly dinner theater, allowing audiences to participate.

CHINATOWN

That ornate and arched gate at Wentwoth Avenue and Cermak Road welcomes locals and visitors alike to one of the largest Chinatowns in America. This iconic structure is an apt symbol for the neighborhood, where the local population is still predominantly Chinese-American and history happily co-exists with contemporary life. The two-story outdoor **Chinatown Square** mall encompasses everything from restaurants and small boutiques to big banks, thereby giving the community a buzzing culinary and cultural introduction. Many of the restaurants here offer classic Chinese-American fare that is an amalgam of Sichuan and Cantonese cuisines, but for a homemade spread stock up on all things authentic from **Chinatown Market**. This large and "super" store is outfitted with endless rows of Lee Kum

Kee sauces, fresh seafood, fresh produce, and more. At local standby **Go 4 Food**, a Sichuan beef lunch combo or wok-fried and hundred-spiced chicken continue to sate those pungent palates. Let the kids pick out a few intriguing Japanese sweets at **Aji Ichiban**, housed in the Chinatown Square mall, where bins filled with rainbows of foil-wrapped Japanese candy offer opportunities for tricks or treats. Unless you can read the characters on the wrappers, you're in for a surprise—though the store offers samples before charging by the pound.

Home cooks as well as haute chefs know Chinatown isn't just a destination for dining out. It's also great for filling up on all the good eats necessary for a great home-cooked meal. In fact, the entire neighborhood is a specialty marketplace of sorts: find a mind-boggling array of fresh-pulled noodles at **Mayflower Food**; while

Hong Kong-based tea shop, **Saint's Alp Teahouse**, serves quick snacks and a variety of tea-based drinks including the widely popular milk tea and taro milk tea—with or without tapicola pearls. Freshly baked fortune and almond cookies are a revelation at **Golden Dragon Fortune Cookies**, but those craving a wider range of sweets, may pour over the cases at **Chiu Quon Bakery** filled with cakes and other cream- or custard-filled pastries. Meanwhile, additional inspiration can be found by perusing a cookbook (or ten) from the Chinese Cultural Bookstore. Finally, pay homage to the perennial city pastime by watching the White Sox do their thing on U.S. Cellular Field, or the "Monsters of the Midway" take the gridiron inside Soldier Field's formidable walls.

Museums and learning centers showcase Windy City's heritage from all angles. Apart from the stately collection of historic buildings in Grant Park's Museum Campus, this neighborhood is also home to Willie Dixon's Blues Heaven Foundation, whose mission is to preserve its musical legacy. With swooping green roof ornaments, the Harold Washington Library Center is impossible to miss, but an equally worthy site is the glass-ceilinged winter garden hidden inside. **Iron Street Farm**, a seven-acre urban field in Bridgeport, is part of Chicago's focus on eradicating food deserts within city limits. Here, local residents grow vegetables, raise chickens, and cultivate bees as part of the farm's educational programs. Respect!

Acadia ⌘ ⌘

Contemporary XxX

B3

1639 S. Wabash Ave. (bet. 16th & 18th Sts.)

Phone: 312-360-9500   Dinner Wed – Sun
Web: www.acadiachicago.com
Prices: $$$

Dining here is like being let in on a secret, uncovered along this rather unfortunate strip of no-man's land. The unexpected yet grand space employs nothing but neutral grays that extend from the concrete façade to the cushioned chairs and silvery beads dividing the center of this lofty room in half. Service is gracious and professional—the kind we should all expect but is hard to find.

Unusual and artful presentations may begin with canapés arriving in a box of moss or along a branch. Follow this with hamachi served as a brilliant study of flavor and balance, showcasing silky and beautifully marbled fish, placed on a bed of coconut-infused rice pudding with dabs of black garlic, bits of finger lime, and lemongrass-spiced chutney. Genius and luxury are at play in the sinfully rich Australian Wagyu beef, served red and fleshy with classic Bordelaise, roasted maitake to magnify the umami, chunks of sweet lobster, and lobster foam to lend an ocean-like airiness to the plate.

Finish meals on a smooth and fudgy note with chocolate pudding cake accompanied by coconut gelée for striking visual contrast, a swipe of caramel, rum ice cream, candied black walnut, and toasty little slivers of fresh coconut.

Ahjoomah's Apron

Korean 🍴

A4

218 W. Cermak Rd. (bet. Archer & Wentworth Aves.)

Phone: 312-326-2800   Lunch & dinner daily
Web: www.ahjoomahchicago.com
Prices: 💰💰   🚇 Cermak-Chinatown

Thanks to this modern, casual space, southside Chicagoans no longer need to head uptown for their fix of authentic Korean food. While there are no tabletop grills smoking up the dining room, the picnic-style tables fill quickly with generous portions of kitchen-grilled *bulgogi*, warming stews, and *banchan*.

A crimson kimchi *jjigae* broth, seamlessly balanced between sour and spicy, bobs with soft chunks of tofu and pork. *Bibimbap* sizzles in a stone bowl, letting the requisite crispy crust form on the bottom while diners dig into a mountain of glistening sweet soy *kalbi*, crunchy vegetables, and fried egg. Want to feel virtuous about your meal? Wall posters tout the health benefits of traditional Korean ingredients like *doenjang*, an umami-rich soybean paste.

A10 👻

Italian 🍴🍴

C5

1462 E. 53rd St. (at Harper Ave.)

Phone: 773-288-1010   Lunch Sun
Web: www.a10hydepark.com   Dinner nightly
Prices: $$

A10 is a highway that winds through the Italian Riviera, but its detour through Hyde Park comes courtesy of prolific restaurateur, Matthias Merges. University of Chicago students and staff populate this split space, building a buzz over marble-topped rounds in the low-key bar area or dark wood tables in the convivial dining room.

Like the décor, the menu deftly balances comfort and sophistication. A single fresh pasta ribbon folded back and forth becomes lasagna filled with succulent veal osso bucco, fresh baby oregano leaves, and both quark and *Parmigiano* cheeses tucked within each layer. Tender chunks of octopus, Niçoise olives, and saffron-tinged slaw dress a chickpea fritter; and rustic chocolate beignets with toasted meringue triangles sweeten the finish.

Brasserie by LM

French ✕✕

800 S. Michigan Ave. (bet. 8th & 9th Sts.)

Phone: 312-431-1788
Web: www.brasseriebylm.com
Prices: $$

Lunch & dinner daily

🚇 Harrison

Taking its cue from the neighborhood cafés that dot the boulevards of Paris, Brasserie by LM brings a bit of stylish French spirit to Michigan Avenue. Despite its chi-chi surroundings at the Essex Inn across from Grant Park, this is an understated modern diner, serving up affordably priced bistro fare from morning to night.

The croque monsieur is a totem of indulgence, layered with ham and béchamel, then lavishly buttered for grilling and blanketed with melted cheese. Skin-on pommes frites pair pleasantly with the sandwich, but grilled Caesar salad drizzled with a garlicky dressing is slightly more inculpable. Splurge on the signature *teurgoule*, a classic rice pudding from Normandy made with plump, toothsome grains and heaps of cinnamon.

Cai

Chinese ✕✕

2100 S. Archer Ave. (at Wentworth Ave.)

Phone: 312-326-6888
Web: www.caichicago.com
Prices: 🍪🍪

Lunch & dinner daily

🚇 Cermak-Chinatown

Cai rolls out the red carpet for a lavish experience on the second floor of Chinatown Square, making it the local choice for celebratory seafood dinners or quick midday dim sum. The banquet hall-style room is grand and formal, complete with crystal chandeliers and professional service.

To say there's a lot to choose from is an understatement, as there are nearly 100 rolled, crimped, steamed, and fried dim sum options alone. Highlights include flaky puff pastry turnovers filled with sweet and savory barbecue pork; and large lotus leaves that envelope tender sticky rice mixed with chicken, liver, and crab. When the dim sum parade ends at 4:00P.M., the menu shifts to an equally vast selection of Cantonese dishes like crunchy stir-fried lotus root with ginger.

Chicago Curry House

Indian XX

B2

899 S. Plymouth Ct. (at 9th St.)

Phone: 312-362-9999
Web: www.curryhouseonline.com
Prices: 💲💲

Lunch & dinner daily

🚇 Harrison

Maybe you sniff the wafting aromas of ginger, garlic, and cumin first; maybe you hear the sitar music tinkling its welcoming notes as you enter. Either way, you know immediately that Chicago Curry House is a commendable showcase of Indian and Nepalese cuisine.

The lunch buffet lets you eat your fill for under $12, with crispy *pappadum*, baskets of fresh naan, and must-have curries like the Nepalese *khasi ko maasu* with chunks of bone-in stewed goat in a velvety cardamom- and black pepper-sauce. Indian butter chicken, creamy and rich in a tomato- and *garam masala*-spiced stew, is equally sumptuous. À la carte offerings are even more extensive.

The staff has helpful suggestions for dealing with the area's draconian parking restrictions, so call ahead for tips.

Connie's Pizza

Pizza XX

A5

2373 S. Archer Ave. (at Normal Ave.)

Phone: 312-326-3443
Web: www.conniespizza.com
Prices: $$

Lunch & dinner daily

🚇 Halsted

No one knows who Connie was, but the name happened to be on the building bought by Jim Stolfe in 1963, and it stuck. Even Chicagoans who've never set foot in this spacious location know about its near-monopoly at White Sox games (including a complimentary shuttle to U.S. Cellular Field) and constant presence at citywide festivals. Those who do step inside the flagship come for the convivial vibe and, of course, pizza.

Of the many options, the deep-dish is Miss Popularity, but it's fun to go one further with a stuffed pizza topped with a buttery crust. The garlic- and oregano-laced sauce is pleasantly tangy, and carnivores sing the praises of Connie's plump fennel sausage. Call ahead to forego the 45-minute cooking time and pick your pie up at the drive-thru.

Eleven City Diner

B2

Deli ✗

1112 S. Wabash Ave. (bet. 11th St. & Roosevelt Rd.)

Phone: 312-212-1112
Web: www.elevencitydiner.com
Prices: 😋

Lunch & dinner daily

🚇 Roosevelt

Nosh on a mile-high sandwich or chocolate malt at Eleven City Diner, a modern revival of the classic Jewish deli. Gleaming subway tiles play off retro leather booths and swiveling barstools, while jazz in the background keeps things moving with chutzpah and finesse.

Diner standards include patty melts, sandwiches piled with corned beef or pastrami, knishes, and latkes. Bubbie's chicken soup comes bobbing with a fluffy matzo ball the size of a baseball; while Junior's cheesecake from Brooklyn or a triple-decker wedge of red velvet cake sates all the sweet-loving guests. A full-service deli counter offers salamis and smoked fish to-go. For a true blast from the past, stop by the candy stand near the entry stocked with Bazooka Joe and other favorites.

Kurah

B3

Middle Eastern ✗✗

1355 S. Michigan Ave. (at 14th St.)

Phone: 312-624-8611
Web: www.kurahchicago.com
Prices: $$

Lunch & dinner daily

🚇 Roosevelt

The phrase "small plates" doesn't always translate to "great value," but Kurah offers an exception to the rule with its affordable selection of shareable, Middle Eastern-influenced dishes. Featuring Arabic-inspired wallpaper and upholstered seats, the setting is as warm and cozy as the open grill blazing away in the kitchen.

Build a meal from hot and cold tapas options like *muthowma*, a blend of silky potatoes and whipped garlic that's perfect for scooping onto warm pita bread. Larger meat platters like a single juicy lamb and beef *kifta kabob*, served with roasted vegetables and golden saffron rice, make a hearty meal for one. For dessert, dark chocolate oozes invitingly between layers of phyllo and crushed walnuts in a tasty twist on classic baklava.

Lao Sze Chuan

A4

2172 S. Archer Ave. (at Princeton Ave.)

Phone:	312-326-5040	Lunch & dinner daily
Web:	www.tonygourmetgroup.com	
Prices:	😊😊	🚇 Cermak-Chinatown

The news clips papering its front windows don't lie: this flagship branch of Tony Hu's mini-chain is a longtime Chinatown hot spot with a second outpost in Streeterville. But hot is a double entendre here, and a crimson-themed décor along with mod acrylic chairs printed with chili peppers clues guests in to the kitchen's propensity for spicing things up.

If the book-length menu seems overwhelming, scan the list of favorites at the beginning for a quick pick—be sure to avoid any items marked with a chili if you'd rather walk on the mild side. As for the hits, chili oil and peppercorns give numbing heat to crunchy, translucent sheets of beef tendon, and succulent Xinjiang-style cumin lamb is generously coated in cumin seeds and tossed with fresh, zippy ginger.

La Petite Folie

C5

1504 E. 55th St. (at Harper Ave.)

Phone:	773-493-1394	Lunch Tue – Fri
Web:	www.lapetitefolie.com	Dinner Tue – Sun
Prices:	$$	

♿ Though its tree-lined courtyard off 55th Street may not be as picturesque as the Tuileries, La Petite Folie remains a transporting Gallic hideaway in Hyde Park. The graceful lace-curtained dining room and curvaceous wood bar draws scholarly types from nearby University of Chicago, with prices that satiate student budgets.

A retinue of French classics like whole trout Grenobloise are refreshed by seasonal market ingredients at the hands of Chef/co-owner Mary Mastricola. Slices of smoked duck drizzled with black currant vinaigrette get an earthy touch from apple-walnut compote in an elegant lunch salad. Even the wine list chosen by Mastricola's husband Michael is an all-French affair, with numerous by-the-glass choices from Bordeaux to Chablis.

Mercat a la Planxa

Spanish XX

B1

638 S. Michigan Ave. (at Balbo Ave.)

Phone: 312-765-0524
Web: www.mercatchicago.com
Prices: $$

Lunch & dinner daily

🚇 Harrison

Within a cavernous space in the Renaissance Blackstone hotel, Mercat a la Planxa recreates the hustle and bustle of a Spanish marketplace with an extensive menu of Catalan tapas. The dining room's tightly packed tables are perfect for grazing, and soaring ceilings along with cathedral windows overlooking Grant Park impress locals and out-of-towners alike.

Plump, crunchy *gambas al ajillo* are bathed in buttery garlic sauce with a hint of lemon, and servers add to the excitement by drizzling jus over skewers of bacon-wrapped lamb loin medallions at the table. This is the kind of place where nary a splash of sauce is left behind, so use those slices of brioche—with a swipe of sweet onion purée for good measure—to sop up every last delicious drop.

MingHin 😊

Chinese XX

A4

2168 S. Archer Ave. (at Princeton Ave.)

Phone: 312-808-1999
Web: www.minghincuisine.com
Prices: 🪙🪙

Lunch & dinner daily

🚇 Cermak-Chinatown

Conveniently situated on the ground level of Chinatown Square, MingHin is a stylish standby that draws a diverse crowd to the neighborhood. Spacious dining rooms separated by wooden lattice panels offer seating for a number of occasions, from casual booths and large banquet-style rounds to specially outfitted tables for hot pots.

Dim sum is a popular choice even on weekdays, with diners making selections from photographic menus rather than waiting for a passing cart. Among the numerous options, juicy *har gao*, stuffed with plump seasoned shrimp, always hit the spot. Pan-fried turnip cakes are simultaneously crispy and creamy, studded with bits of pork and mushroom, and fluffy, subtly sweet Malay steamed egg cake is a rare find for dessert.

Phoenix

A4

Chinese ✖️✖️

2131 S. Archer Ave. (bet. Princeton & Wentworth Aves.)

Phone: 312-328-0848   Lunch & dinner daily
Web: www.phoenixchinatownchicago.com
Prices: 🍴   🚇 Cermak-Chinatown

Dim sum lovers get the best of both worlds at Phoenix, a comfortable room that boasts a grand view of the Chicago skyline. Here, stacks of bamboo baskets are wheeled to tables on signature silver trolleys for a classic dim sum experience—yet each diner's selection is cooked to order for truly fresh and steaming hot bites. The proof is in the soft and poppable shrimp-and-chive dumplings and the fluffy white buns stuffed with chunks of barbecue pork.

Those looking for larger portions will appreciate the meandering menu, which also boasts Hong Kong-style stir-fry and clay pot dishes alongside Americanized Chinese classics. Fillets of steamed sea bass swim in soy oil on a large oval platter, sprinkled with a touch of slivered scallion to brighten the delicately flaky fish.

The Promontory

C5

American ✖️✖️

5311 S. Lake Park Ave. West (bet. 53rd & 54th Sts.)

Phone: 312-801-2100   Lunch & dinner daily
Web: www.promontorychicago.com
Prices: $$

Equal parts restaurant, watering hole, and music venue, The Promontory brings a much-needed gathering place to the Hyde Park community. Under lofty ceilings trimmed with black iron beams and sleek wood accents, urbanites sip hand-crafted cocktails around a central bar.

A white-hot fire blazes away in the open kitchen, providing the "hearth to table" food trumpeted on the menu. Smoky roasted feta arrives in a pool of balsamic vinegar and oil with a generous assortment of briny olives, while shatteringly crisp black trumpet mushrooms and pickled shallot add piquant crunch to Nantucket bay scallops. For dessert, sweet brûléed marshmallow and a scoop of graham cracker ice cream sit atop a moist chocolate soufflé, a reverse take on s'mores.

Gold Coast

GLITZ & GLAMOUR

The moniker says it all: the Gold Coast is one of the Windy City's most posh neighborhoods, flaunting everything from swanky high-rises along Lake Shore Drive to dazzling boutiques dotting Michigan Avenue. Stroll down the Magnificent Mile only to discover that money can indeed buy it all. Then, head over to Oak Street for yet another spree and watch millionaires mingle over Manolos and heiresses rummage for handbags.

APPLAUDING THE ARTS

Through all this glamor, Gold Coast architecture is not just notable but stunning. And, mansions crafted in regal Queen Anne, Georgian Revival, or Richardsonian Romanesque styles are unequivocally breathtaking. However, this neighborhood is not all about the glitz; it is also deeply committed to the arts, housing both the Museum of Contemporary Art as well as the world-leading Newberry Library. Culture vultures are sure to uncover something edgy and unique at A Red Orchid Theater, after which the exotic Indian lunchtime buffet at **Gaylord** seems not only opportune, but perhaps obligatory? This prized subterranean location, with its spelled-out menu items and well-stocked bar, is sought by both aficionados as well as anyone hungering for free appetizers during happy hour. Nearby, Le Cordon Bleu College of Culinary Arts houses **Technique**, a student-run restaurant where diners get to glimpse the next food fad in Chicago kitchens.

RAUCOUS NIGHTS

It's a well-known fact that the Gold Coast also knows how to party. Visit any nightclub, pub, or restaurant along Rush and Division to get a sense of how the cool kids hold it down—untill well after dawn. By then, find breakfast on the burner at the **Original Pancake House**. This may seem like a lowbrow treat for such a high-brow neighborhood, but really can there be anything more rewarding than fluffy pancakes, towering waffles, and sizzling skillet eggs after a late-night spree? Another perfect place to start your day is at Italian deli **L'Appetito**, which also serves up hearty breakfasts, baked goods, and Italian-style sammies. But, rest assured as there is also some darn good junk food to be had in this white-gloved capital of prosperity. American comfort classics like sliders, burgers, and mac and cheese find their way into the menu at **LuxBar**, a dynamic lounge and bar with some of the best people-watching. Need some sweet?

Surely these robust eats should be sealed by a cup that revives? **TeaGschwendner** is just the spot where locals lose themselves in a world of exotic selections. And, if you don't feel like steeping your own "Sencha Claus" blend, then snag a seat at **Argo Tea** where clouds of whipped cream and flavorful iced drinks are all part of the carte—it's just like Starbucks without the coffee! Serious cooks and gourmands make a beeline for **The Spice House**, where a spectrum of high quality and often esoteric spices, seasonings, and rubs (ground and blended in-house) make for an integral part of any delightful dinner party at home.

Make your way to to one of **Teuscher's** outposts for decadent dark chocolate or even **Corner Bakery Cafe** for a fleet of bakery fresh treats—the golden-brown cinnamon crème cake topped with crumbles of cinnamon streusel and powdered sugar has been drawing residents for over two decades and is dubbed a signature for good reason.

A QUICK FIX

With so many awards under its belt and boasting the best ingredients in town, **Gold Coast Dogs** is packed to the gills (er, buns), perpetually. Inside, everyone is either a regular or on the verge of becoming one, mainly due to their deliciously charred dogs, usually topped with gooey cheddar. Or, simply humor your hot dog hankering by joining the constant queue outside **Downtown Dogs**.

HEAVEN ON EARTH

In keeping with its quintessentially elegant and old-world repute, the Gold Coast allows you to don Grandma's pearls for afternoon tea at **The Drake's Palm Court**. Daintily sip, not slurp, your tea while listening to the gentle strumming of a harp and sampling a tasty selection of sandwiches, pastries, and scones. If it's good enough for the Queen, it will certainly do. Also housed in The Drake Hotel, warm and luxurious **Cape Cod Room** is famous for seafood specials and old-world cocktails, presented in oversized brandy snifters. And, over on Delaware Place, first-class wines and cocktails aren't the only thing heating up the scene at **Drumbar**—a rooftop hot spot at the Raffaello Hotel that lets the fashionable crowd frolic alfresco at night (and during the day on Sunday).

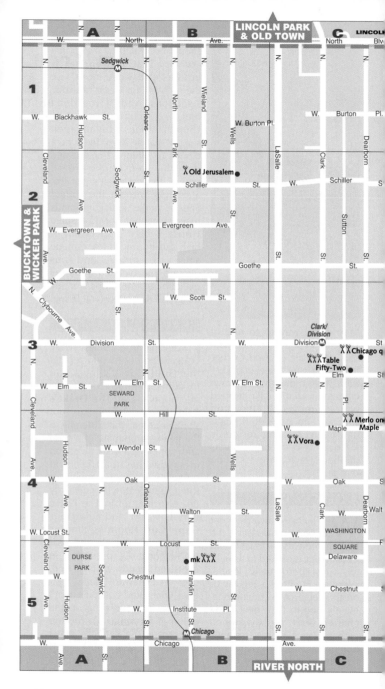

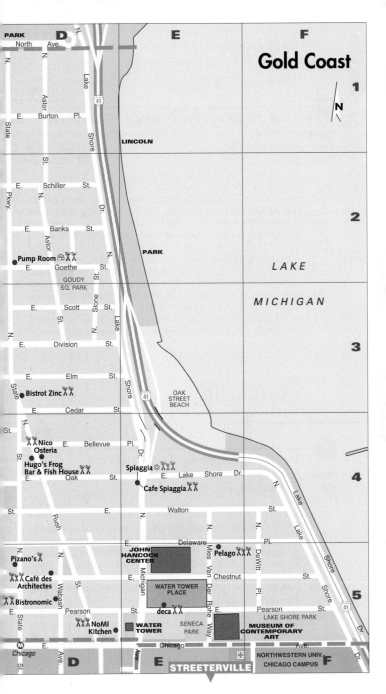

Gold Coast

N

PARK
North Ave.

LINCOLN

PARK

LAKE

MICHIGAN

E. Burton Pl.

E. Schiller St.

E. Banks St.

● Pump Room ⚬ X X

E. Goethe St.

GOUDY
SQ. PARK

E. Scott St.

E. Division St.

E. Elm St.

● Bistrot Zinc X X

E. Cedar St.

OAK
STREET
BEACH

X X Nico
Osteria ●

Hugo's Frog
Bar & Fish House X X

Spiaggia ⚬ X X X
E. Lake Shore Dr.

Cafe Spiaggia X X

E. Bellevue Pl.

E. Oak St.

E. Walton

E. Delaware

● Pelago X X X

● Pizano's X

JOHN
HANCOCK
CENTER

X X X Café des
Architectes

E. Chestnut

X X Bistronomic

WATER TOWER
PLACE

Pearson

X X X NoMI
Kitchen ●

deca X X

E. Pearson St.

LAKE SHORE PARK

WATER
TOWER

SENECA
PARK

MUSEUM OF
CONTEMPORARY
ART

Ⓜ Chicago

E. Chicago Ave.

STREETERVILLE

NORTHWESTERN UNIV.
CHICAGO CAMPUS

83

Bistronomic

French

D5

840 N. Wabash Ave. (bet. Chestnut & Pearson Sts.)

Phone: 312-944-8400
Web: www.bistronomic.net
Prices: $$

Lunch Wed – Sun
Dinner nightly
Chicago (Red)

Tucked away from the buzz of the Magnificent Mile, Bistronomic is a great place to cool your tired heels. Jaunty red awnings beckon brightly, and the revolving door spins guests into a warm room that's focused on the bonhomie of dining with friends. Oxblood walls, gray banquettes, and a central bar play up the bistro feel, while the kitchen conveys creativity with fresh renditions of tasty classics.

Rusticity and elegance come together in a fillet of Lake Superior whitefish that is pan-seared to golden-brown and matched with spring ratatouille, preserved lemon, and puréed eggplant. Exquisitely crisp *feuilletine* is a glamorous upgrade to the classic Kit Kat bar, folded with hazelnuts, bittersweet chocolate, and finished with a sweet-tart orange sauce.

Bistrot Zinc

French

D3

1131 N. State St. (bet. Elm & Cedar Sts.)

Phone: 312-337-1131
Web: www.bistrotzinc.com
Prices: $$

Lunch & dinner daily

Clark/Division

If you couldn't tell from the bright red exterior and hand-painted windows, Bistrot Zinc is indeed a classic dressed in mosaic-tiled floors, lemon-tinted walls hung with mirrors, woven rattan chairs, and yes, that curvaceous zinc bar. Suits, locals, and Gold Coast power shoppers populate the tables from lunch through dinner, as white-aproned waiters happily uncork bottles of *rouge et blanc*.

Don't look for modern surprises on the menu; contentment here is attained through uncomplicated but expertly prepared French dishes from frites to frisée. Whole trout, pan-fried until golden and napped with butter sauce, hits all the right notes; while daily standards like croque monsieur or French onion soup are enhanced by more ambitious monthly specials.

Café des Architectes

Contemporary XxX

D5

20 E. Chestnut St. (at Wabash Ave.)

Phone: 312-324-4063
Web: www.cafedesarchitectes.com
Prices: $$$

Lunch & dinner daily

Chicago (Red)

European sophistication lends extra polish to this shimmering contemporary spot in the Sofitel Hotel, where "Bonjour" is passed around freely by the mostly French staff. The dining room is just as chic, with crimson banquettes, black-and-white portraits of the city's architectural marvels, and floor-to-ceiling windows with striking steel accents.

The seasonally shifting lineup of small plates is simple but creative, like a single Wianno oyster dabbed with fennel cream and crowned with spoonfuls of both sturgeon and faux citrus caviar. Market-inspired entrées include butternut squash ribbons curling over tender beef short rib and vanilla-tinged salsify purée.

For a more casual, small bites affair, move to Le Bar, the hotel's chic watering hole.

Cafe Spiaggia

Italian XX

E4

980 N. Michigan Ave. (at Oak St.)

Phone: 312-280-2750
Web: www.spiaggiarestaurant.com/cafe
Prices: $$

Lunch & dinner daily

Chicago (Red)

After an extensive renovation, Cafe Spiaggia is sporting a sophisticated, contemporary new look, with beautiful white tufted leather banquettes, dark wood tables, and black-and-white photos gracing the wall. Towards the back, leather stools line a long white marble bar, and majestic floor-to-ceiling windows offer views of Magnificent Mile.

The menu is solid and approachable Italian—a decidedly less formal alternative to sophisticated older sister, Spiaggia, next door. Kick things off with the *piadini*, a thin Romagna-style flatbread, grilled and folded around delicious fillings like mortadella, maybe a caprese, or even chicken and honey. Then, slide on over to the kitchen's focus—*gemelli* humming with summer beans, preserved lemon, Pecorino Romano, and Prosciutto di Parma.

Chicago q

Chicago ▲ Gold Coast

C3

Barbecue ✗✗

1160 N. Dearborn St. (bet. Division & Elm Sts.)

Phone: 312-642-1160   Lunch & dinner daily
Web: www.chicagoqrestaurant.com
Prices: $$ Clark/Division

American barbecue is anything but honky tonk in this gorgeous Gold Coast setting. Everything within the bright, bi-level space seems to gleam, from the colossal contemporary light fixtures and sun-splashed skylights to the shimmering open kitchen and myriad bottles of whiskey at the bar.

Elegant preparations elevate traditional barbecue elements, like a spicy pairing of cornmeal-dredged fried green tomatoes and habañero-glazed pork belly with red onion-mango relish. Baby back ribs—so tender they're practically falling off the bone—are served with a trio of house-made sauces for dipping and slathering. And pig lovers planning for a large party can order a whole pork shoulder carved tableside with a picnic-worthy spread of slaw, beans, and cornbread.

deca

E5

Contemporary ✗✗

160 E. Pearson St. (at Water Tower Place)

Phone: 312-573-5160   Lunch & dinner daily
Web: www.decarestaurant.com
Prices: $$ Chicago (Red)

Part of the Ritz-Carlton's expansive 12th floor lobby, deca is a casual haunt that still keeps a few high-end accents around. Paintings hung in gilded frames add to the attractiveness in the seated dining area; and a gently trickling sculptural fountain (illuminated by a skylight) offers an auditory escape from the lobby's background buzz.

The well-edited menu features light, seasonal dishes that are skillfully prepared. Two large pillows of freshly made squash ravioli are garnished with hearty kale pistou, pickled wild mushrooms, and toasted pepitas. Wild salmon with a crunchy mustard crust is bathed in luxurious garlic-red wine jus. Finish in style with a wedge of tangy lemon tart decorated with fresh raspberries and set atop a neat pool of coulis.

Hugo's Frog Bar & Fish House

American ✕✕

D4

1024 N. Rush St. (bet. Bellevue Pl. & Oak St.)

Phone: 312-640-0999
Web: www.hugosfrogbar.com
Prices: $$

Lunch Sat – Sun
Dinner nightly
Clark/Division

Housed in a sprawling setting adjacent to big brother Gibson's, Hugo's always seems packed. The vast dining room sets white linen-topped tables amidst dark polished wood and pale walls decorated with a mounted swordfish, fish prints, and model ships. Hugo's bar draws its own crowds with abundant counter seating.

The menu focuses on a selection of fish preparations as well as steaks and chops. These are supplemented by stone crab claws, oysters, crab cakes, chowders, and sautéed frog's legs. Speaking of frog's legs, the restaurant takes its name from the nickname of owner Hugo Ralli's grandfather, General Bruce Hay of Her Majesty's Imperial Forces.

Bring a football team to share a slice of the Muddy Bottom Pie, a decadent (and enormous) ice cream cake.

Merlo on Maple

Italian ✕✕

C4

16 W. Maple St. (bet. Dearborn & State Sts.)

Phone: 312-335-8200
Web: www.merlochicago.com
Prices: $$$

Dinner nightly

Clark/Division

Inside a graciously decorated Victorian townhouse, Chef/owner Luisa Silvia Marani proudly showcases the bounty of her native Bologna with an Emiliana-inflected accent and delicious Northern Italian fare. Her frequently changing roster of luscious dishes are edible billboards for the foods of the region—think *mortadella di Bologna* and *tartufi neri del'Umbria*.

Rabbit ragù clings to delicate parsley-flecked bow tie pasta tossed with *Parmigiano-Reggiano* and copious handfuls of butter. Wine-braised bone-in lamb shank, served in its own rich sauce, needs little else to shine. Signature *budino di mascarpone, cioccolato e caffé* is the standard-bearer for proper tiramisù, accompanied by tart sugar-coated red currants to offset the creamy sweetness.

mk

 American XxX

B5

868 N. Franklin St. (bet. Chestnut & Locust Sts.)

Phone: 312-482-9179   Dinner nightly
Web: www.mkchicago.com
Prices: $$$ 🚇 Chicago (Brown)

After nearly two decades in business, larger than life "mk" still welcomes all to Chef/owner Michael Kornick's eponymous flagship. Rich brown tones warm up the former paint factory's lofty interior, which features a skylit space that's beloved citywide for big nights and romantic evenings.

There's a seasonal dish here to sate every appetite, whether diners are seated at linen-draped tables or perched on sleek stools in the lounge area. Bar bites offer upscale indulgences like bison sliders tucked into bone marrow-buttered focaccia, while a dual preparation of tartares—yellowfin tuna with Moroccan olives complementing Scottish salmon with charred red onion—could be a meal on its own. For dessert, citrusy "Where troubles melt like lemon drops" is every bit as charming as its name.

Nico Osteria

Italian XX

D4

1015 N. Rush St. (bet. Bellevue Pl. & Oak St.)

Phone: 312-994-7100   Lunch & dinner daily
Web: www.nicoosteria.com
Prices: $$$ 🚇 Chicago (Red)

Buzz around Nico Osteria has already reached deafening levels, especially since this Paul Kahan spot isn't tucked into a gentrifying corner of the city, but situated smack dab in the center of the chic Gold Coast. Communal bar seating keeps the space humming with energy, but moody lighting conspires to keep the vibe relaxed.

Though billed as Italian-inspired cooking, the kitchen takes liberties with traditional dishes on the seafood-heavy menu. Well-grilled and generously oiled sourdough *fett'unta* topped with combinations like *baccalà* and Dungeness crab are rustic introductions to the meal. Ask for more bread to soak up the Neapolitan-style ragù—a skillet bubbling with goodies like a swordfish meatball and slabs of grilled pork belly in a tomato gravy.

NoMI Kitchen

American

D5

800 N. Michigan Ave. (entrance on Chicago Ave.)

Phone: 312-239 4030   Lunch & dinner daily
Web: www.nomirestaurant.com
Prices: $$$ Clark/Division

A hushed aerie awaits on the seventh floor of the Park Hyatt at NoMI Kitchen. Let the dapper staff whisk you through the hotel lobby and elevator to a glassed-in dining room with Water Tower views. A semi-open kitchen doesn't detract from the lush but restrained décor, and a breezy terrace offers an alfresco option with a different menu.

Chef Ryan LaRoche's impressive, ingredient-driven dishes are equally inspired by Eastern and Western cuisines. Fresh fish makes for a seaworthy selection of sushi and maki, while pickled pepper jam and sweet pine nut streusel pair with orbs of fried caponata-style eggplant that are crispy on the outside and perfectly silky within. End with a parade of house-made ice cream flavors like toasted vanilla marshmallow.

Old Jerusalem

Middle Eastern

B2

1411 N. Wells St. (bet. North Ave. & Schiller St.)

Phone: 312-944-0459   Lunch & dinner daily
Web: N/A
Prices: ☜☜   Sedgwick

Set on a charming and centrally located stretch of Old Town, this family-run Middle Eastern favorite has been eagerly accommodating its happy customers for years.

The menu focuses on Lebanese classics, such as tabbouleh with cracked wheat, scallions, and tomatoes, seasoned with lemon, olive oil, and plenty of crisp, green parsley. Hummus arrives rich with tahini, perhaps accompanying the likes of grilled chicken kebabs and traditional flatbreads. Finish with flaky-sweet baklava.

While the décor may not impress, Old Jerusalem manages to make its well-worn look feel cozy and comfortable for everyone. Very reasonable prices, family-friendly service, and generous portions make this *the* neighborhood go-to, whether dining in or taking out.

Pelago

Italian Italian XXX

E5

201 E. Delaware Pl. (at Mies van der Rohe Way)

Phone: 312-280-0700
Web: www.pelagorestaurant.com
Prices: $$$

Lunch & dinner daily

Chicago (Red)

Adjacent to Hotel Raffaello, the elegance of this brick structure is accentuated by large arched windows. Inside, the bi-level room wears a crisp style à la high ceilings, eminently comfortable leather seats, and a soft azure-blue color scheme.

If the décor doesn't transport you to the Mediterranean in a flash, look to the regional Italian menu with ingredients imported directly. A salad of plum tomatoes topped with creamy burrata and fragrant basil in a light dressing is as inherently satisfying. So, too, are pasta signatures including rich *risotto alle verdure* or creamy ricotta-filled ravioli swimming in a vibrant sauce of spinach and showered with slivers of nutty parmesan. Swap dessert for a fine selection of imported cheeses, and never look back.

Pizano's

Pizza X

D5

864 N. State St. (bet. Chestnut St. & Delaware Pl.)

Phone: 312-751-1766
Web: www.pizanoschicago.com
Prices:

Lunch & dinner daily

Chicago (Red)

While Chicago may be hailed as home of the deep-dish pizza, the thin-crust pies at Pizano's have justly earned their own devoted following. This refreshing and cozy local spot recalls Italian-American style without feeling like a chain-restaurant cliché; even the waitstaff's genuine warmth is palpable.

Of course, the crowds come for the crust—here it is flaky, buttery, thin (by local standards), and perfectly crisp. As unexpected as it sounds, their pizzas are some of the best in town. And yet, it should be no surprise as pizza has long been the family calling: owner Rudy Malnati's father founded Pizzeria Uno.

The "thinner" offspring at Pizano's sates its growing fan-base from three locations, and even ships to those far from the Second City.

Pump Room ⑨

American ✗✗

D2

1301 N. State Pkwy. (at Goethe St.)

Phone: 312-229-6740   Lunch & dinner daily
Web: www.pumproom.com
Prices: $$ 🚇 Clark/Division

Back when the Public Hotel was known as the Ambassador East, scores of celebrities clinked glasses and forks in the Pump Room. Though these memories are preserved in black-and-white photos hung throughout the hotel, today the sunken dining room is a classy, updated space where cushy circular booths, mod orbital lights, and brown kraft paper placemats meld flawlessly.

Under the direction of Jean-Georges Vongerichten, the seasonal American menu is as casually riveting as the décor. An amply sized boneless fried chicken breast is moist and flavorful beneath its shatteringly crisp coating, ready to sop up habanero-infused butter sauce. In an elegant sundae, handfuls of candied peanuts and caramel popcorn top three neat quenelles of salted caramel ice cream.

Table Fifty-Two

Southern ✗✗✗

C3

52 W. Elm St. (bet. Clark & Dearborn Sts.)

Phone: 312-573-4000   Lunch Sun
Web: www.tablefifty-two.com   Dinner Tue – Sat
Prices: $$$ 🚇 Clark/Division

Chef Art Smith's drawl floats overhead like a warm breeze as he chats up guests inside Table Fifty-Two's cozy white row house, a stately survivor of the Great Chicago Fire. Southern charm permeates every inch of the room, from the pressed-copper ceiling to the white sideboards to a wood-burning oven churning out the restaurant's signature biscuits.

The meal might get started with an amuse-bouche of deviled eggs topped with pickled mustard seeds, and if it's a Sunday or Monday, the famous fried chicken will be making an appearance on many plates. Plump fried green tomatoes and thick pork chops are on order, but for a true down-home taste, get a tall wedge of hummingbird cake, fragrant with banana and pineapple and slathered in cream cheese frosting.

Spiaggia ❀

Italian ✕✕✕

980 N. Michigan Ave. (at Oak St.)

Phone: 312-280-2750
Web: www.spiaggiarestaurant.com
Prices: $$$$

Dinner nightly

🚇 Chicago (Red)

This modern bi-level dining room showcases subdued shades of gray, an intricately tiled marble floor, and spacious seating that only money can buy. Its views of the lake and Magnificent Mile are just as priceless. Glass "caves" for wine and cheese, and charcuterie served at the bar whet the appetite.

The kitchen reflects its elegant surrounds in treating each meticulously sourced ingredient with care, respect, and talent. Modern twists are clear throughout the menu, yet Spiaggia remains a very classic Italian restaurant. This is immediately evident in pasta courses such as the springy and resilient fresh *tajarin*; the thin and pale yellow noodles are twirled with a none-too-buttery sauce and generous shaving of fragrant white truffles. "Little hats" or *cappelletti* are stuffed with duck confit, leeks, and Parmigiano, then served in a rich duck consommé amid poached egg and dehydrated hen of the woods mushrooms. Venison with white truffles, chestnut purée, and tart macerated mulberries is amazingly delicate on all levels. Finish with puffs of blood orange meringue with pine-rosemary essence and pine-nut brittle.

Ignore the occasional trip-ups and upsells; dining here is a true culinary journey.

Vora

Asian XX

C4

1028 N. Clark St. (bet. Maple & Oak Sts.)

Phone: 312-929-2035
Web: www.vorachicago.com
Prices: $$

Lunch & dinner daily

🚇 Clark/Division

Whether you're a carnivore, herbivore, or somewhere in between, Vora's plethora of Asian offerings aims to please. The modern space puts nature at the forefront with vine-like clusters of light bulbs snaking above bars, room dividers punctuated with floral cutouts, and sprightly lime-green banquettes.

Can't choose from the health-oriented lineup of Taiwanese dim sum, Indian curries, or Chinese classics? The dim sum box is actually a bento offering a dizzying array of multi-cultural tastes: soft shrimp *siu mai*, juicy *xiao long bao*, steamed pork buns, and miso soup, as well as other bites. Slices of Sichuan beef and vegetables stir-fried with chili sauce can be amped up to match Chinatown's level of heat, or toned down to suit milder tastes.

Look for the symbol 🍳 for a brilliant breakfast to start your day off right.

93

A fascinating pair of lively North Side neighborhoods, Humboldt Park and Logan Square have for long been revered as Chicagoland's heart and soul. They may reside a few steps off the beaten path, but locals here still live to eat and can be found perusing the wares of global grocers, secret bodegas, and those fine falafel shops. **Smalls** is one such tasty smoke hut that churns out familiar barbecue dishes alongside Asian comfort food. Here, hickory-smoked brisket on Texas toast with Thai-style "tiger cry" sauce has earned an army of devotees for good reason. **Koreatown** is a prized thoroughfare spanning miles along Lawrence Avenue and preparing faithful meals that commence with *banchan*, followed by *galbi*, *bulgogi*, or *bibimbap*. **JungBoo Market** is a gem in Avondale flaunting specialties from rice cakes and ground red pepper flakes, to dried vegetables and seaweed snacks. Stroll further along these tree-lined streets dotted with quaint buildings and trendy shops, until you land upon **Bang Bang Pie Shop**. Here, handmade, buttery biscuits are likely to keep you inside—indefinitely. But, make sure to step out and into **Global Garden**, a community venture (or "refugee training farm") where immigrants grow produce for sale at local farmer's markets or CSAs. Other like-minded operations include **Campbell Co-op** or **Drake Garden** whose harvest of vegetables and plants unite the neighborhood's diverse groups while ensuring gorgeous greenery amid the city. Humboldt Park is also home to a vibrant Puerto Rican community—just look for

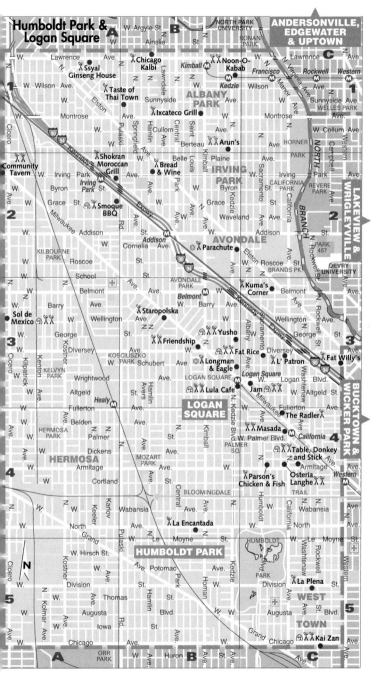

Humboldt Park & Logan Square

W. Argyle St.

NORTH PARK UNIVERSITY

RONAN PARK

ANDERSONVILLE, EDGEWATER & UPTOWN

W. Lawrence Ave.

Ꭶ Ssyal Ginseng House

Ꭶ Chicago Kalbi

Kimball

ꭶꭶ Noon-O-Kabab

Francisco

Rockwell

Western

Ainslie

St.

W. Lawrence Ave.

C

1 W. Wilson Ave.

Kedzie

Wilson

Manor

Sunnyside Ave.

1

Ꭶ Taste of Thai Town

Sunnyside

ALBANY PARK

Ave.

WELLES PARK

W. Montrose Ave.

W.

Montrose

Ave.

W. Collum Ave.

Elston

Ꭶ Ixcateco Grill

Springfield

Hamlin

Central

Saint

Cullom

Berteau

Ave.

HORNER PARK

NORTH

Cicero

Ꭶ Arun's

Campbell

Western

ꭶꭶ Community Tavern

Ꭶ Shokran Moroccan Grill

Belle

Louis

Kimball

Plaine

Ave.

Irving Park

CALIFORNIA PARK

REVERE PARK

W. Irving Park St.

Ꭶ Bread & Wine

Plaine

Ave.

Irving Park

Ave.

BRANCH

Ave.

Irving Park Rd.

W. Byron

Byron

Sacramento

2 W. Grace St.

Milwaukee

ꭶꭶ Smoque BBQ

Grace

St.

Kedzie

Grace

Ave.

California

St.

PARK 457

Rockwell

2

W. Addison

Addison

St.

Waveland

Ave.

DEVRY UNIVERSITY

W. Cornelia

Addison

ꭶ Parachute

AVONDALE

Elston

Roscoe

St.

Rockwell

W. Roscoe

KILBOURNE PARK

Ave.

BRANDS PK.

W. School

St.

AVONDALE PARK

W.

Belmont

ꭶꭶ Sol de Mexico

Belmont

Ave.

Belmont

ꭶ Kuma's Corner

Belmont

W. Barry Ave.

Ꭶ Staropolska

W. Barry

Ave.

Wellington

Rockwell

3 W. George

George

St.

Ꭶꭶ Friendship

ꭶꭶ Yusho

Albany

Wellington

George

St.

3

Diversey

KOSCIUSZKO PARK

ꭶꭶ Fat Rice

Diversey

Ꭶ L' Patron

ꭶꭶ Fat Willy's

Cicero

Kilpatrick

Kostner

W. Schubert

Ꭶ Longman & Eagle

Logan Square

Logan Blvd.

Altgeld St.

W. Wrightwood

KELVYN PARK

Hamlin

Myers

Ave.

LOGAN SQUARE

Jam ꭶꭶ

Washtenaw

W. Altgeld

Kenton

Ave.

ꭶꭶ Lula Cafe

W. Fullerton Healy Ave.

LOGAN SQUARE

Milwaukee

Fullerton

Ave.

4 W. Belden

HERMOSA PARK

Belden

Ave.

The Radler ꭶ

4

Palmer

ꭶꭶ Masada

California

Dickens

MOZART PARK

W. Palmer Blvd.

Kimball

PALMER SQ.

ꭶꭶ Table, Donkey and Stick

HERMOSA

Armitage

Ave.

Armitage

Western

W. Cortland

Ꭶ Parson's Chicken & Fish

Osteria Langhe ꭶꭶ

TRAIL

BLOOMINGDALE

Karlov

Keeler

Wabansia

Central

Humboldt

Wabansia

Ave.

W. North Ave.

Ꭶ La Encantada

California

North

Ave.

Grand

Le Moyne St.

Cicero

Pulaski

N

W. Hirsch St.

HUMBOLDT PARK

HUMBOLDT PARK

Washtenaw

Rockwell

Western

W. Potomac

Kostner

Hamlin

Ave.

Homan

Kedzie

Ave.

W. Division St.

Division

Ꭶ La Plena

St.

5 W. Thomas

5

W. Augusta

Augusta

Blvd.

WEST

Augusta

St. Blvd.

W. Iowa

Kolmar

Grand

TOWN

W. Chicago Ave.

ORR PARK

Chicago

Ave.

ꭶꭶ Kai Zan

Ave.

W. Huron St.

A

B

C

Paseo Boricua, the flag-shaped steel gateway demarcating the district along Division Street. These storefronts are as much a celebration of the diaspora as the homeland, with an impressive array of traditional foods, rare ingredients, and authentic *pernil*. In fact, the annual **Puerto Rican Festival** features four days of festivity, fun, and great food. You can also get your fill of Caribbean cuisine in these parts, but for serious Latin food, dash over to **Café Colao**, a Puerto Rican coffee shop selling pastries and sandwiches. Get here before the crowds for a cheese-and-guava *pastelillo* or Cuban sandwich with *cafe con leche*, of course.

Bill Dugan's **The Fishguy Market** has been serving Michelin-starred restaurants for decades, while also renting space to **Wellfleet**, a popular luncheonette named after the Cape Cod fishing town. Here fish fans are always in good hands thanks to the kitchen's creative renditions of fresh crustaceans. If steaming hot dogs are a custom in Chicago, then **Jimmy's Red Hots** is the standard bearer of this neighborhood. Meanwhile,

the great value found at **Dante's Pizzeria** may only be exceeded by its larger-than-life, exceedingly tasty pies. **Pierogi Street** is another popular stop among residents now that it has morphed into a solid storefront preparing every Polish delight under the sun. And, if those *paczki's* don't have you hooked for good, look to **Grandma J's Local Kitchen** for a breakfast spread with deliciously unique sides—think French toast sticks or kale chips. Pastries take the cake at **Shokolad** and the staff at this Ukrainian haunt know how to keep your eyes on the prize: a stacked-to-the-top glass bakery case showcases its wares to great effect. Their signature cheesecake lollipops may not hail from the Old Country, but be assured that they are very tasty.

LOGAN SQUARE

An eclectic mix of cuisines combined with historic buildings and charming boulevards attracts everybody from hipsters and working-class locals, as well as artists and students to this lovely quarter. Within the culinary community, a blend of home chefs, star cooks, and staunch foodies can be found plunging into the products at **Kurowski's Sausage Shop**, a respected butcher specializing in handmade cuts of Polish meats. Novices take note: pair a flavorful sausage with toasted rye before picking up some pickles to-go from the old-school and always reliable **Dill Pickle Food Co-op**. Carrying on this cultural explosion, Logan Square is also home to **4 Suyos**, a well-regarded Peruvian favorite cooking the classics but with a creative twist. Find a plethora of regulars who practically reside here for the soft, creamy tofu marinated in *anticuchos* sauce, coupled with quinoa, and crested with *queso fresco*. Also of epicurean note is **Logan Square Farmers Market** selling everything ingestible from raw honey to organic zucchini; while the uniquely sourced and beautifully packaged brews at **Gaslight Coffee Roasters** is a caffeine junkie's real-life fantasy. Just as kids delight in a day spent at **Margie's Candies** for homemade chocolates, adults eagerly await a night out at **Scofflaw** for potent, gin-infused libations and secret menu combinations. On the opposite end, students prepare for an impromptu dinner with *nonna* by buying up all things authentic from **Half Italian Grocer**. Food wonks however, know to shop till

they drop at **Independence Park Farmers Market** for a divine dinner back home. Over in German-centric Lincoln Square, **Mirabell's** stays true to her Bavarian roots with big bites and bold brews. Less locally traditional but just as tantalizing is **Jimmy's Pizza Café**, justly mobbed for its mean rendition of a New York-style slice. Albany Park is another melting pot of global foods and gastronomic retreats minus the sky-high price. Plan your own Middle Eastern feast with a spectrum of cheeses, spreads, and flatbreads from **Al-Khyam Bakery & Grocery**, tailed by perfect baklava from **Nazareth Sweets**. But, if meat is what you're craving, then join the crowds of carnivores at **Charcoal Delights**, a time-tested burger joint.

Arun's

Thai Thai ✕✕

B1

4156 N. Kedzie Ave. (at Berteau Ave.)

Phone: 773-539-1909   Dinner Tue – Sun
Web: www.arunsthai.com
Prices: $$$$ 🔲 Kedzie (Brown)

Dining at Arun's feels like attending a dinner party hosted by a well-traveled friend. Covered wall-to-wall in rich carpeting and filled with artwork and figurines, the dining room feels homey and intimate. Adding to the ambience, the kitchen offers a choice of seven- ten- or 12-course chef's tastings nightly in lieu of à la carte.

The dishes on each tasting menu shift according to the chef's whims, and some are more successful than others. Courses range from the familiar and comforting to the innovative: crisp, shattering light batter coats two thin strips of pork belly; a hearty chunk of beef tenderloin melts into rich spice-infused *massaman* curry; and a squirt of lemon balances the fragrant coconut broth and crushed chili peppers of *mee kati* noodles.

Bread & Wine

International ✕

B2

3732 W. Irving Park Rd. (at Ridgeway Ave.)

Phone: 773-866-5266   Lunch Sat – Sun
Web: www.breadandwinechicago.com   Dinner Tue – Sat
Prices: $$ 🔲 Irving Park (Blue)

Bread & Wine's mix of American bistro fare and international flair mirrors the cultural melting pot of surrounding nabe Humboldt Park, and the former laundromat's parking lot fills quickly. Solo diners perch at the 10-seat counter to watch the chefs at work, while groups crowd around tables made from cross-sections of fallen trees, snacking on barbecue *chicharrónes* or house-made charcuterie.

Plates like the mortadella sandwich smeared with olive pesto and stacked with tasso and pancetta further showcase the kitchen's prowess with cured meat. A substantial beet and barley salad is loaded with feta cheese and fresh arugula. Before you leave, browse the small market for bread, wine, and artisanal treats; diners receive a discount on same-day purchases.

Chicago Kalbi

B1

3752 W. Lawrence Ave. (bet. Hamlin & Lawndale Aves.)

Phone: 773-604-8183 Dinner Wed – Mon
Web: www.chicago-kalbi.com
Prices: $$

Take me out to the ballgame—or the Korean barbecue joint where a ballplayer would feel right at home. At this quirky spot, autographed baseballs line the shelves, while photographs and posters of ballplayers paper the walls. But the cluttered décor doesn't deter locals from frequenting this modest yet welcoming joint.

Gas grills at each table give off an intoxicatingly savory perfume as patrons take their time searing their choice of well-marbled marinated beef, including the always-popular *bulgogi* or *kalbi*, and then cool their mouths with a traditional array of *banchan*. For those who prefer their meat raw, beef tartare assumes an interesting twist of flavor and texture when folded with Asian pears, sesame seeds, and sesame oil.

Community Tavern

A2

4038 N. Milwaukee Ave. (bet. Cuyler Ave. & Irving Park Rd.)

Phone: 773-283-6080 Dinner Tue – Sun
Web: www.communitytavern.com
Prices: $$

Created by restaurateur Quay Tao as a lively respite with a touch of sophisticated comfort, Community Tavern is true to its title. Inside, Portage Park locals take up every inch of space at the modern wooden bar and communal tables.

A bistro-inspired menu takes luxurious liberties with tradition, as evidenced in the foie gras-whipped butter served with biscuits or pound cake made even richer with brown butter. Steak frites are no less appealing for their straightforward plating—a classic combination of juicy skirt steak and thin-cut potatoes with garlic aïoli for dipping. To really indulge, pair it with a side of cremini mushrooms, quartered, roasted, and sautéed in umami-spiked steak jus with a sprinkle of fried sweet shallots.

Fat Rice

Macanese **XX**

C3

2957 W. Diversey Ave. (at Sacramento Ave.)

Phone: 773-661-9170
Web: www.eatfatrice.com
Prices: $$

Lunch Wed – Sun
Dinner Tue – Sat
Logan Square

Not familiar with the food of Macau? Not to worry—Fat Rice turns the uninitiated into believers nightly. A wooden pergola shelters hardy souls braving the infamous wait for a table. Bar seating around the open kitchen gives a bird's-eye view of the mélange of ingredients used in each dish, though servers are happy to walk any guest through the intoxicating mashup of Portuguese and Asian cuisine.

Sharing is recommended for platters like the namesake *arroz gordo*, a paella-esque blend of meat, shellfish, and pickles. Pillowy bread sops up chunky olive-and-*bacalhau* spread in a pool of verdant olive oil. Shredded dried pork and fried shallots are intriguing but successful dessert components, when paired with salted caramel, sesame and crispy rice.

Fat Willy's

Barbecue **X**

C3

2416 W. Schubert St. (at Artesian Ave.)

Phone: 773-782-1800
Web: www.fatwillys.com
Prices: $$

Lunch & dinner daily

With piles of hickory and applewood stacked at the entrance and the sweet-spicy aroma of smoke filling the air, Fat Willy's telegraphs an authentic barbecue experience from the outset. Vintage hand mixers decorate one wall, but this isn't a precious farmhouse bakery—the meat is front and center, as indicated by the rolls of paper towels and sheets of Kraft paper laid out over gingham tablecloths.

Signature baby back ribs are pink and glistening with fat after a slow smoke, and a duo of house-made barbecue sauces lets diners kick things up as desired. Minced fresh garlic adorns the pulled pork sandwich, with a few shakes of seasoned vinegar for extra oomph. After those savory indulgences, a slice of cool, creamy peanut butter mousse cake is just the ticket.

Friendship

Chinese

B3

2830 N. Milwaukee Ave. (bet. Dawson & Kimball Aves.)

Phone: 773-227-0970   Lunch & dinner daily
Web: www.friendshiprestaurant.com
Prices: $$ Logan Square

Innovative Chinese cuisine and sophisticated cocktails make this hip Logan Square venue worth seeking out. Inside the dimly-lit space, wood-lined walls, sleek banquettes, linen-draped tables, and polished cooper accents play off a palette of rich neutrals to lend a modern, upscale vibe.

Friendship's spirited menu offers both traditional cuisine and enticing departures. Fruit juices and liquors enhance items like Barbarian beef with a chili-cabernet sauce. Then, Champagne lemon chicken, XO brandy beef *chow fun*, and sizzling Xi'an pork with a red chilli-and-black bean sauce all boast salty, sweet, and spicy notes. Chocolate fortune cookies are a sweet finish, but if in need of more, you're in luck: there's a second outpost downtown on the lakefront.

Ixcateco Grill

Mexican

B1

3402 W. Montrose Ave. (bet. Bernard St. & Kimball Ave.)

Phone: 773-539-5887   Dinner Tue – Sun
Web: N/A
Prices: $$ Kedzie (Brown)

Servers stand erect as soldiers at Ixcateco Grill, their pressed white shirts tucked into immaculate black pants. It's a sight you wish you'd see more often—the unmistakable feeling that the staff cares deeply about your experience at this delicious Mexican hot spot. The colorful space, painted in bright shades of orange, green, and fuchsia, only adds to the bonhomie.

Chef Anselmo Ramírez, a veteran of Frontera Grill and Topolobampo, knows his way around Southern Mexican food. Try the irresistible *picaditas*, a pair of tender little masa canoes filled with savory chicken carnitas, pickled cactus, avocado cream, and *queso fresco*; or the wonderfully complex and authentic *pollo en mole negro*, sporting that perfect, complex blend of sweet and spicy *mole*.

Jam

American **XX**

C3

3057 W. Logan Blvd. (at Albany Ave.)

Phone: 773-292-6011   Lunch Thu – Tue
Web: www.jamrestaurant.com
Prices: 😑   🖥 Logan Square

Hiding in plain sight on a residential Logan Square block, Jam remains the sweetheart of brunch-o-philes who won't settle for some greasy spoon. Clean white walls and gray stone tables punctuated by lime green placemats give a gallery-like feel to the space; a friendly welcome and wide-open kitchen keep it homey.

Their brunch standards like French toast are nothing short of luxurious: think brioche soaked in vanilla- and malt-spiked custard cooked sous vide to absorb every drop, then caramelized in a sizzling pan and garnished with lime leaf-whipped cream and pineapple compote. Braised beef, tangy tomato *crema*, and smoked Gouda are rolled into lacy buckwheat crêpes and topped with a sunnyside egg for an elegant take on the breakfast burrito.

Kai Zan 😑

Japanese **XX**

C5

2557 ½ W. Chicago Ave. (at Rockwell St.)

Phone: 773-278-5776   Dinner Thu – Tue
Web: www.eatatkaizan.com
Prices: **$$**

A recent expansion has doubled the space of Kai Zan's tiny empire on far western Chicago Avenue, adding multi-rooms of wooden tables and benches next to the original sliver of a marble sushi counter. Make a reservation to guarantee a spot at the counter, where it's a pleasure to watch chefs and twin brothers Melvin and Carlo Vizconde work in synchronicity.

Though known for its sushi, grilled items like juicy beef tongue complement the roster of exceptionally fresh bites. Smoky seared *saba* and octopus sashimi are served with typically restrained seasoning, needing nothing more than a dab of soy and dip in pickled wasabi sauce. Monthly specials may include Eskimo clouds, a poetic name for escolar-wrapped kushi oysters with Tabasco-ponzu foam.

Kuma's Corner

American ✗

C3

2900 W. Belmont Ave. (at Francisco Ave.)

Phone: 773-604-8769   Lunch & dinner daily
Web: www.kumascorner.com
Prices: ☜☜

Even vegans know the cult following of Kuma's Corner, though there's absolutely nothing for them on the menu at this heavy metal burger joint on an unassuming Avondale corner. It's not for the faint of heart: between the crowds, the crunching blasts of sound, and the NC-17 artwork. Steady yourself with a beer or Bourbon while waiting for a table and a juicy patty.

The lines wouldn't be stretching out the door if the kitchen weren't cranking out kick-ass burgers. The menu features more than a dozen options of 10-oz. monsters served on pretzel rolls with myriad toppings like roasted garlic mayonnaise, house-made hot sauce, and pepper jack cheese. Almost as famous, mac and cheese with add-ins offers a comparably artery-clogging change of pace.

La Encantada

Mexican ✗

B4

3437 W. North Ave. (bet. Homan & St. Louis Aves.)

Phone: 773-489-5026   Dinner Tue – Sun
Web: www.laencantadarestaurant.com
Prices: ☜☜

Encantada is Spanish for enchanting, and this family-run spot more than lives up to its name. Royal-blue, golden-yellow, and exposed brick walls are hung with gallery-style artwork (most of which is for sale), and contemporary Latin tunes waft through the air. Culinary inspiration begins in the family's hometown, Zacatecas, but pulls from around Mexico with delectable results.

Enchiladas rojas, a Zacatecan specialty, are as authentic as one could wish. Two small, salted beef-filled tortillas are draped with earthy salsa *rojas* for muted chili heat, while avocado and *crema fresca* bring depth to a rustic chicken tortilla soup. The chewy, caramelized crust on pan-fried plantains is textbook perfect, served with a dollop of cinnamon-laced cream.

La Plena

C5

2617 W. Division St. (bet. Rockwell St. & Washtenaw Ave.)

Phone: 773-276-5795 Lunch & dinner Thu – Sun
Web: N/A
Prices: $$

Owners Epi and Soraya Velez have created a warm and welcoming haven for anyone hoping to enjoy a little piece of Puerto Rico in Chicago. Their home-style cooking would make any Boricua proud, offering standards from *mofongo* to *lechon* and even the holiday favorite of *coquito*—with much less of the heaviness often associated with the traditional cuisine.

As the story goes, the *jibarito* was created by Chicago's Puerto Rican community, and La Plena's rendition—featuring thin steak strips, garlicky mayonnaise, and melted cheese between fried flattened plantains—is an exceptional example. For dessert, dig into a slice of dense, eggy flan while you take in the dining room's custom murals that showcase Puerto Rico's beaches and countryside.

L' Patron

C3

2815 W. Diversey Ave. (bet. California Ave. & Mozart St.)

Phone: 773-252-6335 Lunch & dinner Wed – Mon
Web: N/A
Prices: $$

Don't worry—the long line stretching past L'Patron's neon-bright façade isn't cause for concern. Counter service moves quickly at this affordable and popular Diversey Avenue taqueria, as staffers smoothly satiate customers with a concise but tasty array of tortas, tacos, and burritos wrapped in handmade tortillas. The interior décor is just as colorful as the outside, with pulsing Latin music to keep you moving as you munch.

Ultra-fresh dishes are cooked to order, like a grilled burrito stuffed with charred poblanos, caramelized onion, and tomatillo-jalapeño salsa. Carne asada tacos arrive packed with grilled, well-seasoned beef; while crisp tortilla chips, still warm from the fryer, are addictive companions for scooping chunky, garlicky guacamole.

Chicago ▶ Humboldt Park & Logan Square

Longman & Eagle ⌘

2657 N. Kedzie Ave. (at Schubert Ave.)

Phone: 773-276-7110
Web: www.longmanandeagle.com
Prices: $$

Lunch & dinner daily

🚇 Logan Square

Poised along a trendy corner and marked by a single ampersand over the door, this is the ultimate merger of the Old World and New Order. It's the kind of place where remnants of a glorious past live in harmony with more current elements, and where chefs prefer bandanas and beards to toques. Yet, the cuisine is as haute as ever.

Millennials never tire of this local hangout and its numerous dining nooks, including the hip and happening bar that pours an exceptional carte of cocktails; a boisterous front dining room; as well as an exposed brick alcove that flaunts both space and privacy. Open from early to late, the jumping tavern cooks up an exciting lineup of truly extraordinary fare. Make a decadent start with duck (pastrami, confit, and heart) in a jar neatly coupled with rice, beans, and potatoes. Black bass, fried oysters, and green tomato chow chow in a Southern pork broth is another rich dish; while buckwheat cannelloni with chickpeas, French feta, and fennel barigoule in soubise is as wholesome as it is heavenly.

At the end, black sesame doughnuts with tapioca and coconut are creamy, crunchy, and certify nothing short of sweet dreams—perhaps in one of the hotel rooms above the bar?

Chicago ▶ Humboldt Park & Logan Square

Lula Cafe 😊

B3

American ✖✖

2537 N. Kedzie Ave. (off Logan Blvd.)

Phone: 773-489-9554
Web: www.lulacafe.com
Prices: $$

Lunch & dinner Wed – Mon

🔲 Logan Square

Despite a gleamingly renovated kitchen, neighborhood darling Lula Cafe remains the same beloved hangout it's always been. No matter what's on the constantly evolving menu, the fresh, seasonal, and always original fare keeps the casual spot slammed with the creative denizens of Logan Square from morning to night.

The mouthwatering fixings in Lula's Royale breakfast sandwich change with the seasons and might include thin slices of meaty, tender short rib, a sunny-side up farm egg, smoky cumin aïoli and bitter orange jam served alongside a salad of vinegary carrot, daikon, and cilantro. Sweet teeth are satisfied by a tall wedge of double-layered carrot cake complete with crème anglaise and a luxurious spoonful of strawberry preserves on the side.

Masada

C4

Middle Eastern ✖✖

2206 N. California Ave. (bet. Lyndale & Palmer Sts.)

Phone: 773-697-8397
Web: www.masadachicago.com
Prices: ⊖⊖

Lunch & dinner daily

🔲 California (Blue)

Masada Ramli, the mother of owner Shadi Ramli, is the inspiration of this richly adorned spot bedecked with metal lanterns and colorful glazed tiles. A collection of hamsas at the entrance wards off evil, and the lower level lounge pours a bevy of sprits including cocktails, crafts beers, and *arak*.

Although kebabs and wraps can be ordered, there's nothing commonplace about Masada's home-style cooking. Instead, imagine the likes of lamb's kidney and heart sautéed with onions and oyster mushrooms; or *fetit betinjan*, crunchy pita cubes and roasted eggplant dressed with tahini, pomegranate molasses, and lemon. A number of vegan options abound and attract, including *koshari*, a hearty mélange of rice, lentils, and gluten-free pasta, accompanied by spicy tomato sauce and tart pickles.

Noon-O-Kabab

B1

Persian

4661 N. Kedzie Ave. (at Leland Ave.)

Phone: 773-279-9309
Web: www.noonokabab.com
Prices: 💳💳

Lunch & dinner daily

🚇 Kedzie (Brown)

A bustling lunch crowd appreciates the welcoming hospitability at this family-run Persian favorite in the upper reaches of Humboldt Park. Intricate tilework and patterned wall hangings offset the closely set linen-topped tables and add touches of elegance to the homey space.

A basket of warm pita bread and a bowl of salty Bulgarian feta, parsley, and raw onions sate the appetites of those perusing the kababs on the menu. Succulent, hand-formed lamb *koubideh* and beef tenderloin skewers are juicy and charred with a hint of spice, and vegetarian offerings like *tadiq* with *ghormeh sabzi* play up the textural contrast of crispy pan-browned saffron rice against flavorful stewed spinach. Sample a glass of "awesome" house Earl Grey tea steeped with cardamom and ginger.

Osteria Langhe

C4

Italian

2824 W. Armitage Ave. (bet. Mozart St. & California Ave.)

Phone: 773-661-1582
Web: www.osterialanghe.com
Prices: $$

Lunch Sun
Dinner nightly

🚇 California (Blue)

A tapestry-length photograph of the Piemontese countryside is the only nod to tradition in Osteria Langhe's buzzy contemporary space. Lines of glowing bulbs hanging from a sculptural grid bring warmth to bare wood tables and metal chairs. A communal table at the restaurant's entrance, visible through the garage-like glass façade, shines like a beacon of conviviality.

Don't spoil your appetite by eating too many of the complimentary house-made black olive *grissini* before the entrées arrive. Regional specialties abound on the menu: rich, eggy strands of *tajarin* swirl around braised beef ragù or simple butter and sage. Use delicate crêpe-like *crespella*, filled with a variety of seasonal vegetables, to sop up spicy leek *fonduta*.

Parachute ✿

B2

Fusion ✕

3500 N. Elston Ave. (at Troy St.)

Phone: 773-654-1460
Web: www.parachuterestaurant.com
Prices: **$$**

Dinner Tue – Sat

Husband-and-wife chef team Johnny Clark and Beverly Kim have put their little corner of Avondale on Chicago's culinary map with this hip and homey bistro. Young foodies fill the space every night, whether seated at tables lining the wooden banquette or perched on colorful stools dotting a double-sided slab of counter, half of which faces the open kitchen.

Clark and Kim's exemplary cuisine results from a deep understanding of the Korean pantry as well as a brilliant application of au courant technique to seasonal product. Baked potato *bing* bread, the restaurant's signature flaky flatbread carb-bomb, is stuffed with melted scallions and bacon bits, topped with nutty sesame, and served with sour cream butter. Then, cauliflower is deep-fried, set over cool, herbaceous raita, and studded with shards of spicy *tandoori* chicken skin; while *dukbokki*, or Korean rice cakes, are pan-crisped and combined with bits of succulent goat meat sausage and refreshingly bitter wilted rapini.

Desserts are a stellar finish—think silky panna cotta served with a soy sauce-caramel drizzle and topped with popped corn, or a novel take on fruit crisp with buckwheat, Bing cherries, ginger-spiced broth, and scoop of *sakura* ice cream.

Parson's Chicken & Fish

American ✗

C4

2952 W. Armitage Ave. (at Humboldt Blvd.)

Phone: 773-384-3333   Lunch & dinner daily
Web: www.parsonschickenandfish.com
Prices: $$ 🖥 California (Blue)

For the young professionals and new families of gentrifying Logan Square, Parson's Chicken & Fish is a lively but low-key hangout that hits all the bases. It's equally appropriate for a midday snack with the kids or a late-night munchies run, and the stay-and-play vibe extends to on-site activities like a winter ice skating rink or summer ping pong tables.

As per the name, poultry and piscine offerings are house specialties, with signature golden-fried chicken (and equally popular Negroni slushies) on many tables. An aïoli-smeared brioche bun holds a piping-hot fillet of beer-battered fish topped with crisp slaw and house hot sauce. Dessert isn't made in house, but no matter; neighboring Bang Bang Pie Shop provides daily slices of sweetness.

The Radler

German ✗

C4

2375 N. Milwaukee Ave. (at Fullerton Ave.)

Phone: 773-276-0270   Lunch Sat – Sun
Web: www.dasradler.com   Dinner Tue – Sun
Prices: $$ 🖥 California (Blue)

With around 20 suds on tap and more than 95 bottles to sample, The Radler is everything you want a beer hall to be. Though the space is new, it has an old soul: communal benches hearken back to the days of classic Bavarian *biergartens*, and the enormous Bohemian Export beer mural that commands guests' attention is indigenous to the building—a happy discovery during demolition.

A stack of small plates on each table sends the message that everything on the menu is meant for sharing. A German onion pie arrives straight from the oven, topped with shaved asparagus and made-to-order Pilsner soubise. Four types of wurst are available by the link, like Thüringer—served over a bed of spring green peas with authentic marinated cucumber salad and traditional mustard.

Shokran Moroccan Grill

Moroccan ✗

A2

4027 W. Irving Park Rd. (bet. Keystone Ave. & Pulaski Rd.)

Phone: 773-427-9130   Dinner Wed – Mon
Web: www.shokranchicago.com
Prices: ⊜⊜   🚇 Irving Park (Blue)

Ⓢ

BYO

Embrace Moroccan hospitality to the fullest and bone up on your Arabic at Shokran, where the country's culinary culture is displayed in a romantic setting. Nooks and crannies throughout the dining rooms offer intimacy; take a seat among the cozy cushioned banquettes and prepare to say "shokran" (thank you) repeatedly as courses come your way. Traditional dishes offer the most authentic experience, like sweet and savory *bastilla*, a flaky pastry starter that's large enough to serve two, stuffed with spiced chicken and dusted with cinnamon. Famously rustic, the lamb Marrakesh tagine features a meaty bone-in shank adorned with bitter slivers of preserved lemon and surrounded by sweet peas, whole black olives, and tender quartered artichoke hearts.

Smoque BBQ 😊

Barbecue ✗

A2

3800 N. Pulaski Rd. (at Grace St.)

Phone: 773-545-7427   Lunch & dinner Tue – Sun
Web: www.smoquebbq.com
Prices: ⊜⊜   🚇 Irving Park (Blue)

♿

Smoque opens for lunch at 11:00 A.M., but a crowd of devotees can be found lining up for a barbecue fix long before then. Once inside, peruse the chalkboard menu, then order cafeteria-style before staking your claim among the communal seating while waiting (and salivating).

The half-and-half sandwich, piled with pulled pork and brisket, is the best of both worlds, with chunky shreds of tender pork and spice-rubbed slices of pink-rimmed beef spooned with vinegary barbecue sauce. The usual side dish suspects like zingy, crisp coleslaw and deeply smoky baked beans are anything but standard here, complementing the 'cue as they should. For a sweet finish, look no further than pecan bread pudding drizzled with salted caramel-Bourbon sauce.

Sol de Mexico 😊

Mexican ✖✖

A3

3018 N. Cicero Ave. (bet. Wellington Ave. & Nelson St.)

Phone: 773-282-4119   Lunch & dinner Wed – Mon
Web: www.soldemexicochicago.com
Prices: $$

Far more authentic than the average chips-and-salsa joint, Sol de Mexico brightens the scene and palate with a lively atmosphere (cue the mariachi music!) and delectable house specialties. Walls painted in tropical pinks, blues, and oranges are a cheerful canvas for Dia de los Muertos artifacts.

To sample the kitchen's skill, start with *sopes surtidos "xilonen"*—four molded masa cups with a variety of fillings like caramelized plantains doused in sour cream or tender black beans topped with crumbly house-made chorizo. Then, move on to the *pollo en mole manchamanteles*, which translates to "tablecloth stainer." Rich and slightly bitter with a comforting nuttiness, the aptly named mahogany sauce begs to be sopped up with freshly made tortillas.

Ssyal Ginseng House

Korean ✖

A1

4201 W. Lawrence Ave. (at Keeler Ave.)

Phone: 773-427-5296   Lunch & dinner Mon – Sat
Web: www.ssyal.com
Prices: 🥜🥜

With Ssyal Ginseng House's invigorating *samgyetang* at their doorstep, it's a wonder anyone in Albany Park ever gets sick. Since 1993, the sunny spot has served this restorative dish, featuring an entire Cornish game hen stuffed with glutinous rice, jujubes, and whole garlic cloves in an earthenware bowl of delicately flavored ginseng broth.

Equal care and skill goes into the rest of the Korean specialties on offer, all of which are presented with kind, attentive service. *Oden ttuck-bok-gi* is piled high in a chewy mix of thin fish cake strips, glutinous rice cakes, and shredded carrots and cabbage tossed in sweet and spicy red pepper paste. For an immunity boost in your own kitchen, take home some of Ssyal's house-dried ginseng or ginger candies.

Staropolska

Polish ✗

B3

3030 N. Milwaukee Ave. (bet. Lawndale & Ridgeway Aves.)

Phone: 773-342-0779   Lunch & dinner daily
Web: www.staropolskarestaurant.com
Prices: 💰

Fans of traditional Polish cooking know to proceed to this Logan Square mainstay. If a stroll past nearby Kurowski's Sausage Shop doesn't put you in the mood for some meaty, belly-busting cuisine, then one step inside this Old World-style sanctum certainly will.

Polish pilsners and lagers are poured at the bar and pair perfectly with the stuffed and slow-cooked plates sent out by the kitchen. Pierogies are a staple, and are offered here with a variety of sweet and savory embellishments. Stuffed cabbage is available with a meatless mushroom filling, and house specialties include the *placek po wegiersku*: a light and tender griddled potato pancake folded over chunks of pork and bell pepper slices, braised in a tomato and sweet paprika sauce.

Table, Donkey and Stick 😀

Austrian ✗✗

C4

2728 W. Armitage Ave. (bet. California Ave. & North Point St.)

Phone: 773-486-8525   Dinner nightly
Web: www.tabledonkeystick.com
Prices: $$ 🏠 Western (Blue)

When American comfort food just won't suffice, look to Table, Donkey and Stick for a helping of cozy Alpine fare. The rustic inn-inspired setting reflects its reputation as a gathering place where friends meet at the inviting bar or settle in at communal tables for whimsical, creative compositions.

Though the food is European-influenced, ingredients from local farms make their way into many dishes. Caraway seeds spice up duck meatballs nestled among springy egg noodles with dehydrated sauerkraut and shaved salted egg yolk, and honeycomb tripe wins new fans when fried to a crisp and topped with house-made giardiniera. For a sweet take on the traditional baked good, try the pretzel-shaped puff pastry sprinkled with candied mustard seeds.

Taste of Thai Town

Thai ✕

B1

4461 N. Pulaski Rd. (at Sunnyside Ave.)

Phone: 773-299-7888
Web: www.tasteofthaitown.com
Prices: 🍴🍴

Lunch & dinner daily

BYO

Well-regarded Thai restaurateur Arun Sampanthavivat expands his influence with this long-awaited second sibling, a casual and welcoming gathering place housed in a former police station. The menu showcases a taste of each of Thailand's diverse regions, though many diners will be familiar with the offerings on hand. The mouthwatering aromas of each dish are matched in many cases by eye-watering spice.

Pad see ew retain their chewy bite when tossed with crisp veggies like *gai lan* and green beans, and is served with a caddy of sugar, pickled jalapeños, and chili sauce to customize your preferred level of heat and sweet. A cup of pepper pork curry, the chef's specialty, bobs with tender pork belly in a balanced and sumptuous turmeric-tinged sauce.

Yusho 😊

Japanese ✕✕

B3

2853 N. Kedzie Ave. (bet. Diversey Pkwy. & George St.)

Phone: 773-904-8558
Web: www.yusho-chicago.com
Prices: $$

Lunch Sun
Dinner Wed – Mon
🚇 Logan Square

Just off the beaten (and quickly gentrifying) path from its Logan Square brethren, Yusho quietly draws a crowd. A narrow façade hides a deceptively expansive room done up in a rustic-chic mix of weathered wood planks, cement floors, plaid-upholstered booths, and Danish midcentury chairs.

Diners show up in droves for a rotating selection of steamed buns, crispy chicken bits, and slurpable noodle bowls. "Logan Poser Ramen" showcases Chef/owner Matthias Merges' house-made noodles, a swirl of thick, al dente strands in spicy *tonkatsu* broth. A poached hen egg and crispy pig's tail croquette take it over the top. Vegetarians delight in an elegant pickled gobo root salad with translucent Asian pear and black plum slices and a silky tofu-*tobanjan* dressing.

113

Lakeview is the blanket term for the area north of Lincoln Park, including Roscoe Village and Wrigleyville (named after its iconic ball field). Keeping that in mind, enjoy a boisterous game with maximum conveniences at a Wrigley Field rooftop like **Murphy's Bleachers**, where hot dogs and hamburgers are washed down with pints of beer. When the beloved Cubs finish their season each October, don't despair, as these American summertime classics continue to shape the neighborhood's cuisine. Thanks to a large Eastern European population, a sumptuous supply of sausages and wursts can be found in a number of casual eateries or markets, including **Paulina**—a local institution where expected items like corned beef and lamb are offered beside more novel items like ground venison and loin chops. This is also a hot spot among local Swedish families, who come for time-tested plates of pickled Christmas ham or even cardamom-infused sausages. Other Swedes may opt to sojourn to **Ann Sather**, a sweet brunch spot branded for its baseball glove-sized cinnamon buns.

CLASSIC CHICAGO

Diners are all the craze in this area, starting with **Glenn's** whose menu reads like a seafaring expedition with over 16 varieties of fish on offer. And, between its kitchen's savory egg specialties, 30 types of cereal, and a blackboard menu that makes Egyptian tombs look brief, this is a veritable big city sort of spot and flaunts something for everyone. Similarly, the Windy City's passion for the humble hot dog is something to bark home about, and Lakeview offers plenty of proof. Case in point—the dogs and burgers at **Murphy's Red Hots**, which may be relatively simple in presentation, are totally amazing in taste. But, keep in mind that this location has outdoor picnic tables and no inside seating.

BAKING IN BAVARIA

Even Chicagoans can't survive on hot dogs alone. Thankfully, Lakeview has an antidote for practically every craving imaginable. Should you have a hankering for Bavarian baked goods, for instance, **Dinkel's Bakery** is right around the corner. Originally opened by a master baker from Bavaria in 1922, this family-run business (in its current locale since 1932) is renowned for faithful renditions of strudels, *butterkuchen*, and stollen. Their big breakfast sandwich, Dinkel's Burglaur, may be less traditional but is just as tasty—not unlike those decadent donuts. Items here can be purchased fresh, but are also available frozen for shipping to lucky out-of-town fans.

FASCINATING FOOD FINDS

For a different type of high, stop by south-of-the-border sensation, **5411 Empanadas**. This food truck-turned-storefront sells Argentinian empanadas with such inventive fillings as malbec beef or chorizo with *patatas bravas*. It also showcases impressive Latin sweets like *alfajores* to go with good, strong coffee. Connoisseurs of quality-baked goods will want to pop into **Bittersweet Pastry Shop**, where Chef/owner Judy Contino has been whipping up luscious desserts for almost two decades. It's a one-stop shop for everything from breads, pastries, and cupcakes, to exquisitely sculpted wedding confections. Those seeking a classic American experience should proceed to **Fritz Pastry** for a soulful breakfast spread that unveils bakery specials like banana bread, cinnamon rolls, hand pies, and macarons. Another laudation, even if it comes in buttery and sugary packages to these neighborhoods, is **City Caramels**—home to some lip-smacking treats. Settle in before making your way through Bucktown (by way of coffee-inspired caramels with chocolate-covered espresso beans); Lincoln Square (toasted hazelnuts anybody?), and Pilsen (Mexican drinking chocolate with ancho chili) with their respective caramel and candy cuts.

If savory bites are more your style, trek to **Pastoral**, commonly hailed as one of the country's top destinations for cheese. Their classic and farmstead varietals, fresh breads and olives, as well as intermittently scheduled tastings are a local treasure. An offbeat yet quirky vibe is part and parcel of Lakeview's fabric and testament to this fact can be found at **The Flower Flat**, boasting a comforting breakfast or brunch repast in an actual flower shop. Meanwhile, **Uncommon Ground** is as much a restaurant serving three square meals a day as it is a coffee shop revered for its live music talent and performances. During the months between June and September, stop by at any time to admire their certified organic sidewalk garden before tasting its bounty on your plate, inside. And a few more blocks north, aspiring young chefs with big dreams proudly present a wholesome grab-n-go restaurant called **Real Kitchen**. Here on the menu, home-style items like baked Amish chicken are paired with a unique and crusty pork belly sandwich to reflect each chef's take on a favored classic.

ROSCOE VILLAGE

Everyone loves a rollicking street fair, and this nabe's **Shock Top Oyster Fest** with an incredible music and beer selection as well as worthy guests of honor (maybe a certain mollusk believed to have aphrodisiac qualities) doesn't disappoint. Nostalgic New Yorkers and transplants take note: Roscoe Village is also home to **Apart Pizza**, Chicago's very own homage to the thin-crust pie. (Just remember, you're in deep-dish land, so you might want to refrain from admitting just how much you enjoyed it!) And because no feast is complete without gelato, bide some time at **Black Dog** whose creamy concoctions count renowned local chefs among their fans.

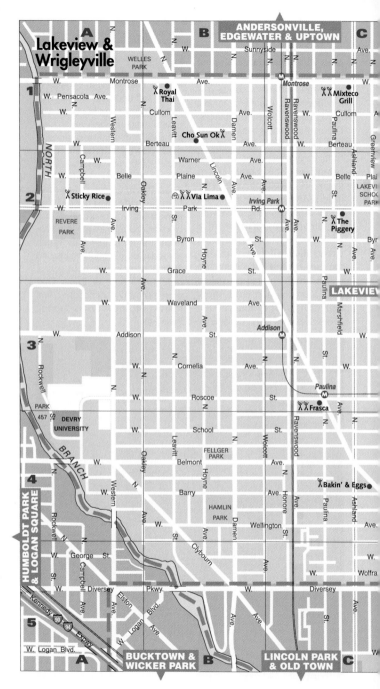

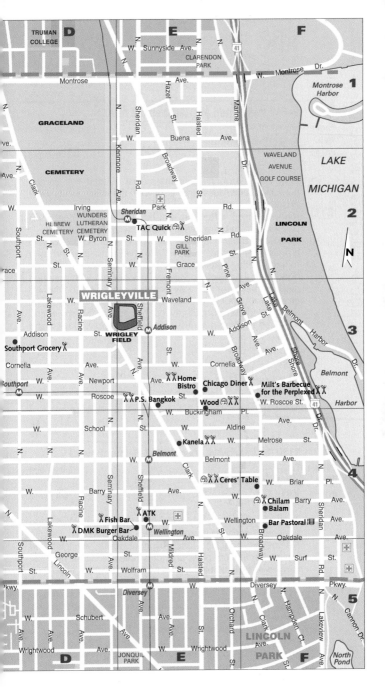

ATK

E4

Thai ✗

946 W. Wellington Ave. (at Sheffield Ave.)

Phone: 773-549-7821
Web: www.andysthaikitchen.com
Prices: $$

Lunch & dinner daily

🚇 Wellington

Chef Andy Aroonrasameruang's Thai kitchen has earned numerous accolades and a devout following in its brief existence. Bring friends and settle in to the slender, spotless room arranged with ebony-finished tables and accent walls painted with hues evocative of turmeric and purple onion.

Cooked-to-order creations are spicy, sour, crunchy, and aromatic—as in the snappy Isaan-style sausage sided by a mouthwatering dipping sauce. The *kao soy* features thin egg noodles in a rich golden-yellow curry stocked with pounded chicken, bean sprouts, raw cabbage, and pickled mustard greens—all topped by a nest of crunchy fried noodles. The duck in red curry is chili-revved, redolent of five-spice, and balanced by the sweetness of diced pineapple, grapes, and tomato.

Bakin' & Eggs

C4

American ✗

3120 N. Lincoln Ave. (bet. Barry & Belmont Aves.)

Phone: 773-525-7005
Web: www.bakinandeggschicago.com
Prices: 🍳🍳

Lunch Thu – Mon

🚇 Paulina

A pastry case chockablock with cupcakes, cookies, and brownies entices passersby into this relaxed Lincoln Avenue breakfast and lunch hangout. Inside, whitewashed repurposed church pews provide ample seating for both big families as well as solo hipsters who can be seeen sipping on Intelligentsia coffee, which is on hand for a pick-me-up.

As the sibling of Wicker Park's Lovely Bake Shop, it's no wonder the moist, generously frosted cupcakes take the cake. Flavors like pumpkin spice, peanut butter and jelly, and red velvet make it hard to pick a favorite. Latin influences on the savory menu mean carb-loaded and dense *chilaquiles* with avocado and tomatillos. A kids' menu offers mini breakfast burritos or buttermilk pancakes with whipped cream smiles.

Bar Pastoral

International

 F4

2947 N. Broadway (bet. Oakdale & Wellington Aves.)

Phone:	773-472-4781	Lunch Sat – Sun
Web:	www.barpastoral.com	Dinner nightly
Prices:	$$	Wellington

When Wrigleyville denizens want to say cheese, they head to Bar Pastoral, the rustic bistro companion to an artisan cheese and wine shop. Subtly styled like a cave for aging, the restaurant's barrel-vaulted ceilings and exposed brick walls evoke intimacy. A glossy half-moon bar, marble-topped cheese counter, and rustic wood tables inlaid with wooden wine box details let guests gather and sample.

As expected, many dishes feature cheese, though shareable plates run from house-made charcuterie to bone-in pork chops. Thick slices of bacon-wrapped country pâté are generously studded with pistachios. A succinct wine list offers a number of by-the-glass selections for pairing with cheese—such as the raw cow's milk Kentucky Rose served with caramelized onion chutney.

Ceres' Table

Italian ✗✗

F4

3124 N. Broadway (bet. Barry Ave. & Briar Pl.)

Phone:	773-922-4020	Lun Sat – Sun
Web:	www.cerestable.com	Dinner nightly
Prices:	$$	Belmont (Brown/Red)

Rounding out a second year in its Lakeview home, Ceres' Table continues its reign as a stylish setting for enjoying the kitchen team's rustic Italian cooking. Whether waking up with brunch, snacking at aperitivo hour, or filling up with the $22 trio (pizza, beer, and dessert), there's an excuse to stop in for any occasion or budget.

Regional Italian favorites from Tuscany to Sicily are represented throughout the menu. A wood-burning oven brings cannellini beans to creamy consistency in a broth for meaty monkfish osso buco. Then oversized orecchiette cups chunks of tender pork sugo, balanced by bitter rapini; and Tuscan *torta della nonna* is sweet simplicity, with buttery baby pine nuts coating a wedge of vanilla-tinged custard pie.

121

Chicago Diner

E3

3411 N. Halsted St. (at Roscoe St.)

Phone: 773-935-6696
Web: www.veggiediner.com
Prices: ⊜⊜

Lunch & dinner daily

🚇 Addison (Red)

"Meat free since '83" is the slogan at Chicago Diner, where servers have been slinging creative, healthy fare to grateful vegetarians and vegans for decades. The ambience evokes a neighborhood diner with fire engine-red tables trimmed in chrome, shiny black vinyl chairs, and raised booths. And the food? It looks and tastes the part.

Convincingly crispy seitan buffalo wings cool down the spice factor with vegan ranch dressing; while *flautas* filled with mashed potato, faux cheese, and jalapeños are served with tons of flavorful fixings so that the meat is not missed at all. With a popular brunch menu, numerous gluten-free choices, and a stronghold on the local vegan scene, you can expect a line. So, get there early or hope for good Karma—and a seat.

Chilam Balam 😊

F4

3023 N. Broadway (bet. Barry & Wellington Aves.)

Phone: 773-296-6901
Web: www.chilambalamchicago.com
Prices: $$

Dinner Tue – Sat

🚇 Wellington

Chilam Balam's cozy subterranean space feels like an undiscovered hideaway, but the secret of this lively Mexican hot spot is out. Though waits can be long, the accommodating staff goes the extra mile to mix up margaritas with BYO tequila or walk guests through the rotating roster of shared plates.

Familiar favorites and seasonal specials make for a festive mix of adventurous, yet universally pleasing dishes. Flat corn tortillas form a sandwich-style enchilada, stuffed with fork-tender beef brisket and topped with crunchy strands of sweet potato slaw. Salty chorizo and green papaya *tlacoyos* show that opposites attract, and peanut butter empanadas— primed for dipping in Oaxacan chocolate sauce and dulce de leche—take a childhood favorite to new heights.

Cho Sun Ok

K o r e a n ✗

B1

4200 N. Lincoln Ave. (at Berteau Ave.)

Phone: 773-549-5555
Web: www.chosunokrestaurant.com
Prices: 💰💰

Lunch & dinner daily

🚇 Irving Park (Brown)

BYO

As tempted as you might be to judge this book by its brisk, unsmiling cover, don't. Instead, enter the cozy, wood-paneled den and raise that first delicious forkful to your mouth.

Take a cue from the regulars and start with *galbi*, a crave-worthy signature that glistens from a soy- sugar- and garlic-marinade and warrants good old-fashioned finger-licking. *Haemul pajeon* stuffed with squid and scallions is a crisp, golden-fried delight; and *kimchi jjigae* is a rich, bubbling, and nourishing broth packed with soft tofu and tender pork. Summer calls for a taste of the *bibim naengmyeon*—a chilled broth floating with buckwheat noodles, fresh veggies, Asian pear, and crimson-red *gochujang* all tossed together for a delicious reprieve from the city's sweltering heat.

DMK Burger Bar

A m e r i c a n ✗

E4

2954 N. Sheffield Ave. (at Wellington Ave.)

Phone: 773-360-8686
Web: www.dmkburgerbar.com
Prices: 💰💰

Lunch & dinner daily

🚇 Wellington

Outside, towering neon "DMK" letters shine like a beacon for burger fanatics; inside, craft beers gush from taps and attentive, accommodating servers sling mile-high piles of fries. With blaring music and church pew-lined banquettes, it's a cool and modern hang for families and friends of all ages.

Sate salt cravings with a batch of batter-fried okra pods and tangy pickle spears dipped in creamy herbed ranch; then order by number to get the creative grass-fed burger of your choice. The #3 takes on a Reuben with pastrami, sauerkraut, and Gruyère; while #9 is the platonic ideal of a patty melt, with smoked Swiss, caramelized onions, and chewy bacon between caraway-studded slices of rye bread. Save room for #15—the always-interesting daily special.

Fish Bar

Seafood ✗

Seafood ✗

E4

2956 N. Sheffield Ave. (at Wellington Ave.)

Phone: 773-687-8177
Web: www.fishbarchicago.com
Prices: $$

Lunch & dinner daily

🚇 Wellington

Chicago may not be known for local seafood, but Fish Bar makes sure to handpick the best from both the Atlantic and Pacific coasts to fill its chilled coffers. A blackboard above the semi-open kitchen lists the fresh daily fish and oyster offerings, ready to be shucked, steamed, fried, and grilled for guests lining up at the wood bar that snakes around the room. The casual menu pays homage to classic coastal fish shacks, yet throws in a few gussied-up items like tartare and octopus à la plancha. Bowls of gumbo stick to the classic recipe with zippy andouille sausage, okra, and chunks of blue crab. The Satchmo po'boy is a mouthful, combining fried rock shrimp and crawfish tails along with slaw and sweet pickles in a traditional, buttery split-top roll.

Frasca

Italian ✗✗

C3

3358 N. Paulina St. (at Roscoe St.)

Phone: 773-248-5222
Web: www.frascapizzeria.com
Prices: $$

Lunch Sat – Sun
Dinner nightly
🚇 Paulina

The warmth of the wood-burning brick oven and the list of generously priced wines is enough to entice Lakeview's young professionals into the friendly confines of Frasca. Amidst décor inspired by the restaurant's name ("branch" in Italian), lively groups and intimate dates sample wine flights and split appetizers like charred Brussels sprouts and cauliflower florets tossed with bacon and briny capers.

Chewy pizza crusts blistered from the heat of the oven are laden with market-fresh toppings. The salsiccia adds shaved pickled fennel and delicate, wispy fronds to handfuls of crumbled fennel seed sausage and pools of melted Havarti. Grab extra forks for the moist tiramisù with a generous inch-thick layer of cocoa-dusted mascarpone mousse.

Home Bistro

A m e r i c a n ✖️✖️

E3

3404 N. Halsted St. (at Roscoe St.)

Phone:	773-661-0299	Lun Sun
Web:	www.homebistrochicago.com	Dinner Tue – Sun
Prices:	$$	Belmont (Brown/Red)

BYO

Home dishes up loads of charm with a healthy dash of humor in the heart of Boystown. Flickering tea lights on the closely packed bistro-style tables faintly illuminate cozy orange walls painted with food-related quotes. Chef Victor Morenz's eclectic menu picks up influences from around the globe, but each dish is consistently gratifying.

Southern meets south of the border in crisp fried oyster tacos with pickled pepper remoulade. Candied kumquats and olive tapenade contrast pleasantly with buttery seared duck breast, and a dense cube of warm, fudgy chocolate cake placed over a swipe of coconut peanut butter is a decadent finale. Plan for an early evening if you're looking forward to a quiet meal; at peak hours, those orange walls really reverberate.

Kanela

A m e r i c a n ✖️✖️

E4

3231 N. Clark St. (bet. Belmont Ave. & School St.)

Phone:	773-248-1622	Lunch daily
Web:	www.kanelabreakfastclub.com	
Prices:	🪙	Belmont (Brown/Red)

A comfortable, lived-in setting makes this breakfast club more like a home away from home for many Lakeview residents. The cozy chocolate-brown dining room packs in hungry brunchers on weekends, but the flung-open front windows, efficient kitchen (and a Bloody Mary or two) keep everyone happy.

Since Kanela is Greek for "cinnamon," the signature pastry is appropriately loaded with spiced sugar, vanilla frosting, and blueberries. A flight of four kinds of French toast sweetens the deal for indecisive types. But savory brunchers have a host of options too, including the Lorraine scramble with Gruyère, peppered bacon, and sprightly scallions. Brunch cocktails, fresh-squeezed juices and smoothies, as well as Julius Meinl coffee cover all the beverage bases.

125

Milt's Barbecue for the Perplexed

F3

Barbecue ✖✖

3411 N. Broadway (bet. Hawthorne Pl. & Roscoe St.)

Phone: 773-661-6384
Web: www.miltsbbq.com
Prices: 🍴

Lunch Sun – Fri
Dinner Sun – Thu
🚇 Addison (Red)

The full name of this kosher spot is Milt's Barbecue for the Perplexed, but even without pork (or dairy) on the menu, there's no sign of "confusion" among patrons, as the catalog of smoky barbecue and Jewish deli delights are bound to appease one and all. Additionally, 100% of their profits go to charity, so get in here and get your craving on. The room is simple, with dark wood furnishings and floors, but the kitchen is all sparkle.

Tender chopped brisket on a toasted hamburger bun arrives with a trio of barbecue sauces—mustardy Carolina, smoky Memphis, and sweet Kansas City—and fries in a wire fryer basket; while pulled smoked chicken makes its way into the homemade soup. Don't expect to take your Friday night date here as Milt closes at sundown out of respect for the Sabbath.

Mixteco Grill

C1

Mexican ✖✖

1601 W. Montrose Ave. (at Ashland Ave.)

Phone: 773-868-1601
Web: www.mixtecogrill.com
Prices: $$

Lunch Sat – Sun
Dinner nightly
🚇 Montrose (Brown)

Floor-to-ceiling windows that wrap around the corner of Montrose and Ashland are flanked by cheerful orange curtains that imitate Mixteco's fiery and flavorful Mexican fare. A large open kitchen splits the casual dining space, giving the front room's patrons a firsthand look at the mesquite-fired grill and from-scratch preparations.

Non-traditional menu items might miss the mark here and there, but familiar dishes don't disappoint—and neither do the reasonable prices that pull in crowds of regulars. Shredded chicken enchiladas (wrapped with house-made tortillas) balance earthy, complex *mole negro* with a burst of brightness from radish matchsticks, cilantro, and raw onion; and thick and creamy refried black beans ensure that no one leaves hungry.

The Piggery

American ✗

C2

1625 W. Irving Park Rd. (at Marshfield Ave.)

Phone: 773-281-7447
Web: www.thepiggerychicago.com
Prices: $$

Lunch & dinner daily

Irving Park (Brown)

The bacon is back—as well as the ham, the shoulder, and the rest of the pig too. This Lakeview sports bar and shrine to all things porcine pays homage to its whimsical ways by way of kitschy pig paraphernalia that shares shelf and wall space with flat-screens tuned to Cubs and Sox games, naturally.

The menu may be hell for vegans, but it's a pork lover's paradise: cuts from every part of the animal find their way into nearly each dish, from hearty ham-stuffed burgers to the signature bacon-wrapped jalapeño poppers. Gently charred slabs of ribs basted with the Piggery's own heady barbecue sauce are teeth-sinkingly tender. Even salads may give you the meat sweats, with pulled pork or buffalo chicken—and bacon, of course—offered as toppings.

P.S. Bangkok

Thai ✗✗

E3

3345 N. Clark St. (bet. Buckingham Pl. & Roscoe St.)

Phone: 773-871-7777
Web: www.psbangkok.com
Prices:

Lunch & dinner Tue – Sun

Belmont (Brown/Red)

Even first-timers are part of the family at P.S. Bangkok, a charming Lakeview retreat run by a trio of sisters. Wind chimes ring softly as Sue (who runs the front of the house) graciously welcomes each guest. Linen-draped tables, wooden arches, and bamboo accents lend subtle elegance to the space.

Diners do double takes at intriguingly titled dishes that depart from the usual Thai menu. "Love me tender" duck is a sweetheart of a meal, featuring fanned duck breast slices with crackling, sugary skin in a citrus-tinged sauce. "Beef paradise" is marinated in garlic and spices, and served with Thai barbecue dipping sauce. Stir-fried entrées named for flavor profiles like pungent, tangy, or peppery let guests cater to their own taste buds.

Royal Thai

Thai

B1

2209 W. Montrose Ave. (bet. Bell Ave. & Leavitt St.)

Phone: 773-509-0007
Web: www.royalthaichicago.com
Prices: ⊜⊜

Lunch & dinner Wed – Mon

🖵 Western (Brown)

BYO

Stately elephants march down the silk runners on each linen-draped table at this age-old Lakeview Thai spot, adding a regal air to the already-polished dining room. Glossy bamboo floors, dark wood high-backed chairs, and ceiling fans atop light walls hung with mirrors make the space look larger than it is.

What this minuscule spot lacks in size, it makes up for in big and bold flavors. Be mindful of your spice tolerance, as the kitchen is known to turn up the heat. They're not fooling around so don't plan on kissing anyone after sucking on plump Royal Thai prawns topped with a potent mix of minced, fresh garlic, dried red chillies, and fragrant cilantro. Ask for a second bowl of rice to sop up the homemade peanut curry in spicy *rama* chicken.

Southport Grocery

American

D3

3552 N. Southport Ave. (bet. Addison St. & Cornelia Ave.)

Phone: 773-665-0100
Web: www.southportgrocery.com
Prices: ⊜⊜

Lunch daily

🖵 Southport

Equal parts specialty grocery and upscale diner, this Southport Corridor hot spot draws quite a crowd. Local products and in-house goodies are stocked in the front of the narrow space, while the rear offers comfortable banquettes for a casual sit-down meal.

Breakfast is served as long as the sun shines, with options like a freshly baked and buttered English muffin stuffed with ginger-sage sausage, a vibrant orange sunny side-up egg, and sweet pepper jelly. A side of red bliss potatoes sweetens the deal, but if you're really looking for something sugary, the grilled coffee cake is a double-layered cinnamon and cream cheese delight. Craving more of your meal? You're in luck: certain menu items, denoted with an asterisk, are available for purchase up front.

Sticky Rice

Thai ✗

A2

4018 N. Western Ave. (at Cuyler Ave.)

Phone: 773-588-0133

Web: www.stickyricethai.com

Prices: ☺☺

Lunch & dinner daily

🚇 Irving Park (Blue)

BYO
There's no dearth of Thai joints in this neighborhood, but Sticky Rice stands out—not only for its focus on Northern Thai specialties, but also for the quality and abundance of dishes made to order. Sunny and citrus-hued, it's the kind of place where those who dare to step outside their satay-and-pad Thai comfort zone will be greatly rewarded.

Luckily, the extensive menu makes it easy to do just that. Tender egg noodles absorb the fragrant coconut curry in a bowl of *kow soy* that's redolent of citrusy coriander and served with pickled greens and cilantro. *Larb* duck is zippy and full of spice, with an unforgettable tart-and-sweet dressing. Hint: use the spot's namesake sticky rice to temper the heat while soaking up every last drop.

TAC Quick ☺

Thai ✗

E2

3930 N. Sheridan Rd. (at Dakin St.)

Phone: 773-327-5253

Web: N/A

Prices: ☺☺

Lunch & dinner Wed – Mon

🚇 Sheridan

♿

BYO
The focus at this Wrigleyville institution is on speedy, authentic Thai food—and that's exactly what you'll get. Colorful orchids brighten up the minimal space, where solo diners sit at the narrow center bar and people-watchers keep an eye on the hustle and bustle outside from high tables near the windows.

Two laminated menus—one with standard fare, and another "secret" listing with more traditional dishes—ensure there's something for everyone. It's hard to resist double-dipping a stack of glistening, charred *moo ping* pork skewers in sour, spicy, and sweet sauce, or finishing every flaky morsel of *pad ped pla duk* (fried catfish with creamy green curry). Spice crazed? You're in luck; TAC Quick's heat level is perhaps the most authentic around.

Via Lima

B2

Peruvian XX

4024 N. Lincoln Ave. (bet. Cuyler Ave. & W. Irving Park Rd.)

Phone: 773-348-4900

Web: www.vialimachicago.com

Prices: $$

Lunch Sun

Dinner Tue – Sun

Irving Park (Brown)

Via Lima infuses a chic, contemporary personality into the typical rustic atmosphere of a Peruvian restaurant. Here, Lakeview residents pack themselves into comfortable booths upholstered in colorful fabrics, sharing dishes from a refined menu of familiar classics or tucking into larger entrées at bare wood tables.

A bracingly sour *leche de tigre* broth infused with fiery South American *rocoto* chile adds zing to market-fresh fish ceviche, while starchy corn kernels and a scoop of creamy sweet potatoes tame the heat. *Choclo* soufflé blends a fluffy, mildly sweet corn cake with meltingly tender duck confit to balance sweet and savory; while Lucuma mousse subtly showcases the vibrant marigold-hued Peruvian fruit, topped with a spoonful of fresh vanilla whipped cream.

Wood

E3

Contemporary XX

3335 N. Halsted St. (at Buckingham Pl.)

Phone: 773-935-9663

Web: www.woodchicago.com

Prices: $$

Lunch Sun

Dinner nightly

Belmont (Brown/Red)

The décor at this Boystown spot might be all grown-up with rich wood tones set against pale tufted booths and a glossy cream bar, but witty winks to the gay community pop up throughout the menu. Cocktails like a "manhandled sour" are as suggestively named as they are superbly prepared. Heck, even Sunday brunch is titled "Morning Wood."

That said, the menu is incredibly refined. Choose from seasonal American food like roasted venison with creamed spinach as well as homemade sausage and spaetzle. Or opt for the country ham flatbread topped with creamy raclette and charred black kale, presented in squares for easy sharing. The bar continues to pour long after the kitchen closes, so night owls sample from the "Backwoods" menu of Belgian frites and sauces.

Lincoln Park & Old Town

The congregation of history, commerce, and nature is what makes Lincoln Park and Old Town one of Chicago's most iconic districts. Scenically situated on Lake Michigan's shore, the eponymous park offers winter-weary locals an excuse to get out. And if that isn't enticing enough, the park also keeps its patrons happy with a spectacular array of cafés, restaurants ranging from quick bites to the city's most exclusive reservations, and takeout spots offering picnic-perfect products. Populated by college grads, young families, and wealthy upstarts, as well as home to more than a handful of historic districts, museums, shopping, music venues, and the famous (not to mention, free) zoo, Lincoln Park flourishes as a much sought destination year-round.

DELICIOUS DINING

Wallet-happy locals and well-heeled gourmands make reservations to come here and dine at some of the most exclusive restaurants in town. But beyond just glorious, white-glove restaurants, there's more delicious eating to be done in this area. During the weekend, these streets are jumping thanks to a combination of plays, musicals, bars, and scores of high-rises housing affluent and brash yuppies. On Wednesdays and Saturdays during the **Green City Market**, the south end of the park is transformed into hipster chef-foodie central. With the aim to increase availability of top produce and to improve the link between farmers and local producers with restaurants and food organizations, this market

works to educate the Windy City's masses about high-quality food sourcing. (In winter it is held across the street inside the Peggy Notebaert Nature Museum).

Lincoln Park's outpost of **Floriole Café & Bakery** brought about much jubilation, and along with it, a regular fan following. In fact, the aromas wafting from freshly baked breads, pastries, and cookies never fail to tempt onlookers. For more savory goodness, try the heartwarming **Meatloaf Bakery**, where meatloaf and mashed potatoes are crafted into all types of dishes. Leaving aside their quirky titles ("loaf-a-roma" or "no buns about it burger loaf"), this may just be some of *the* best baked goods in town. Like many foods (Juicy Fruit, Cracker Jack, and Shredded Wheat, for example), it is said that the Chicago-style dog may have originated at the Chicago World's Fair and Columbian Exhibition in 1893. Others credit the Great Depression for its birth. Regardless of its

origin, one thing is for certain—chef-driven **Franks 'n' Dawgs** is this city's most desirable hot dog destination. By cooking with only fresh, locally sourced ingredients, these hand-crafted creations are sure to hit the spot. Similarly, **The Wieners Circle** is as known and loved for its delicious dogs and fries, late hours (as late as 5:00 A.M.), and intentionally rude service. Red meat fiends may choose to carry on the party at **Butcher & the Burger** as they do their part to stay at the helm of the burger game, or linger at **Gepperth's Meat Market**, which was established in 1906 when the neighborhood was comprised of mostly Hungarian and German settlers. Old-world butchery is the dictum here with knowledge that has been passed down for generations. If prime cuts and all the trimmings come to mind, you know you've arrived at the right place. Meanwhile the ocean's bounty can be relished in all its glory at **Half Shell**. Here the cash-only policy has done nothing to deter crowds from consuming platters of crab legs and briny oysters. Wash down these salty delights with a cool sip from a choice selection at **Goose Island Brewery**, makers of the city's favorite local beers. Keep up this alcohol-fueled fun at **Barrelhouse Flat**, which is always hip and happening thanks to a litany of hand-crafted punches. Then wind up in time—for brunch perhaps?—at **The Drinkingbird**. From a sweet and stirring sake punch to spicy house-made sausages, the carte du jour is nothing less than satisfying.

Lincoln Park is also one of the most dog-friendly areas around, but then what else would you expect from a neighborhood named after a huge expanse of grass? Big bellies and bold palates with Fido in tow are forever filling up on artisanal goods at **Blue Door Farm Stand**. This particularly edgy grocery-cum-café also doubles up as a watering hole and breakfast hot spot for

lunching ladies who can be found picking at kale salads or induling in grilled cheese sammies. If that doesn't bring a smile, deep-fried oreos at **Racine Plumbing** or decadent popcorn from **Berco's** boutique will certainly do the trick. It's a whole different ballgame at **Karyn's Raw Bistro** where a full vegan menu keeps devotees raving year-round. Adjacent, **Karyn's Fresh Corner Café** has the raw movement in fine fettle by selling a host of meals-to-go. These include "meatballs" made from lentils or even soy-protein "sloppy Joes."

OLD TOWN

The Old Town quarter has a few quaint cobblestoned streets that are home to the Second City comedy scene (now with a Zanies, too, for even more laughs). Also nestled here is June's annual must-see (and must-shop) Old Town Art Fair; the Wells Street Art Fair; as well as places to rest with beers and a groovy jukebox—maybe the **Old Town Ale House**? Wells Street is the neighborhood's main drag, and is really where browsing should begin. Any epicurean shopping trip should also include **The Spice House** for its exotic spice blends, many named after local landmarks; or **Old Town Oil** for hostess gifts like infused oils and aged vinegars. Prefer a sweeter vice? **The Fudge Pot** tempts passersby with windows of toffee, fudge, and other chocolate-y decadence. Lastly, you may not be a smoker, but the Up Down Cigar is worth a peek for its real cigar store Indian carving.

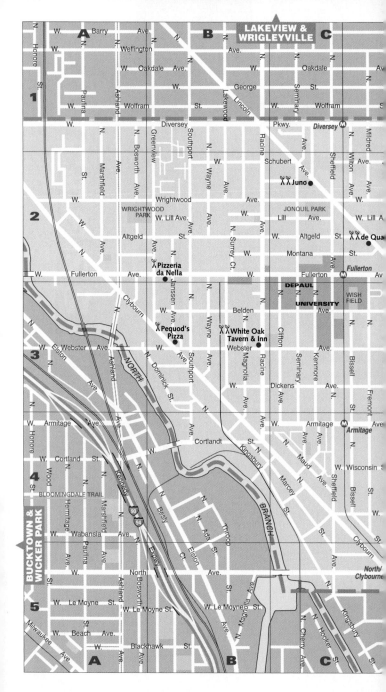

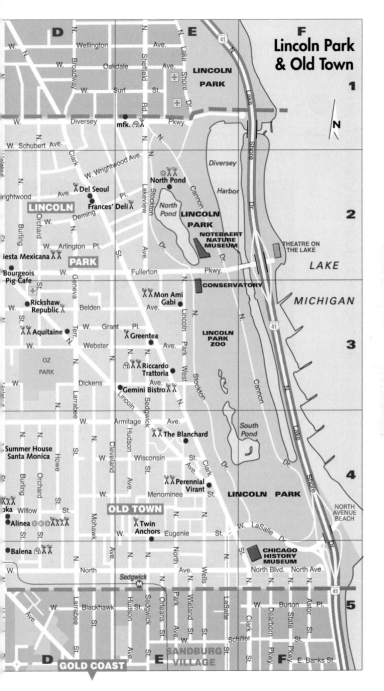

Lincoln Park & Old Town

D **E** **F**

1

Lake Shore Dr.

41

LINCOLN PARK

W. Wellington Ave.

W. Oakdale Ave.

Sheffield St.

W. Surf St.

N. Broadway

W. Diversey Pkwy.   mfk.

N. Clark

W. Schubert Ave.

W. Wrightwood Ave.

Diversey Harbor

North Pond

Del Seoul

N. Lakeview Ave.

Frances' Deli

Stockton Dr.

LINCOLN

N. Orchard

W. Deming Pl.

North Pond

LINCOLN PARK

NOTEBAERT NATURE MUSEUM

THEATRE ON THE LAKE

2

N. Burling

rightwood Ave.

W. Arlington Pl.

St. Geneva

PARK

iesta Mexicana

Fullerton Pkwy.

LAKE

Bourgeois Pig Cafe

CONSERVATORY

MICHIGAN

Rickshaw Republic

W. Belden Ave.

Mon Ami Gabi

N. Lincoln Ave.

Aquitaine

Terr.

W. Grant Pl.

Greentea

N. Park

LINCOLN PARK ZOO

3

W. Webster Ave.

N. Stockton Dr.

OZ PARK

W. Dickens Ave.

Riccardo Trattoria

Gemini Bistro

N. Larrabee

N. Lincoln

N. Sedgwick

Cannon Dr.

41

W. Armitage Ave.

N. Hudson

The Blanchard

Summer House Santa Monica

N. Howe

N. Cleveland

Wisconsin St.

N. Clark St.

South Pond

4

N. Burling

N. Orchard

W. Menominee St.

Perennial Virant

LINCOLN PARK

oka

W. Willow St.

N. Mohawk

OLD TOWN

Twin Anchors

Alinea

W. Eugenie St.

N. Wells St.

N. LaSalle Dr.

NORTH AVENUE BEACH

Balena

W. North Ave.

Sedgwick M

CHICAGO HISTORY MUSEUM

North Blvd.   North Ave.

41

5

W. Larrabee

Blackhawk

N. Hudson

N. Sedgwick

N. Park

N. Orleans St.

N. Wieland St.

N. LaSalle St.

W. Burton Pl.

N. Clark St.

N. Dearborn St.

N. State St.

Astor St.

N. Dearborn Pkwy.

St. Schiller

SANDBURG VILLAGE

E. Banks St.

GOLD COAST

D **E** **F**

Alinea ✿ ✿ ✿

Contemporary XXXX

1723 N. Halsted St. (bet. North Ave. & Willow St.)

Phone: N/A   Dinner Wed – Sun
Web: www.alinearestaurant.com
Prices: $$$$ North/Clybourn

Who needs a meal followed by a show when you can have both together? That's because eating at Alinea, which involves around 20 courses over about three hours, is more than simply dinner—it's culinary theater. Perhaps it could qualify for a Tony Award along with its Michelin stars, because you're even invited backstage afterwards to meet the talented protagonists in the kitchen. Alinea provides such a vivid, visceral experience, that you'll even forget about the somewhat painful and entirely inhospitable booking procedure.

Neophytes have nothing to fear here as there's a veritable army of charming, clued-up helpers and servers to guide you effortlessly through each and every dish. And guidance is certainly needed because the only menu you'll see is the one presented to you like an award certificate as you leave.

The cooking is strikingly original and very clever. It can surprise but it can also challenge; at times dishes can be playful or even whimsical. But underpinning all those clever techniques and all those dazzling arrangements and quite striking presentations is an inherent understanding of flavor— and this is what gives the cooking such great depth.

Aquitaine

 American **XX**

D3

2221 N. Lincoln Ave. (bet. Belden & Webster Aves.)

Phone: 773-698-8456 Dinner nightly
Web: www.aquitainerestaurant.com
Prices: $$ Fullerton

When Lincoln Park locals want French-inspired cuisine, they head to Aquitaine for a taste of Chef/owner Holly Willoughby's refined cooking. Dim lighting and subtle brocade details on the walls keep the long, narrow dining room casually romantic, with enough simple sophistication to swing a Saturday night date or weekday post-work dinner. A well-priced wine list only adds to the elegant appeal.

Large chunks of succulent lobster are a luxe touch in a ramekin of tender potato gnocchi bathed in creamy sauce. Eggplant, olive, and tomato relish give double-cut lamb chops a Provençal spin, heightened by a drizzle of basil pesto. Textbook-perfect crème brûlée needs only a tap of the spoon to send its delicate sugar crust splintering into the silken custard.

Balena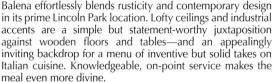

D5

Italian **XX**

1633 N. Halsted St. (bet. North Ave. & Willow St.)

Phone: 312-867-3888 Dinner nightly
Web: www.balenachicago.com
Prices: $$ North/Clybourn

Balena effortlessly blends rusticity and contemporary design in its prime Lincoln Park location. Lofty ceilings and industrial accents are a simple but statement-worthy juxtaposition against wooden floors and tables—and an appealingly inviting backdrop for a menu of inventive but solid takes on Italian cuisine. Knowledgeable, on-point service makes the meal even more divine.

Start with a choice from the large vermouth selection and a round of burrata with pickled mustard seeds and fresh mint, ready to be piled on *lardo*-brushed toast. Or sink your teeth into wood-fired pizza with a parade of toppings like pistachio pesto and crisp mortadella. For dessert, brandy-soaked cherries add boozy warmth to caramel *budino* with salty-sweet praline crumble.

The Blanchard

E4

1935 N. Lincoln Park W. (bet. Lincoln Ave. & Wisconsin St.)

Phone: 872-829-3971   Dinner Tue – Sun
Web: www.theblanchardchicago.com
Prices: $$$

In a minimalist but elegant space that complements its picturesque Lincoln Park environs, The Blanchard serves up sophistication with a side of well-executed French bistro food. Petite portions still satiate thanks to the richness of classic dishes like rillettes, duck à l'orange, and foie gras preparations.

Escargots à la Bourguignonne start the meal on a luxurious note, with each of six plump curls sitting on a knob of mushroom duxelles and bathed in garlic butter, parsley, and breadcrumbs. Lightly caramelized capers and a brown butter sauce garnish two thin fillets of Dover sole meunière, with a streak of green pea tendril pommes purée alongside. Lush passion fruit curd and a sprinkle of lavender buds enhance a moist and chewy coconut financier.

Bourgeois Pig Cafe

D2

738 W. Fullerton Pkwy. (at Burling St.)

Phone: 773-883-5282   Lunch & dinner daily
Web: www.bpigcafe.com
Prices: Fullerton

Scholarly types from nearby DePaul University adore this bookish café on a quiet block of Fullerton. Choose from a litany of salads, sandwiches, and drinks from oversized chalkboard menus behind the counter; then stake out one of the premium second-floor tables. Upstairs, chandeliers, cozy couches, and scattered antiques (not to mention frequent study groups guzzling caffeine and homemade cookies) lend character.

Many sandwiches take names from literary works, like *The Old Man and the Sea* (tuna salad) or *Catcher in the Rye* (reuben). The muffuletta is a lightly pressed panini rendition of the New Orleans standard, stacking a deli's worth of ham, salami, mortadella, provolone, and mild giardiniera in fresh focaccia for a hearty yet delicate bite.

Boka

Contemporary ✗✗✗

D4

1729 N. Halsted St. (bet. North Ave. & Willow St.)

Phone: 312-337-6070   Dinner nightly
Web: www.bokachicago.com
Prices: $$$ North/Clybourn

Housed in an affluent part of town, find a small walkway that leads into this elaborate, handsome, and very sultry dining room. There are three different seating areas and each exudes class with a bit of romance, whimsy, and occasional quirk (note the escutcheon-covered doorway and capricious paintings). Against dark pebbled walls, find oversized horseshoe booths, long banquettes, and mirrored light bulbs casting funky shadows. The semi-outdoor solarium has a living wall of moss and ferns. Servers are friendly and genuine without a hint of pretense.

This is the kind of place where one can sink in and not care to leave.

Chef Lee Wolen's menu may be modern, but it is widely appealing with a Mediterranean edge. Begin with translucent slivers of fresh sea bass that get a pleasant chew from almond crumble and perfect flavor from a subtle dab of citrusy *yuzu kosho*. Then, deliciously tender and evenly pink Colorado lamb is served with a harmonious hodgepodge of creamy yogurt, charred lettuce, and nearly sweet baby potatoes. For dessert, an airy and whipped mound of praline-flavored mousse is set beside milk ice cream, which serves as a cooling counterpoint to the nutty flavors throughout and makes for a fine ending.

de Quay

Fusion

C2

2470 N. Lincoln Ave. (bet. Altgeld & Montana Sts.)

Phone: 872-206-8820   Dinner Tue – Sun
Web: www.dequay-chicago.com
Prices: $$ 🚇 Fullerton

Given its history as a former colony, the Dutch have developed a great deal of appreciation for Indonesian culinary tradtions. And, Chef/owner David de Quay pulls from his family heritage to bring the two together at his eponymous restaurant. Delft pottery houses and sleek teak wood wall accents are visual mementos of this union.

On the menu, sweet-and-sour *babi panggang* departs from its traditional pairing with roast pork to heighten succulent grilled shrimp and fragrant lemongrass *lumpia*. Crisp-edged dumplings enclose a creamy potato-and-Gouda filling that is studded with bacon and English peas. Chewy house-made *stroopwafels* sandwich warm spiced caramel with vanilla bean-flecked ice cream for an unforgettable *finis*.

Del Seoul

Korean ✗

D2

2568-2570 N. Clark St. (bet. Deming Pl. & Wrightwood Ave.)

Phone: 773-248-4227   Lunch & dinner daily
Web: www.delseoul.com
Prices: 🚇 Diversey

♿ Korean street food makes its way from the trendy trucks to a fast-casual space that gives the people what they crave. All the intoxicating flavors of Korean cuisine are here in finger food form, perfect for sharing or creating your own personal buffet. Choose from the video screens above the counter, take a number, and grab a seat.

Bite-sized barbecue tacos are the star of the menu, filled with a variety of meats including *kalbi*-style braised beef short ribs or panko-breaded sesame-chili shrimp. Both get a topping of bright cilantro-onion slaw on grilled white corn tortillas. Canadian poutine crosses a number of borders when topped with more of those tender short ribs, house-made kimchi, pickled red onions, and a trio of melted cheddar, jack, and *crema*.

Fiesta Mexicana

D2

2423 N. Lincoln Ave. (bet. Fullerton Ave. & Halsted St.)

Phone: 773-348-4144   Lunch & dinner daily
Web: www.fiestamexicanachicago.com
Prices: 🚇 Fullerton

Cheerful and bright, Fiesta Mexicana is truly a party for the eyes and tastebuds. High-ceilinged rooms are lined with colorful murals of small-town life, and wide-open front windows invite in warm evening breezes. Live mariachi bands turn up the heat on weekends.

Creative Mexican fare begins with the usual suspects like tacos *al pastor* and piquant, spunky house-made salsa, but unique dishes broaden the offerings. Here, a bowl of *fundido* is a Latin cousin to spinach-and-artichoke dip, with a blend of tangy cheeses and plenty of roasted poblanos for extra heat. Pan-fried pork tenderloin medallions come smothered in tomatillo sauce alongside drunken beans, bacon-wrapped shrimp, and a side of smashed red potatoes with oozing *Chihuahua* cheese.

Frances' Deli

D2

2552 N. Clark St. (bet. Deming Pl. & Wrightwood Ave.)

Phone: 773-248-4580   Lunch daily
Web: www.francesdeli.com
Prices:

Frances' Deli is the type of quaint, lived-in diner everyone dreams of having just around the corner from home. Lucky Lincoln Park residents get that wish fulfilled at this authentic pre-war haunt packed with American antiques and memorabilia—where weekend waits are the norm as half the neighborhood vies for a place at one of the closely spaced tables.

As with any good diner, breakfast, lunch, and dinner all know how to hit the spot. The deli roasts its own meats and does Jewish-American staples right, from flavorful, crisp-tender potato pancakes to oversized pastrami and brisket sandwiches with all the fixings (slaw, fries, and potato salad). As long as you're going for the full nostalgia trip, slurp down a made-to-order milkshake or malt.

Gemini Bistro

American ✗✗

E3

2075 N. Lincoln Ave. (at Dickens Ave.)

Phone: 773-525-2522
Web: www.geminibistrochicago.com
Prices: $$

Lunch Sun
Dinner Tue – Sun
🚇 Armitage

Opposites attract at this delightful neighborhood bistro that offers the best of both worlds: a chic, upscale setting with a casual, approachable attitude. Dark Venetian blinds and awnings remove outside distractions, letting guests focus their attention on the white marble bar and the lychee martinis shaken there. Most street parking in the area is permit only, so consider the valet.

Seasonal American cooking pulls inspiration from the Mediterranean in dishes like plump double-boned pork chop Lyonnaise, cooked to a juicy medium, draped in herbed demi-glace, and nestled with *cipollini* onions and roasted fingerling potatoes. Smaller bites like a trio of seared scallops are paired with the timeless flavors of brown butter, capers, and lemon zest.

Greentea

Japanese ✗

E3

2206 N. Clark St. (bet. Belden & Webster Aves.)

Phone: 773-883-8812
Web: N/A
Prices: $$

Lunch Tue – Sat
Dinner Tue – Sun

BYO

Regulars would rather your eyes glaze past Greentea's nondescript storefront so they can keep this secret to themselves. The bento box-sized room isn't glitzy, so the scene is limited to a few lucky cat sculptures and plants to punctuate the seafoam green walls. Otherwise, the focus is kept on the *itamae* in colorful chef's coats and the pristinely fresh seafood they're preparing.

Purists love the well-priced nigiri, sashimi, and manageably sized rolls showcasing silky hamachi or glistening uni with a touch of minerality. Tiger Eyes salad is a visual showstopper: squid stuffed with smoked salmon, julienned cucumber, and marinated carrots sliced into thin rounds are a clever and flavorful resemblance to an orange-pupiled eye.

Juno

C2

Japanese ✗✗

2638 N. Lincoln Ave. (bet. Seminary & Sheffield Aves.)

Phone: 773-935-2000
Web: www.junosushichicago.com
Prices: $$$

Dinner Tue – Sun

🚇 Diversey

🍶

Raw fish with a side of creativity differentiates Juno from the rest of this city's sushi brethren. With a plain, tavern-like bar up front as well as a bright, inviting dining room and counter (the best seat in the house) in back, this low-key spot is popular for a casual meal. The menu offers cool bites like the Juno queen, a special nigiri of salmon topped with spicy scallop and potato crunch; and hot treats like honey-glazed quail.

Chef B.K. Park's omakase must be ordered 48-hours in advance, but with cleverly spun morsels like briefly torched prawn with pineapple salsa, pickled garlic oil-drizzled New Zealand King salmon, soy-marinated sea eel dabbed with ground sesame seeds, and spicy octopus *temaki*, it's a feast well worth the extra effort.

mfk. 😊

E1

Spanish ✗

432 W. Diversey Pkwy. (bet. Pine Grove Ave. & Sheridan Rd.)

Phone: 773-857-2540
Web: www.mfkrestaurant.com
Prices: $$

Lunch Tue – Sun
Dinner nightly

🚇 Diversey

"First we eat, then we do everything else," said M.F.K. Fisher, the food writer who serves as both the inspiration and namesake for this young neighborhood darling. Thanks to large windows, whitewashed brick walls, and gleaming silver-and-white tilework, the subterranean space manages to evoke a breezy seaside oasis. And with a seafood-centric menu featuring modern interpretations of Iberian-inspired plates, the food follows suit.

The ocean's bounty is showcased in simple but flavorful dishes, like crispy fried prawn heads served with a nutty *salbitxada* sauce for dipping; and bowls of cataplana stew with fresh clams, crunchy shrimp, and grilled cobia collar. A crumbly slice of Basque cake and an expertly pulled *cortado* ends the meal on a high note.

Mon Ami Gabi

E3

2300 N. Lincoln Park West (at Belden Ave.)

Phone: 773-348-8886   Dinner nightly
Web: www.monamigabi.com
Prices: $$

A real French bistro can give an American steakhouse a run for its money in the meat department any day, and the 11 different steak preparations on Mon Ami Gabi's menu (all served with crispy golden frites) are justly impressive. Beyond the butcher case, a selection of satisfying Francophile classics keeps the sophisticated Chicago contingent returning to this cozy, stylish standby.

Tradition reigns in the kitchen, where the emphasis is on flavorful and unpretentious dishes like seafood *pot-au-feu* bobbing with scallops and pepper-crusted cod fillet in a tasty fennel broth. Pickled cornichons and warm toast points make a meal out of house-made country pâté. And for an indulgent finish, split a plate of warm caramel-drizzled pineapple crêpes.

Pequod's Pizza

B3

2207 N. Clybourn Ave. (at Webster Ave.)

Phone: 773-327-1512   Lunch & dinner daily
Web: www.pequodspizza.com
Prices: ⊜⊜   🚇 Armitage

Ditch your diet, grab your fellow Blackhawks fans, and head to this Lincoln Park stalwart for some of the best pies in town. Christened for Captain Ahab's sailing ship, Pequod's menu promises smooth sailing for sports bar noshers, featuring a lineup of shareable bar snacks such as wings and mozzarella sticks, hearty sandwiches like tender Italian beef, and both thin-crust and deep-dish pan pizzas.

Grab that cutlery before digging into the buttery crust of each deep-dish pie, ringed with blackened cheese at the edges. Then toppings like pepperoni, fresh garlic, and crunchy sautéed onions are generously layered between tart tomato sauce and handfuls of cheese for an oozy jumble in every bite. A towering wedge of fudge cake awaits those with room for dessert.

North Pond ✿

Contemporary ✗✗

2610 N. Cannon Dr.

Phone: 773-477-5845
Web: www.northpondrestaurant.com
Prices: $$$

Lunch Sun
Dinner Tue – Sun

Sitting just north of the pond, this former warming house for ice skaters has been reconceived as a chic Craftsman-style cottage with windows overlooking the shimmering water. Flickering candles and wood accents make it feel like a remote forest lodge, and a quote from Chaucer over the wine rack enhances the overall historic feel.

Both the reasonably priced à la carte and fixed menus appear simple, listing one or two main seasonal ingredients often repeated with new insight throughout a meal. However, each dish elevates farm-to-table cooking with creative exploration. This is at once clear in the "egg, bacon," its velvety yolk ready to spill over and lushly sauce the roasted rapini, bacon confit, and dark slice of toasted pumpernickel beneath. This may be followed by pearly white fluke set over deep-green kale braised with bacon and paired with shards of crisped kale, juice-like kale foam, as well as bacon bits, purple potato slices, sweet apple balls, toasted hazelnuts, and a single, succulent Gulf shrimp.

Finish with a quenelle of unique smoked olive oil sorbet paired with torn pieces of herbaceous rosemary cake, cinnamon-laced apple, spiced pecans, puffs of apple foam, and salt-pepper crumble. Then breathe a sigh of supreme satisfaction.

Perennial Virant

E4

American ✕✕

1800 N. Lincoln Ave. (at Clark St.)

Phone:	312-981-7070
Web:	www.perennialchicago.com
Prices:	$$

Lunch Sat – Sun
Dinner nightly

Housed along tony Lincoln Avenue and packed with patrons to match, this Paul Virant operation is a "perennial" hit. Take the time to truly appreciate the philosophy followed at his haute farm-to-table spot, where local, sustainable cuisine combines with a minimalist décor featuring lush earth tones and chandeliers crafted from repurposed jars.

Each ingredient-driven dish honors farmers and seasonality. Crisp pan-fried spaetzle, vivid green with mint, steals the show from a duo of mild but meaty lamb sausages, while a pickled pair of golden beets and diced onion provide a light, refreshing counterpoint to Arctic char. Chèvre ice cream rounds out an arrangement of velvety chocolate pavé, buttery graham cracker, salty-sweet caramel, and chewy coconut macarons.

Pizzeria da Nella

B2

Italian ✕

1443 W. Fullerton Ave. (bet. Greenview & Janssen Aves.)

Phone:	773-281-6600
Web:	www.pizzeriadanella.com
Prices:	$$

Lunch & dinner daily

🚇 Fullerton

Though it calls itself a pizzeria, this cheerful and vast Italian hang near DePaul University is so much more. A mosaic-tiled wood-burning oven gleams from the rear of the dimly lit space, brightened by sunny yellow and Mediterranean blue walls. Craft beer nerds should take a seat at the bar for a sampling from the varied list of artisanal Italian brews.

Authentic Neapolitan pizzas share menu space with modern stuffed "bomba" pies like the Ciotta Ciotta, which mounds a deli case's worth of *salumi* and cheeses between two pizza dough rounds. Pasta selections are equally sprawling, and include fresh combinations like pappardelle with plump mussels, black truffles, and pecorino. Limoncello-soaked strawberries over homemade sponge cake keep the finale light.

Riccardo Trattoria 🐷

Italian ✗✗

E3

2119 N. Clark St. (bet. Dickens & Webster Aves.)

Phone: 773-549-0038
Web: www.riccardotrattoria.com
Prices: $$

Dinner nightly

The timeless wood-and-cream décor doesn't resemble an Italian *nonna's* kitchen, but no matter—the soulful personality of Chef/owner Riccardo Michi and his cache of family recipes make his eponymous restaurant a second home to nearly half the neighborhood. It's a spot that's suited for flirty date nights, boisterous dinners, and every occasion in between.

As befits the word "trattoria," rustic Italian preparations take precedence, but the simplicity satisfies. Chunks of pork sausage add heft to a heaping bowl of hand-rolled cavatelli bathed in a light tomato cream sauce, and curls of grilled calamari need only a squirt of lemon, splash of olive oil, and sprinkle of parsley to sing. For dessert, a thin, buttery tart shell cradles tender wine-poached pears.

Rickshaw Republic

Indonesian ✗

D3

2312 N. Lincoln Ave. (bet. Belden Ave. & Childrens Plz.)

Phone: 773-697-4750
Web: www.rickshawrepublic.com
Prices: 🐽🐽

Lunch Sat – Sun
Dinner Tue – Sun
🚇 Fullerton

The captivating flavors of Southeast Asian street food are matched by the creative design at this friendly, family-run Lincoln Avenue space. Color and pattern collide as parasols, puppets, and bird cages vie for attention with abstract Indonesian wood carvings. Once the food arrives, though, the spotlight shifts to the aromatic plates.

Start with crisp *martabak* crêpes that behold a savory combination of beef, onions, and egg. Then move on to lemongrass-braised chicken thighs in a turmeric-tinged coconut curry with sweet and spicy tamarind *sambal* and pickled cabbage. Surprise your palate with *es cendol*, a mix of coconut milk and green *pandan* jelly in palm sugar syrup. Finally, take one of Mama Setiawan's homemade *sambals* home to bring color to your cooking.

Summer House Santa Monica

American ✕✕

D4

1954 N. Halsted St. (bet. Armitage Ave. & Willow St.)

Phone: 773-634-4100   Lunch & dinner daily
Web: www.summerhousesm.com
Prices: $$ 🚇 Armitage

Sunny days and southern California come to Lincoln Park in the form of this bright and breezy restaurant that resembles a beach house, albeit an enormous one with lots of house guests. It's the perfect choice for a summer's day—and not a bad one in the colder months either, if you're having a quick bite before the theater or want to shake off those winter blues for a while. There's even a countdown showing the number of days till summer.

The menu proves a good fit for the surroundings by keeping things easy. There are sandwiches, tacos, and salads, but it's the meat and fish from the wood-fired oven that stand out. For dessert, choose a big cookie from the counter by the entrance. There's also a pizza restaurant and bar attached.

Twin Anchors

Barbecue ✕

E4

1655 N. Sedgwick St. (at Eugenie St.)

Phone: 312-266-1616   Lunch Sat – Sun
Web: www.twinanchorsribs.com   Dinner nightly
Prices: $$ 🚇 Sedgwick

Within the brick walls that have housed Twin Anchors since 1932, generations have made their way across the checkerboard linoleum floor to throw a quarter in the jukebox and get saucy with a slab of their legendary ribs in one of the curved booths. Though the bar is wall-to-wall on weekends, most weekdays are low-key, with families and groups ready for a casual night out.

Fall-off-the-bone baby back ribs are the real deal, made with a sweet and spicy rub, served with their own "zesty" sauce or the newer Prohibition version, with brown sugar and a hint of ghost-pepper heat. Classic sides like onion rings, baked beans, or hearty chili round out the meal. If there's a wait at this no-reservations spot, try the beer of the month while cooling your heels.

White Oak Tavern & Inn

1200 W. Webster Ave. (at Racine Ave.)

Phone: 773-248-0200
Web: www.whiteoakchicago.com
Prices: $$

Dinner Tue – Sat

🚇 Armitage

Though there was a late summer (2015) transition in chefs, a creative sense of flavor combinations and technical finesse continue to flourish at this appealingly rustic restaurant and inn. Midwestern hospitality and bounty are at the forefront here, and every ingredient on each section of the multi-category menu is of irreprehensible quality.

The in-house cheese-making and bread programs are on full display as evidenced in a bowl of *stracciatella*, where mozzarella mingles with pickled shallot rings next to fluffy, griddled focaccia sticks. A whiff of smoke uplifts moist, meaty sturgeon, simply seared and surrounded by candied hickory nuts and nutty crème fraîche; while a refined and clever root vegetable tartare is deliciously crowned by a sous vide duck egg.

Look for our symbol 🍺,
spotlighting restaurants
with a notable beer list.

foodies and visitors can contact the Chicago Cultural Center's "culinary concierges" with any food tourism-related queries.

SENSATIONAL SPREADS

Start your voyage here by exploring **Block 37**, one of the city's original 58 blocks. It took decades of hard work and several political dynasties, but the block now houses a five-story atrium with shopping, restaurants, and entrances to public transportation. Next up: **Haute Sausage**, a food truck-turned-brick-and-mortar venture boasting numerous creations infused with Middle Eastern and South African flavors. Top off these savory bites with a bit of sweet at the Chicago outpost of New York City hot spot, **Magnolia Bakery**. As per tradition, folks get in line here for treasures such as banana pudding and melt-in-your-mouth cupcakes. For those watching their waistline, probiotic **Starfruit Cafe**—with a spectrum of delicious frozen yogurts—is like heaven on earth. And, catering to the clusters of office types in the Loop, are several fast food options on the Pedway level (a system of tunnels that links crucial downtown buildings underground, which is a godsend during those brutal Chicago winters.) For a quick grab-and-go lunch, **Hannah's Bretzel** is top-notch. Lauded

The relentless pace and race of Chicago's main business district is named after the "El" tracks that make a "loop" around the area. Their cacophony may be an intrinsic part of the soundtrack of the Windy City, but that isn't to say that this neighborhood doesn't have a culinary resonance as well. In fact, it is one that is perpetually evolving with the region. It wasn't that long ago that the Loop turned into no-man's land once the business crowd headed home for the night. However thanks to a revitalized Theater District, new residential high-rises, sleek hotels, and student dorms, the tumbleweeds have been replaced with a renewed dining scene, wine boutiques, and gourmet grocery stores that stay open well past dusk. In fact, as a testament to the times, local as "über sandwich makers," their version of the namesake crafted from freshly baked German bread, features ultra-tasty fillings (imagine a grass-fed sirloin sammie spread with nutty Gruyère, vine tomatoes, and spicy horseradish aïoli). While summer brings a mélange of musical acts to Millennium Park, Grant Park, and the Petrillo Music Shell that are just begging for a picnic, winter evenings are best spent at **The Walnut Room**. Besides fantastic people-watching, a family-friendly vibe, and stunning Christmas décor,

this Marshall Fields favorite also warms the soul with delicious comfort food like Mrs. Hering's Chicken Pot Pie—the recipe for which dates back to 1890. Foodies can also be found feasting at **Park Grill**, a full-service restaurant flanked by an ice rink in the winter. Of course, no trip to Chicago, much less the Loop, would be complete without munching on Italian specialties from **Vivere**—a longtime, local institution mixing formality with spirited charm in a handsome wood-toned space.

TOURING & CAROUSING

Calling all sweet tooths: with flavors like maple-bacon and pistachio-Meyer lemon, you will be hard-pressed to stop at just one donut variety at the ever-delicious **Do-Rite**. But, if dessert doesn't do it for you, eat your way through the Windy City by way of **Tastebud Tours'** Loop route, whose stops include hot dogs, pizza, and **The Berghoff**, the city's oldest restaurant known for enormous steins of beer. Word on the street is that none of the "slices" in Chicago are considered legit without a deep-dish. So, it's no wonder that the popular **Chicago Pizza Tour** is also headquartered here. From visiting restaurant kitchens, getting schooled on top ingredients, ovens, the physics of pizza-making, and digging into deep-dish pies (naturally!), this expedition is designed to showcase the true essence behind Chi-town's most notable food. During warmer months,

several farmer's markets cater to the downtown crowd and may include the ones at Federal Plaza on Tuesdays or Daley Plaza on Thursdays. Though concession carts dot the streets in nearby Millennium Park, home cooks are in for a treat at **Mariano's Fresh Market**. This gourmet emporium proffers everything from gluten-free lemon bars for stiletto-clad socialites, to holiday gift ensembles popular among local businesses. Moving from food to wine, **Printers Row Wine Shop's** carefully curated, all-embracing wine selection, and weekly wine tastings (every Friday at 5:00 PM.) make it the district's go-to wine spot, intent on equipping real folks with the right amount of relevant information. This city also sees its fair share of coffee connoisseurs, and tourists who are tired of sightseeing should be sure to stop in for a pick-me-up at **Intelligentsia Coffee**—a local coffee chain with an emphasis on direct trade. Locations can be found all over town, but the **Millennium Park Coffeebar** is especially convenient and quite delicious.

TASTE OF CHICAGO

One of the Windy City's biggest events (and the second largest attraction in the state of Illinois), **Taste of Chicago** is a five-day summer extravaganza in Grant Park. For the last 30 years, the festival's never-ending maze of real food booths and live music has attracted hordes of hungry diners from all over. It may be hot and crowded, but that's just part of the fun—or torture.

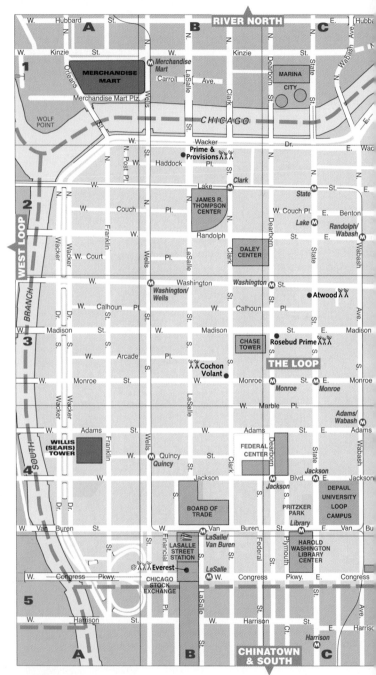

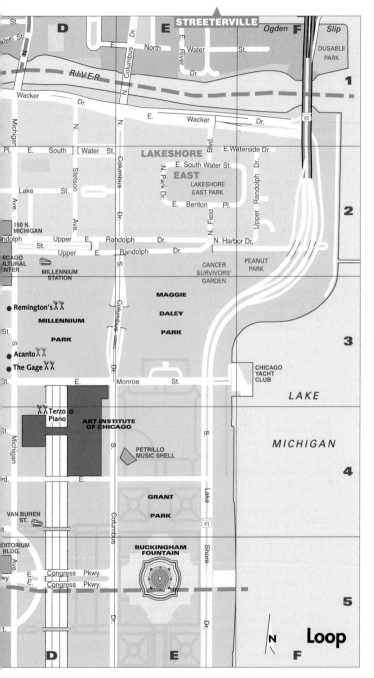

STREETERVILLE

Ogden

Slip

DUSABLE
PARK

D

E

F

St.

ter St.

Dr.

North

E.

Water

St.

River

N.

RIVER

Columbus

Dr.

1

Wacker

Dr.

E.

Wacker

Dr.

41

Michigan

Pl.

N.

E.

South

[Water

St.

E. Waterside Dr.

LAKESHORE

N.

Columbus

Dr.

E. South Water St.

N. Park Dr.

EAST

Upper Randolph Dr.

Lake

St.

Stetson

Ave.

LAKESHORE
EAST PARK

Ave.

E.

Benton

Pl.

2

150 N.
MICHIGAN

Upper

E.

Randolph

Dr.

N. Field St.

N. Harbor Dr.

andolph

St.

Upper

E.

Randolph

Dr.

CANCER
SURVIVORS'
GARDEN

PEANUT
PARK

CHICAGO
ULTURAL
ENTER

MILLENNIUM
STATION

S.

Columbus

Dr.

● Remington's ✕✕

MAGGIE

MILLENNIUM

DALEY

St.

PARK

PARK

3

S.

● Acanto ✕✕

● The Gage ✕✕

Dr.

St.

E.

Monroe

St.

CHICAGO
YACHT
CLUB

LAKE

✕✕ Terzo
Piano ●

Michigan

ART INSTITUTE
OF CHICAGO

S.

MICHIGAN

St.

PETRILLO
MUSIC SHELL

S. Lake

4

rd.

E.

VAN BUREN
ST.

GRANT

PARK

Columbus

Dr.

41

S. Shore

t.

DITORIUM
BLDG.

BUCKINGHAM
FOUNTAIN

Ave.

E.

Congress

Pkwy.

5

wy.

E.

Congress

Pkwy.

Dr.

Dr.

N

Loop

D

E

F

Acanto

D3

Italian ✕✕

18 S. Michigan Ave. (bet. Madison & Monroe Sts.)

Phone: 312-578-0763
Web: www.acantochicago.com
Prices: $$

Lunch & dinner daily

🚇 Monroe

Overseen by Billy Lawless, this Italian reincarnation set in the former Henri space knows how to make an impression: its prime location across from Millennium Park would be a looker any day, but it goes the extra mile with style and sociability. The dining room is striking with angular light fixtures and orange banquettes; a luminous marble bar and matching tables lend a masculine, sophisticated vibe.

The carte's Italian standards are amped up to luxurious levels, like the Treviso and white bean salad with fennel, golden raisins, and crispy pancetta; or house-made duck egg spaghetti drenched in cream sauce and twirled around rapini, spicy pork sausage, and caramelized onions. For dessert, a fresh ricotta tart is highlighted by bittersweet orange marmalade.

Atwood

C3

Contemporary ✕✕

1 W. Washington St. (at State St.)

Phone: 312-368-1900
Web: www.atwoodrestaurant.com
Prices: $$

Lunch & dinner daily

🚇 Washington

This corner restaurant's 19th century façade may be historic, but its soaring dining room is a strikingly modern vision of white marble-topped tables, glossy beveled subway tiles, and low-slung black leather chairs and banquettes. The crimson bar stools fill with patrons meeting for business and pleasure all week, while brunch gets the place buzzing on weekends. Atwood's brasserie menu isn't exactly full of surprises, but its familiar foods are given first-class upgrades—think pancetta-studded mac and cheese; lamb chops with basil and preserved lemon; and an omelet with crunchy bacon, creamy Brie, and verdant asparagus. For a real wake-up call, the Inferno Virgin Mary has more than enough of a kick (plus more of that bacon as a garnish).

Cochon Volant

French XX

B3

100 W. Monroe St. (at Clark St.)

Phone: 312-754-6560   Lunch & dinner daily
Web: www.cochonvolantchicago.com
Prices: $$ Monroe

Though it's attached to the Hyatt, Cochon Volant is quickly entrenching itself as a favorite with Loop locals and sightseers alike for its timeless warmth. Round bistro tables and bentwood chairs are clustered across the mosaic-tiled floor, while a broad, marble-topped bar is bustling with patrons from lunch to happy hour.

French brasserie favorites dominate the menu, ranging from rustic French onion soup to lavish raw seafood *plateaus*. Steak frites are juicy and flavorsome with a tender prime cut of bavette, offered with five sauce options like a classic béarnaise or rich Roquefort. Breakfast is delicious, but for those who don't have time to sit and stay a while, the café and takeaway bakery lets commuters snag a pastry and coffee to go.

The Gage

Gastropub XX

D3

24 S. Michigan Ave. (bet. Madison & Monroe Sts.)

Phone: 312-372-4243   Lunch & dinner daily
Web: www.thegagechicago.com
Prices: $$ Madison

For 10 years, this expansive, eclectic gastropub has catered to the Millennium Park crowds. Handsome banquettes and columns wrapped in celadon tiles lend a clubby allure, but the space's buzzy vibe never feels overwhelming. While a bar stretching half the length of the restaurant gets its fair share of happy-hour crowds, the rear dining rooms offer a more relaxed setting.

Pub classics with flair define the menu, like malt-battered cod with creamy tartar sauce and parsley-dusted thick-cut fries—a solid rendition of fish and chips. Keep it light with crunchy watercress and sugar snap pea salad with house-made burrata, or go all out with a plate of chocolate-toffee cream puffs garnished with tender cocoa-dusted marshmallows.

Everest ✿

French 🍴🍴🍴

B5

440 S. LaSalle St. (bet. Congress Pkwy. & Van Buren St.)

Phone: 312-663-8920   Dinner Tue – Sat
Web: www.everestrestaurant.com
Prices: $$$$ LaSalle/Van Buren

Summit the historic Chicago Stock Exchange building via a private elevator to reach the sophisticated—though not outdated—scene at Everest on the 40th floor. The sunken-level dining room stays dimly lit by contemporary circular metal light fixtures, all the better to gaze admiringly at the views from the windows framing the formal space. Heavy white linens and abstract bronze sculptures adorn each table, at which smartly dressed guests take it all in.

Alsatian chef Jean Joho keeps to the French tradition on his degustation and prix-fixe menus, with nods to local ingredients among the classical techniques and pairings presented nightly. Where other chefs may feel the need to update and tweak time-honored dishes, Everest celebrates its classics.

Subtle hints of ginger in a rich Gewürztraminer butter sauce complement succulent chunks of fresh Maine lobster. Two thick, bone-in lamb chops, ringed elegantly with flavorful fat, are tender but never too chewy, their richness amplified by delicate, silken spring garlic flan and a bed of crisp green beans that soak up the thyme jus. Cap it all off with tart and sweet pistachio vanilla *succès* dabbed with ruddy rhubarb jam.

Prime & Provisions

B2

Steakhouse ✗✗✗

222 N. LaSalle St. (at Wacker Dr.)

Phone: 312-726-7777
Web: www.primeandprovisions.com
Prices: $$$

Lunch Mon – Fri
Dinner nightly
🚇 Clark/Lake

Though it would also feel at home in Las Vegas, this glitzy oversized steakhouse fits right in with its swanky Chicago riverfront neighbors. The polished, masculine interior makes its priorities clear from the get-go, showcasing a two-story wine tower and a peek into the dry-aging room under bold barrel-vaulted ceilings and chandeliers.

A starter of chewy rosemary-sea salt monkey bread whets the palate, while rosy pink slices of slow-roasted bone-in prime rib, rubbed with a crust of fragrant herbs, take a classic hoagie to new heights. When paired with house-cut fries and creamy horseradish dip, it's a meal to rival a Porterhouse, but save room for dessert: a single-serving banana cream pie with loads of whipped cream is a whimsical final bite.

Remington's

D3

American ✗✗

20 N. Michigan Ave. (bet. Madison & Washington Sts.)

Phone: 312-782-6000
Web: www.remingtonschicago.com
Prices: $$

Lunch & dinner daily

🚇 Madison

This shiny gem arrives courtesy of the 4 Star Restaurant Group behind Crosby's Kitchen, Dunlay's, and Frasca. Guests can choose from a few great seating options in the enormous space: a table by the large windows up front, thrown open on temperate days for people-watching; the U-shaped bar, chockablock with televisions airing the latest games; or the intimate, glassed-in dining room lined with wine bottles at the back.

The restaurant features an elevated roster of American classics including steaks, rotisserie chicken and seafood—not to mention a raw bar with Kansai-style box-pressed sushi. It's hard to go wrong here, but don't miss the No. 8 Tuna, which is a ruby-red slice of ahi wrapped in crispy nori and tempura, then paired with kimchi-studded rice.

Rosebud Prime

Chicago ▲ Loop

C3

Steakhouse

1 S. Dearborn St. (at Madison St.)

Phone: 312-384-1900
Web: www.rosebudrestaurants.com
Prices: $$$

Lunch Mon – Sat
Dinner nightly
🚇 Monroe

A member of Chicago's longstanding Rosebud Restaurants, this Loop darling plays the part of a throwback American steakhouse to the hilt. Crimson-hued, faux-alligator chairs and banquettes punctuate a sprawling wood-paneled dining room, where tuxedoed servers weave expertly among suited bankers. A winding staircase leads to a lofty mezzanine.

Classic cuts and chops abound, but Rosebud Prime does all of its dishes with panache. Double-cut bone-in lamb chops sport a plump ribbon of fat encircling their delicate, rich centers. Two strips of grilled skirt steak remain juicy and tender, complemented by a pile of caramelized Bermuda onions; and rich beef and veal ragù makes penne Bolognese a lovely surprise, finished with a dollop of fresh ricotta.

Terzo Piano

D4

Italian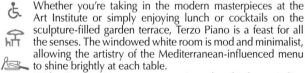

159 E. Monroe St. (in the Art Institute of Chicago)

Phone: 312-443-8650
Web: www.terzopianochicago.com
Prices: $$$

Lunch daily
Dinner Thu
🚇 Monroe

Whether you're taking in the modern masterpieces at the Art Institute or simply enjoying lunch or cocktails on the sculpture-filled garden terrace, Terzo Piano is a feast for all the senses. The windowed white room is mod and minimalist, allowing the artistry of the Mediterranean-influenced menu to shine brightly at each table.

With Tony Mantuano overseeing the kitchen, Italian influences find their way into many seasonal dishes. Charred tomato crème fraîche lends luxurious smokiness and a tart streak to tender chicken Milanese resting on roasted cipollini purée; and agnolotti bursting with a sweet pea-ricotta filling find savory balance with shards of crispy pancetta.

As an added bonus, museum members receive a 10 percent discount on the meal.

Pilsen, University Village & Bridgeport

This cluster of neighborhoods packs a perfect punch, both in terms of food and sheer vitality. It lives up to every expectation and reputation, so get ready for a tour packed with literal, acoustic, and visual flavor. The Little Italy moniker applies to a stretch of Taylor Street that abuts the University (of Illinois at Chicago) Village neighborhood, and it's bigger and more authentically Italian than it first appears. The streets are as stuffed with epicurean shops as an Italian beef is with meat. So, bring an appetite and try this iconic (and messy) Chicago specialty at **Al's No. 1 Italian Beef**. After combing through the supply at **Conte Di Savoia**, an Italian grocery and popular takeout spot, stop for lunch at **Fontano's Subs** (locally famous for their hearty subs) or old-school **Bacchanalia**.

Brunch your way through the day at **Pleasant House Bakery**; then save room for dessert at **Beurrage**, a hip organic bakery-cum-café known for flaky, buttery croissants. But, **Mario's Italian Lemonade** is where you can drown your sorrows—over a frozen fruit slush. Later, consider popping into **Scafuri Bakery** for a sugar refill, some biscotti, or *sfogliatelle*. This charming retreat has been delivering traditional Italian sweets to the community since opening its doors in 1904. Well-loved for fresh-baked breads, pastries,

and cookies, wedding cakes and pies are now also part of their ever-changing repertoire.

UNIVERSITY VILLAGE

Like any self-respecting college "town," University Village is home to a range of warm and toasty coffee shops. Add to that the mélange of doctors, medical students, nurses, and others working in the neighborhood hospital, and you've got a perpetually bustling vibe with great people-watching potential. Take a break from the hustle to quench your thirst at one among a few select locations of **Lush Wine & Spirits**. On Sundays, follow the band of locals to **Maxwell Street Market**. Having relocated to Desplaines Street in 2008, this sprawling bazaar welcomes over 500 vendors selling fresh produce, amazing Mexican eats, and miscellanea. Watch celebrity chef, Rick

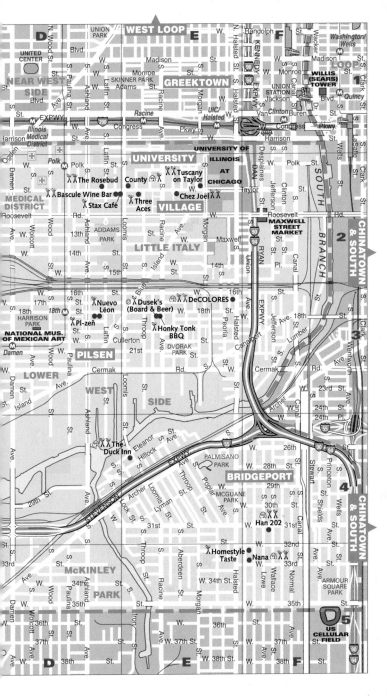

Bascule Wine Bar

Contemporary ✕✕

D2

1421 W. Taylor St. (bet. Laflin & Loomis Sts.)

Phone: 312-763-6912
Web: www.basculewinebar.com
Prices: $$

Lunch Sun
Dinner nightly
🚇 Polk

Among the profusion of Italian-American standbys in Little Italy, Bascule emerges as a rustic and welcoming newcomer. Wide wood plank floors and a windowed façade open up the cozy space, flooding the length of the bar with light—and a semi-open kitchen turning out ambitious seasonal dishes emphasizes that this is much more than a wine bar.

Quality ingredients and technique are on display in compositions like Indiana-farmed rabbit loin tucked with black pepper and glazed with blueberry and rhubarb demi-glace to balance sweetness and spice. Half portions let guests enjoy tastes of heady dishes like truffle *cavatappi* with cheddar crackling and roasted crumpled parsley. Stuffed? Order a slice of the olive oil cake for an ethereally light finale.

Chez Joël

French ✕✕

E2

1119 W. Taylor St. (bet. Aberdeen & May Sts.)

Phone: 312-226-6479
Web: www.chezjoelbistro.com
Prices: $$

Lunch & dinner Tue – Sun

With tables covered in archetypal butcher's paper, butter-yellow walls, and red velvet window dressings, Chez Joël adds a touch of *je ne sais quoi* to Little Italy. The cozy, romantic setting is filled with expats and locals reliving memories of their trips to the City of Light. Taxidermied pheasants keep watch over the room from their high perches, like a Deyrolle curiosity.

The kitchen gives classic French cuisine a soupçon of international embellishment. Three plump scallops spooned with basil pesto are set over a pool of tomato coulis for a Franco-Italian take on *coquilles St. Jacques*. A simple Caesar salad benefits from fresh ingredients like tender grilled chicken and crisp romaine lettuce in a garlicky dressing. Tasty pastas round out the menu.

County

Barbecue 🍴

1352 W. Taylor St. (bet. Ada & Loomis Sts.)

Phone: 312-929-2528
Web: www.dmkcountybarbeque.com
Prices: 💰💰

Lunch & dinner daily

🚇 Polk

As its name implies, this urban 'cue joint celebrates barbecue in all its lip-smacking regional varieties. A flannel-lined wall stretches behind wooden tables set with an array of sauces for sampling, and beer and Bourbon take precedence on the drinks menu.

Ensuring that no barbecue briquette goes unturned, the menu's spice rubs, brines, and smoking methods honor the regional styles of the Carolinas, west Texas, Kansas City, and Memphis. Take a gander at the nightly "smokin' specials" or choose from an already impressive lineup of slow-smoked ribs, wings, and other tasty bits. For extra impact, add a pile of tender pulled pork to a smoked bacon and fried green tomato sandwich—and order a slice of sensationally sweet pecan pie from Scafuri Bakery for dessert.

DeCOLORES 👻

Mexican 🍴🍴

1626 S. Halsted St. (bet. 16th & 17th Sts.)

Phone: 312-226-9886
Web: www.decolor.us
Prices: $$

Lunch Sat – Sun
Dinner Tue – Sun

This family-owned Mexican restaurant in Pilsen's art district appropriately doubles as a gallery, with locals' works rotating frequently on the coffee-colored walls. If the pieces for sale don't strike a chord, just admire the bar's halting design of stylized metal branches snaking between shelves of colorful sugar skulls and paper flags.

Recipes passed down through generations highlight fresh vegetables and healthy fare. The salsa with house-made corn chips as a starter changes every day, but each variety is a pleasure. Hominy stew with roast pork is traditionally garnished with shaved raw cabbage, radish, and red onion in pozole and then sprinkled with cucumber salsa for a fresh take; while boneless *guajillo*-marinated pork loin chops gain sweetness from grilled pineapple.

The Duck Inn 😊

✗✗

E4

2701 S. Eleanor St. (at Loomis St.)

Phone: 312-724-8811   Dinner nightly
Web: www.theduckinnchicago.com
Prices: $$

Grab a taxi and head to the warehouses of Bridgeport, where this stylish, modern tavern—from neighborhood native Kevin Hickey—feels like a diamond in the rough. Through a set of French doors, the hubbub brought on by intricate cocktails in the retro globe-lit lounge leads to a decorous dining room with wide wooden tables and curvy midcentury seating.

Beyond the kitchen's signature rotisserie duck for two, the menu spreads its wings with a focused but diverse selection of small plates and entrées. Briny sea beans are the crowning touch to a winning dish of uni butter-slathered spot prawns and creamy risotto, while a duo of pickle- and beer-brined chicken thigh and drumstick glisten with a tableside finish of smoked paprika jus.

Han 202 😊

✗✗

F4

605 W. 31st St. (bet. Lowe Ave. & Wallace St.)

Phone: 312-949-1314   Dinner Tue – Sun
Web: www.han202.com
Prices: $$

BYO

In a neighborhood dominated by sports bars and Irish pubs, Han 202 stands apart as a sophisticated pan-Asian alternative for White Sox watchers. Bare wood tables and high-backed coffee-and-cream leather seats convey polish—an attitude reinforced by the skilled chefs and servers. Dramatic driftwood sculpture and framed art play against pale walls.

The $35 four-course prix-fixe menu is a true bargain, with each course punctuated by precisely cut fresh bites of sushi. Jeju Island *hirame* is lightly brushed with mirin and kissed with wasabi. Lobster tail arrives warm and buttery with a dollop of fresh ricotta and tender red beet halves, drizzled with olive oil. Seared duck breast adds juicy flavor to standard steamed vegetables in a fermented bean sauce.

Dusek's (Board & Beer) ❀

E3

1227 W. 18th St. (at Allport St.)

Phone: 312-526-3851
Web: www.dusekchicago.com
Prices: $$

Lunch Sat – Sun
Dinner nightly
🚇 18th

Dusek's brings the party to Pilsen thanks to its palpable energy, groovy beats, and good-looking bar pouring an exceptional beverage program. Then consider the fact that the owners of Longman & Eagle are behind this operation and know that you're in for some seriously unique and outstanding eats.

Housed in a booming, hipster-centric corner of the lower west side, this stylish public hall has major cool factor and enough real estate to be a triple threat.

Framed by windows, the dining room is on the main floor while the upstairs (Thalia Hall) is a live music venue. Service throughout is very cordial, so settle in and await a spread of quirky American food. The menu changes daily so don't get hung up on favorites. However, smash-hits may include a wood-roasted cheese-stuffed pretzel coupled with wasabi dipping sauce as well as an ultra-decadent blue crab dip paired with artichoke relish and crusty, house-made pain d'epi. Live out your gourmet gastropub fantasy with slow-cooked salmon sporting a salty crust and spiced with salsa verde; or gnocchi tossed with lamb Bolognese and creamy ricotta. Portions should necessitate a doggie bag, but all the better to save room for an inventive fruit loop donut or even roasted chili churros with dulce de leche.

EL Ideas ✿

C2

2419 W. 14th St. (at Western Ave.)

Phone:	312-226-8144
Web:	www.elideas.com
Prices:	**$$$$**

Dinner Tue – Sat

🔲 Western (Pink)

BYO

Free your mind, keep your expectations high, and ignore the hand-made sign and desolate locale that make this undeniably edgy restaurant feel like a David Lynch movie.

No one comes here for high-end pampering. Rather, the interior is an amalgam of heavy wood timber, zinc ductwork, abstract art, and a homespun curtain made of wine corks. The open kitchen and its team of freewheeling anti-heroes lend a dinner-party vibe, with guests bringing bottles of Bourbon as gifts for the chefs and others getting up to mingle. Woe to those who come here to dine alone.

This prix-fixe is an all-embracive antithesis to highfalutin fine dining, with courses that the chef might describe as salty-sweet stoner food. Envision golden-fried potatoes in a piping hot leek soup, topped with liquid nitrogen-prepared vanilla ice cream that pops and crackles when poured overtop. The result is a brilliant playfulness that hits all the right gustatory notes. Seared venison may arrive with plump morels, jicama brunoise, beluga lentils, and wonderfully bright green garlic "slaw." Flavor, texture, and presentation reach their height in the chartreuse cake with candied fennel, wild huckleberries, and white chocolate crémeux.

Homestyle Taste

Chinese ✗

F5

3205 S. Halsted St. (bet. 32nd & 33rd Sts.)

Phone: 312-949-9328
Web: N/A
Prices: ⊖⊖

Lunch & dinner daily

BYO

For more adventurous fare than spicy Sichuan lamb or dim sum, look no further than this family-run favorite. Though the lengthy menu offers plenty of usual suspects (think scallion pancakes and *mapo* tofu), it's also chock-full of authentic Chinese dishes that will make any offal lover's day.

Thin slices of lamb kidney are dry stir-fried, their mild flavor boosted by copious amounts of cumin and red chilies. Then, a sweet and sour sauce offsets the funky flavor of quick-fried intestine, tripe, and liver; and pickled cabbage and pork meatball soup, boosted by tofu and noodles, is a welcome warmer on cold days. The service is friendly and amenable, so don't be afraid to specify your preferred meat or ask for chili oil to amplify the heat quotient.

Honky Tonk BBQ

Barbecue ✗

E3

1800 S. Racine Ave. (at W. 18th St.)

Phone: 312-226-7427
Web: www.honkytonkbbqchicago.com
Prices: $$

Dinner Tue – Sun

🚇 18th

A rousing success since it opened in 2007, Honky Tonk BBQ serves up live music and award-winning Memphis-style treats on the southwest side of the city. Though the rollicking bar up front takes its cues from a swinging Wild West saloon, the rear dining room offers a more sedate—though still eclectic—setting for sipping house cocktails and chowing down on sensational smoked meats.

You'll need two hands to hold homemade empanadas stuffed with combinations like Manchego cheese and shiitake mushrooms, and extra cottony white bread to soak up the juices of bone-in, wood-smoked chicken. Brisket chili is even more robust with a scoop of creamy mac and cheese—and if you're still hungry, soda floats with Bridgeport-made Filbert's root beer are the cherry on top.

La Casa De Samuel

Mexican 🍴

B3

2834 W. Cermak Rd. (bet. California Ave. & Marshall Blvd.)

Phone: 773-376-7474
Web: www.lacasadesamuel.com
Prices: 🪙🪙

Lunch & dinner daily

🚇 California (Pink)

Though the sign over the awning reads "Cocina Internacional," make no mistake: this Mexican restaurant has been bringing tacos and *queso fundido* to Pilsen since 1989. Exposed wood beams, brick walls, and bright oil paintings add a true-blue vibe; while a tortilla station where an *abuelita* works masa into thin discs gets the appetite going. Multi-generational families return time and again to share spicy *molcajete*-crushed salsa.

Along with the freshly made tortillas that arrive swaddled and warm from the grill, the bustling kitchen turns out solid standards like fajitas as well as unusual wild game options like grilled wild boar, rabbit, or alligator. Wash down baby eels sizzling with garlic and chile with an icy lime-infused margarita.

Nana 😊

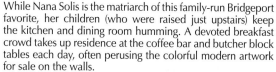

American 🍴🍴

F5

3267 S. Halsted St. (at 33rd St.)

Phone: 312-929-2486
Web: www.nanaorganic.com
Prices: $$

Lunch daily
Dinner Wed – Sun

While Nana Solis is the matriarch of this family-run Bridgeport favorite, her children (who were raised just upstairs) keep the kitchen and dining room humming. A devoted breakfast crowd takes up residence at the coffee bar and butcher block tables each day, often perusing the colorful modern artwork for sale on the walls.

Locally sourced and organic are the guiding principles behind every ingredient here; many dishes also get a little Latin flavor. Soft avocado wedges are tossed in panko, then flash-fried for a crispy exterior and creamy center. "Nanadicts" give a Southwestern accent to eggs Benedict by adding chorizo, corn *pupusas*, and poblano cream. Sunday nights feature family-style fried chicken dinners fit for large groups with larger appetites.

Nuevo Léon

Mexican ✗

D3

1515 W. 18th St. (bet. Ashland Ave. & Laflin St.)

Phone: 312-421-1517   Lunch & dinner daily
Web: N/A
Prices: 💰💰   🚇 18th

Nuevo Leon's colorful trompe l'oeil exterior is almost as loud as the din inside this family favorite in the heart of Pilsen. A jukebox competes with the chatter as it blasts Mexican tunes throughout multiple dining rooms, bouncing off clay tile floors and rattling the hand-painted plates on festive yellow walls.

The crowds come for large portions of straightforward Mexican favorites like slabs of carne asada with warm corn tortillas to wrap the lightly seasoned meat and beans. Munch on a complimentary beef-and-potato soft taco while poring over the extensive menu. Sizzling platters arrive in a heartbeat once the order's been placed. Just add summery tomato salsa or taqueria-style pickled carrots and jalapeños to give each bite a bit more zing.

Pl-zeň

Gastropub ✗

D3

1519 W. 18th St. (bet. Ashland Ave. & Laflin St.)

Phone: 312-733-0248   Lunch Sat – Sun
Web: www.pl-zen.com   Dinner Tue – Sun
Prices: $$ 🚇 18th

The beckoning tentacles of an enormous octopus painted on a brownstone point the way to this quirky subterranean spot. More murals lead diners down a brick-lined alley and into the dining room, where the dim space is lightened by blonde wood bar stools and a hospitable vibe from the cool young staff.

Though both *chilaquiles* and sesame-crusted tilapia tacos find their way on to the menu, Pl-zeň offers a full slate of gastropub fare that steps away from the traditional Mexican bent of the neighborhood. Raisin- and pignoli-studded boar meatballs are simmered in tomato sauce and finished with ricotta and caramelized onions. A poached egg adds richness to crispy pig ear salad with Fresno chili aïoli. Cinnamon-sugar beignets deserve a dip in luscious strawberry-pinot grigio sauce.

175

The Rosebud

Italian **XX**

D2

1500 W. Taylor St. (at Laflin St.)

Phone: 312-942-1117
Web: www.rosebudrestaurants.com
Prices: $$

Lunch & dinner daily

Polk

The Rosebud holds its own among the brass of University Village's Italian thoroughfare. The original location of what is now an extended family of restaurants throughout Chicagoland, it's nothing if not classic with its red neon sign, dark carved wood, and cool but accommodating all-male waitstaff.

Italian wedding soup brings comfort with moist, tiny meatballs, escarole, and *acini di pepe* simmered in broth; while sweet sausage chunks, caramelized onions, and a garlicky white wine sauce make chicken *giambotta* a satisfying choice. Loyal clientele crowd around white tablecloths for platters of their favorite chicken parmesan or linguine topped with a mountain of clams. Also, dessert is not to be missed: a single slice of carrot cake will gratify the whole table.

Stax Café

American **X**

D2

1401 W. Taylor St. (at Loomis St.)

Phone: 312-733-9871
Web: www.staxcafe.com
Prices: ☕☕

Lunch daily

"We're Breakfast Geeks. We take this stuff way too seriously" reads one of the server's T-shirts at Stax Café, and UIC students and staff are grateful for their dedication to heart-warming wake-up delights. From the coffee and fresh juice bar for on-the-go types, to flat-screen TVs for those dying to catch up on sports, this corner restaurant aims to get everyone's day started right.

Breakfast items with tasty twists abound, like ricotta pancakes with strawberry-rhubarb compote; or the Spanish Harlem omelet served frittata-style with chorizo, roasted tomatoes, and poblano peppers. Can't choose? Get a side of mini waffles dusted with powdered sugar alongside your main dish, and don't forget to check out the chalkboards for specials—perhaps breakfast tacos?

Three Aces

1321 W. Taylor St. (bet. Loomis & Throop Sts.)

Phone: 312-243-1577
Web: www.threeaceschicago.com
Prices: $$

Lunch Sat – Sun
Dinner nightly
🚇 Polk

Look past the fact that Three Aces is a bar—a hip, dimly-lit, rock n' roll-loving bar at that—and you'll find a soulful kitchen with a deft hand at turning out Italian riffs on American farm-to-table cuisine. Inventive combinations are the order of the day on both the food and cocktail lists; the Fiery Jalesco gets motors revving with a delicately smoky blend of mezcal, St. Germain, and grapefruit aromatics.

Many dishes beg for sharing, like the Calabrese *pizzetta* that heats things up with spicy sausage and red chili flakes. Roast beef panini takes its cue from Chicago's famous Italian beef, its pressed sourdough slices are slathered with aïoli, packed to the gills with tangy giardiniera and provolone, and served with garlicky beef jus.

Tuscany on Taylor

1014 W. Taylor St. (bet. Miller & Morgan Sts.)

Phone: 312-829-1990
Web: www.tuscanychicago.com
Prices: $$

Lunch Mon – Fri
Dinner nightly
🚇 UIC-Halsted

Italian and Chicago accents co-mingle at Tuscany on Taylor, where the classic cuisine and service are perfectly old-school (no pun intended—the university is a few blocks away). The formal staff tends to diners at white linen-topped tables in the terra cotta-tiled dining room. Chefs in puffy toques man the open kitchen amid shelves of polished copper pans.

A wide-ranging menu of modern Italian interpretations takes guests on a whirlwind tour of the boot. Tiny ravioli stuffed with roasted pears are set in a densely flavorful mascarpone cream sauce with toasted pine nuts and strips of sundried tomatoes. A simple caprese salad arrives as three stacks of thickly sliced heirloom tomatoes, buffalo mozzarella, and basil pesto drizzled with balsamic reduction.

River North

Urban, picture-perfect, and always-happening River North not only edges the Magnificent Mile, but is also set north of the Chicago River, just across the bridge from the Loop. Once packed with factories and warehouses, today this capital of commercialization is the ultimate landing-place for art galleries, well-known restaurants, swanky shopping, and a hopping nightlife. Thanks to all this versatility, the area attracts literally everybody—from lunching ladies and entrepreneurs, to tour bus-style visitors. Tourists are sure to drop by, if only to admire how even mammoth chain restaurants ooze a particular charm here. Among them is **Rock 'n' Roll** **McDonald's**, a block-long, music-themed outpost of the ubiquitous burger chain. This is one of the world's busiest **MickeyD's** with an expanded menu, music memorabilia, and bragging rights to the first two-lane drive-through. Speaking of drive-throughs, River North is also home to the original **Portillo's**, a hot dog, burger, and beer favorite, whose giant exterior belies its efficient service and better-than-expected food. When it comes to size, few buildings can rival **Merchandise Mart** (so large it has its own ZIP code), known for its retail stores, drool-worthy kitchen showrooms, and two great food shops. **Artisan Cellar** is one such gem where in addition to boutique wines and cheeses, you can also purchase Katherine Anne Confections' fresh cream caramels. Locals

also adore and routinely frequent **The Chopping Block** for its expertly taught themed cooking courses; updated, well-edited wine selections; and sparkling knife collection.

From trends to legends, **Carson's** is a barbecue institution. This squat brick box has no windows, but is just the kind of place where wise guys like to do business, with a bib on of course! This old-school treasure features framed pictures of every local celebrity, who can also be seen gracing the walls at seafood superstar, **Shaw's Crab House**. Their nostalgic bar and dining den is dotted with stainless steel bowls to collect the shells from the multitude of bottom-dwellers on offer. Crab is always available of course, but selections spin with the season. For those who aren't down with seafood in any form, this kitchen turns out a few prime steaks as well. Combat the bitter-cold winters and warm your soul with hearty food and easy elegance at **Lawry's Prime Rib**, in the 1890's McCormick Mansion. Inside, the opulent dining room covers all bases from prime rib dinners to seafood signatures. But, true carnivores who like their meat and potatoes done in grand style will find deep comfort in **Smith & Wollensky's** elaborate carte. Another nationwide chain, **Fleming's Prime Steakhouse & Wine Bar** is as well-regarded and recognizable as the aromas wafting from **Bow Truss Coffee Roasters**, where busy commuters pop in for

a robust espresso. Further indulge your dessert dreams at **Firecakes Donuts** where coconut cream-filled buns are chased down by piping-hot chocolate bobbing with soft marshmallows. The Windy City's doughnut craze carries on at **Doughnut Vault**, brought to you by restaurateur Brendan Sodikoff, who appears to have the Midas touch with this morning-fried dough. Formerly the location for the infamous Cabrini-Green government housing, today **Chicago Lights: Urban Farm** showcases organic produce, nutritional education, and workforce training, thereby elevating the level of economic opportunities available to this vibrant community. On the other hand, **Eataly** is an impressive ode to Italian food, employing a massive workforce. This gourmet paradise may present the same delicacies as its NYC flagship, but the Nutella (corner) with its mouthwatering selection is sure to have folks returning for more.

DEEP-DISH DELIGHTS

Thanks to its diverse community, River North is also an excellent destination for various food genres including the local phenomenon of deep-dish pizza. With a doughy crust holding abundant cheese, flavorful sauce, and other toppings, some may say this is closer to a casserole or "hot dish" than an Italian-style pizza. Either way, these pies take a while to craft, so be prepared to wait wherever you go. **Pizzeria Uno** (or sister **Pizzeria Due**), and **Giordano's** are some of the best-known pie makers in town. And, if a little indigestion isn't a concern, chase them down with another local specialty—the Italian beef. At **Mr. Beef's**, these "parcels" resemble a messy, yet super-tasty French dip, wrapping thinly sliced, well-seasoned beef with hot or sweet peppers on a hoagie. If you order it "wet," both the meat and bread will be dipped in pan juices. You could also add cheese, but hey, this isn't

Philly! Distinguished by day, River North pumps up the volume at night with sleek cocktail lounges, night clubs, and authentic Irish bars. Slip into **Three Dots and a Dash**, a retro, tiki-inspired bar featuring some of the city's most well-regarded mixologists. But, for a more rootin'-tootin' good time, stop by the electric **Underground Wonder Bar** whose dangerously tenacious punchbowls and succinct pan-Asian menu make it a favorite for private parties. Meanwhile, happy hour is always hopping at **Green Door Tavern**, which gets its name from the fact that its colored front told Prohibition-era customers where to enter for a drink. To appreciate what all the fuss is about, order their "famous corned beef sandwich" or "the legend burger."

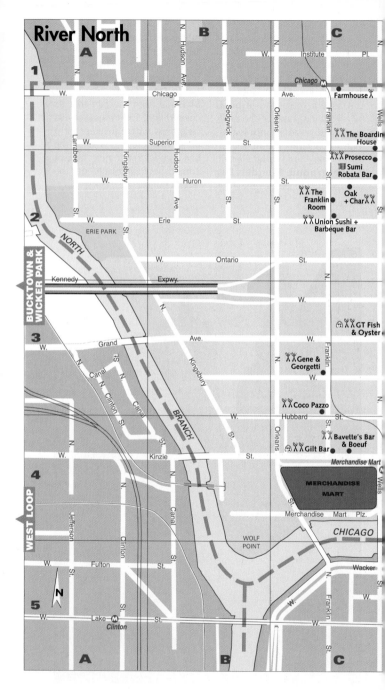

River North

A **B** **C**

1

N. Hudson Ave.

W. Institute Pl.

Chicago Ⓜ

W. Chicago Ave.

🍴 Farmhouse 🍴

N. Larrabee St.

N. Kingsbury St.

W. Superior St.

N. Sedgwick St.

N. Orleans St.

N. Franklin

N. Wells

🍴🍴 The Boarding House

W. Huron St.

N. Hudson Ave.

🍴🍴🍴 Prosecco
🍴 Sumi Robata Bar

2

N.

ERIE PARK

W. Erie St.

🍴🍴 The Franklin Room

Oak + Char 🍴🍴

NORTH

🍴🍴 Union Sushi + Barbeque Bar

W. Ontario St.

Kennedy Expwy.

W.

3

Grand Ave.

W.

🍴🍴 GT Fish & Oyster

N. Canal St.

N. Clinton St.

N. Canal St.

BRANCH

N. Kingsbury St.

N. Franklin

🍴🍴 Gene & Georgetti

W.

🍴🍴 Coco Pazzo

W. Hubbard St.

N. Orleans St.

🍴🍴 Bavette's Bar & Boeuf

W. Kinzie St.

🍴🍴 Gilt Bar

Merchandise Mart

4

WEST LOOP

N. Jefferson St.

N. Clinton St.

MERCHANDISE MART

N. Wells St.

Merchandise Mart Plz.

CHICAGO

W. Fulton St.

WOLF POINT

N. Franklin St.

Wacker

5

W. Lake Ⓜ St.
Clinton

N

A **B** **C**

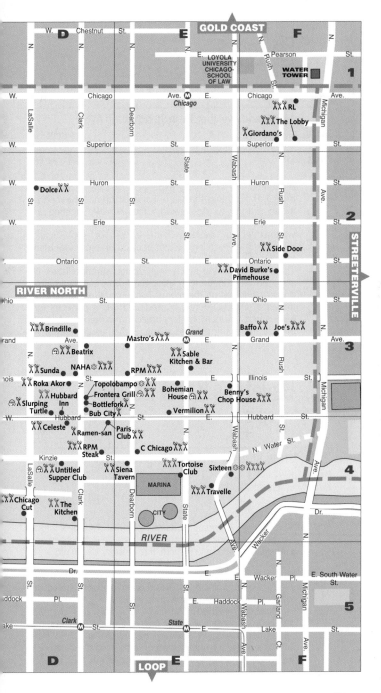

GOLD COAST

W. Chestnut St.

LOYOLA UNIVERSITY CHICAGO-SCHOOL OF LAW

WATER TOWER

W. Chicago Ave. Ⓜ Chicago E. Chicago Ave.

RL

The Lobby

Giordano's

W. Superior St. E. Superior St.

W. Huron Dolce St. Huron E. Huron St.

W. Erie St. Erie E. Erie St.

Ontario St. E. Ontario St.

Side Door

David Burke's Primehouse

RIVER NORTH Ohio St. E. Ohio St.

Brindille Baffo Joe's

Ave. Grand E. Grand Ave.

Mastro's

Beatrix Sable Kitchen & Bar

Sunda NAHA RPM

Roka Akor Illinois E. Illinois St.

Topolobampo Bohemian House Benny's Chop House

Hubbard Inn Frontera Grill

Slurping Turtle Bottlefork

W. Hubbard Bub City St. Vermilion E. Hubbard St.

Celeste

Ramen-san Paris Club

RPM Steak C Chicago

Kinzie St.

Untitled Supper Club Siena Tavern Tortoise Club Sixteen

MARINA Travelle

Chicago Cut The Kitchen CITY

RIVER

Dr.

Wacker Pl. E. South Water St.

Clark St. State Ⓜ Haddock Pl.

Lake Clark Ⓜ St. State Ⓜ Lake St.

LOOP

STREETERVILLE

183

Baffo

Italian XX

44 E. Grand Ave. (bet. Rush St. & Wabash Ave.)

Phone: 312-521-8700
Web: www.bafforistorante.com
Prices: $$$

Lunch Sat – Sun
Dinner nightly
🚇 Grand (Red)

As the flagship fine dining experience of Eataly's mega food mecca, Baffo brings the Mario Batali brand of contemporary Italian cuisine to downtown Chicago. Dim lighting and stylized black-and-white accents add drama to the formal white-tablecloth space, which strives for sophistication despite stutter-start service that needs a bit more fine tuning to shine like a true Batali star.

Thanks to truly top-notch ingredients, simple dishes like poached veal tongue with spicy giardiniera and caramelized onions stand out on the menu. Though pastas can verge on the edge of *too* al dente, braised short rib is perfectly fork-tender with a crunchy, buttery breadcrumb topping and rustic braised greens primed for soaking up the meat's rich jus.

Bavette's Bar & Boeuf

American XX

218 W. Kinzie St. (bet. Franklin & Wells Sts.)

Phone: 312-624-8154
Web: www.bavetteschicago.com
Prices: $$$

Dinner nightly

🚇 Merchandise Mart

Restaurateur Brendan Sokoloff (also of Maude's Liquor Bar and Au Cheval) breathes new life into the tried-and-true steakhouse concept with this swanky destination. The vibe inside may be dark and loud, but that only adds to the bonhomie of the chic and cavernous den, outfitted with exposed brick walls, mismatched dangling light fixtures, and tobacco-brown Chesterfield-style sofas.

Predictably, steakhouse and raw bar standards dominate the menu. Most steaks are wet-aged, and though some may prefer more funk, the cuts are expertly broiled. The kitchen deserves praise for unexpected options like creamy short rib stroganoff featuring hand-cut pasta; buttermilk fried chicken; and sides such as *elote*-style corn in a rich cheese sauce sparked with lime.

Beatrix

D3

519 N. Clark St. (at Grand Ave.)

Phone: 312-284-1377   Lunch & dinner daily
Web: www.beatrixchicago.com
Prices: $$ 🚇 Grand (Red)

From a spartan façade to an industrial décor, Beatrix is the epitome of cool. Then consider its many meal options, popular tunes, and trendy scene rife with hotel guests from the adjacent Aloft, and know why it's jamming. Servers don stylish hairdos and tattoos to match the vibe while attending to the giant room scattered with seats and a coffee bar dispensing excellent local brews.

Meanwhile, the menu veers from creative to quirky with pleasing results. A spring pea soup highlights aroma, flavor, and texture when shot with mint, ricotta, and croutons. Salads may headline, but mains like roasted chili- and chocolate-glazed salmon are a smoky surprise. End with the apple strudel flavored with caramelized brown sugar—it's big in size and faultless in flavor.

Benny's Chop House

E3

444 N. Wabash Ave. (bet. Hubbard & Illinois Sts.)

Phone: 312-626-2444   Lunch & dinner daily
Web: www.bennyschophouse.com
Prices: $$$ 🚇 Grand (Red)

Old-school service meets modern elegance at Benny's Chop House. A far cry from the clubby, masculine steakhouses of yesteryear and just a stone's throw from the Magnificent Mile, this expansive but welcoming space goes for understated glamour, with tasteful inlaid wood and burgundy columns offset by natural stone walls, white birch branches, and a marble bar.

Though Benny's steaks are the draw, those prime cuts of filet mignon and ribeye are matched by fresh seafood like simply roasted bone-in halibut fillet and classic raw bar towers, along with a variety of pastas and salads. A trio of sliders featuring mini portions of Benny's burger, crab cake, and sliced filet with horseradish cream elevate the idea of bar snacks to new heights.

The Boarding House

International ✗✗

C1

720 N. Wells St. (at Superior St.)

Phone: 312-280-0720
Web: www.boardinghousechicago.com
Prices: $$

Dinner Tue – Sat

🚇 Chicago (Red)

The long-awaited passion project from Chicago master sommelier Alpana Singh, The Boarding House has thrown its doors open to four floors of grandeur. The impressively shimmering wine glass clusters dangling in the first floor bar lead way to the upper dining room, which pulls out all the stops by virtue of its arched, mullioned windows and an installation made from more than 4,000 green wine bottles. Small and larger plates make sharing an appealing proposition. House-made *tagliolini* ribbons tossed with fresh peas, mint, and pickled ramps are bright and zesty. Garlic lovers use crispy chicken thighs to sop up every last bit of aromatic green-garlic pistou. Scoops of sour cherry gelée and merlot-chocolate chip ice cream crown rich brownies for dessert.

Bohemian House 😊

Eastern European ✗✗

E3

11 W. Illinois St. (bet. Dearborn & State Sts.)

Phone: 312-955-0439
Web: www.bohochicago.com
Prices: $$

Lunch & dinner daily

🚇 Merchandise Mart

This wickedly stylish "house" is exactly what River North needed to shake it up—a truly unique restaurant serving up delicious Czech, Austrian, and Hungarian cuisines. The stunning beer hall-meets-art nouveau interior (think reclaimed wood beams, stunning tiles arching over a semi-open kitchen, sky-blue tufted leather couches and Persian rugs) is worth a visit alone. No detail is overlooked.

Delightfully, the food is amazingly tasty and just as pretty to look at. Don't miss the open-faced schnitzel sandwich, highlighting juicy pork over apple and kohlrabi slaw, aged Gouda, a fried egg, and drizzle of coarse mustard. Also a must do? The warm blueberry *kolacky*, a traditional Czech cookie filled with blueberry coulis and served with lemon curd and blueberry-sour cream ice cream.

Bottlefork

D3

Contemporary 🍴

441 N. Clark St. (bet. Hubbard & Illinois Sts.)

Phone: 312-955-1900
Web: www.bottlefork.com
Prices: $$

Lunch daily
Dinner Mon – Sat
🚇 Grand (Red)

Bottlefork, Forkbottle—yup, we get it, it's a "bar & kitchen" but, in this case, a very good one. The narrow room is dominated by a 40-foot bar which morphs into an open kitchen. The lights are turned down and the music is turned up—and unless they know Big Audio Dynamite, it's not music for kids. When it comes to the food, "locally sourced and globally inspired" is their USP with the chef, a Four Seasons alumnus, making much of his largely European peregrinations. Expect punchy flavors, teasing combinations, clever twists, and everything from *salumi* and tuna crudo in a jar to "popcorn" sweetbreads, pastas, and Moroccan stews. The terrific cocktail and drinks list covers all bases too. And who isn't tempted to take dessert in liquid form?

Brindille

D3

French 🍴🍴🍴

534 N. Clark St. (bet. Grand Ave. & Ohio St.)

Phone: 312-595-1616
Web: www.brindille-chicago.com
Prices: $$$$

Dinner Mon – Sat
🚇 Grand (Red)

This posh bistro is located just steps away from NAHA, it's impressive sister restaurant from cousins Carrie and Michael Nahabedian. Hushed and intimate, the dining room is awash with a palette of soothing greys and dressed up with herringbone floors along with black-and-white photography. Brindille's menu isn't a sequel to NAHA's contemporary Mediterranean fare, but instead bears a strong Parisian accent influenced by the chef's love of French cuisine. Roasted chestnuts are whirled into a creamy soup and poured over compressed apple, wild mushrooms, and puffed rice. Spot-on Dover sole *meuniere* is plated with a purée of watercress and golden-crisp *pommes rissolées*. And for dessert, preserved cherries are just one option to fill the baked-to-order almond clafoutis.

Bub City

D3

Barbecue

435 N. Clark St. (bet. Hubbard & Illinois Sts.)

Phone: 312-610-4200
Web: www.bubcitychicago.com
Prices: $$

Lunch & dinner daily

Grand (Red)

Bub City isn't as far south as Nashville or Memphis, but the country music vibe comes through just the same at this barbecue- and booze-focused hang. Two bars flank the main stage that hosts nightly live entertainment. One bar is a shrine to over 100 varieties of whiskey, and the other to beer—easily identified by the American flag made from empty cans stacked behind its counter.

Along with the extensive lineup of traditional smoked brisket, ribs, and fried chicken, a raw bar brings chilled seafood refreshment before spicy cheese-stuffed Texas Torpedoes and loaded hot link sandwiches. A bowl of Smokie's chili arrives with a kick from sliced jalapeño, but the caddy of barbecue and hot sauces on each table lets heat fiends intensify the seasoning.

C Chicago

E4

Seafood

20 W. Kinzie St. (at Dearborn St.)

Phone: 312-280-8882
Web: www.cchicago.net
Prices: $$$

Lunch & dinner daily

Merchandise Mart

This spacious looker lands in River North courtesy of the team behind the popular Chicago Cut Steakhouse. At C Chicago, the focus is on fresh—make that really fresh—seafood. This is exciting news: there aren't many seafood restaurants in Chicago, and the few that exist aren't doing it like the talented Chef Bill Montagne, who hails from the piscine temple, Le Bernardin.

Kick things off with a beautiful scallop carpaccio kissed with olive oil, lemon juice, basil, chives and Espelette pepper. Then nibble on an irresistibly chewy farro salad, served warm, tossed with charred corn, mustard greens, and topped with whipped feta. The baked Aleutian cod, arriving in a perfectly subtle Basquaise sauce and dotted with squid ink and red wine vinaigrette is sublime.

Celeste

D4

Contemporary ✗✗

111 W. Hubbard St. (bet. Clark & LaSalle Sts.)

Phone: 312-828-9000 Dinner Tue – Sat
Web: www.celestechicago.com
Prices: $$$ Grand (Red)

Celeste celebrates the city's close relationship with that great American institution—the bar. It is a veritable fun palace evoking the great drinking establishments of the last century and is spread over three floors. On the first floor is a bar with an abbreviated menu. On the second floor is the narrow and nominally named Deco Room where the marble-topped tables face another bar; and upstairs is reserved for private parties.

The food is certainly more than a mere addendum to the terrific cocktail list and the kitchen is clearly a skilled one. Dishes are quite elaborate in their construction—order lamb and you may find it includes the loin, belly and sweetbreads—and they are as flavorsome as they are attractive.

Chicago Cut

D4

Steakhouse ✗✗✗

300 N. LaSalle St. (at Wacker Dr.)

Phone: 312-329-1800 Lunch & dinner daily
Web: www.chicagocutsteakhouse.com
Prices: $$$ Merchandise Mart

Chicago Cut is a steakhouse perfectly suited for the City of the Big Shoulders. The finely tailored locale bustles day and night, thanks to being wrapped in windows along the riverfront, sumptuous red leather furnishings, warm wood trim, and a crackerjack service team cementing its steakhouse vibe.

Non-meat entrées include cedar-planked salmon with a *sriracha*-honey glaze, but make no mistake: beef is boss here. Prime steaks, butchered and dry-aged in-house for 35 days, get just the right amount of time under the flame, as is the case with the perfectly cooked-to-order Porterhouse—pre-sliced and plated for each guest. Sides are a must and should include the dome of hashbrowns, creamed spinach redolent of nutmeg, or tender stalks of grilled asparagus.

Coco Pazzo

Italian **XX**

C3

300 W. Hubbard St. (at Franklin St.)

Phone: 312-836-0900
Web: www.cocopazzochicago.com
Prices: $$

Lunch Mon – Fri
Dinner nightly
🚇 Merchandise Mart

Vibrant blue-and-orange awnings help Coco Pazzo make its mark among the area's stellar restaurants, though their reputation for seasonal Tuscan cuisine has been going strong since 1992. Navy velvet curtains that hang in the wide, welcoming, high-ceilinged room may dampen the din, but not the enthusiasm from regulars ready for a delicious mid-day *tavolata* and bottle from the all-Italian wine list.

Business types fill every seat for the *piatti unici*, a chef-chosen lunch special that changes daily but is always made with expert care. Selections may include Rushing Rivers trout over lentils and spinach paired with speck- and mushroom-studded risotto made with Carnaroli rice. Dinner options like pancetta-wrapped quail with taleggio fondue showcase the kitchen's ambitious side.

David Burke's Primehouse

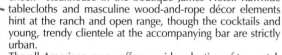

Steakhouse **XX**

F2

616 N. Rush St. (bet. Ohio & Ontario Sts.)

Phone: 312-660-6000
Web: www.davidburkesprimehouse.com
Prices: $$$

Lunch & dinner daily

🚇 Grand (Red)

Banish thoughts of musty wood-paneled rooms from your mind and unwind at this chic—and slightly tongue-in-cheek—steakhouse in the boutique James Hotel. Rawhide tablecloths and masculine wood-and-rope décor elements hint at the ranch and open range, though the cocktails and young, trendy clientele at the accompanying bar are strictly urban.

The all-American menu offers a wide selection of top-notch beef and hearty sides to match. Skewered cubes of maple syrup-smothered, black pepper-dusted bacon are a playful snack to share, a poppable prelude to the carnivorous courses to follow. Bone-in steaks like the 8-ounce filet are juicy and flavor-packed; many cuts are aged in-house in a Himalayan salt-tiled room for prime attention and coddling.

Dolce

Italian ✗✗

D2

127 W. Huron St. (at LaSalle St.)

Phone: 312-754-0700   Lunch & dinner daily
Web: www.dolceitalianrestaurant.com
Prices: $$ Chicago (Red)

With locations in Miami and Atlanta, Dolce's newest outpost lands in Chicago's popular River North neighborhood, tucked into the lobby of the stunning, Cubist-influenced Godfrey boutique hotel. The spacious dining room features a sleek interior with dark wood grain tiles, orange leather furnishings, tweed-lined banquettes, and enormous windows.

Dolce offers a chic take on Italian dining, with a menu featuring pizzas, house-made pastas, and entrées like veal Milanese or fennel pollen-dusted roasted chicken. Try the cool watermelon salad studded with heirloom tomatoes, crumbled goat cheese, pea shoots, mint, and toasted pumpkin seeds. The *pappardelle alla Bolognese* arrives irresistibly silky and dressed in a wickedly good beef, pork, and veal ragù.

Farmhouse

Gastropub ✗

C1

228 W. Chicago Ave. (bet. Franklin & Wells Sts.)

Phone: 312-280-4960   Lunch & dinner daily
Web: www.farmhousechicago.com
Prices: $$ Chicago (Brown)

Like shaking the hand of your local farmer, grab the pitchfork door handles of Farmhouse and you'll be almost as close to the source of your food. Much of the décor is salvaged and much of the menu is procured right from the Midwest. From Indiana chicken to Michigan wine, local is more than a buzzword. Exposed brick, rough-hewn wood, and wire-encased filament bulbs make it the quintessential modern tavern.

Highlights of the harvest headline each course. Whole-grain mustard dresses up a vibrant (and requisite) beet salad. Nueske's bacon is the star in a rustic BLT, accompanied by Klug Farms peaches tossed with balsamic dressing. Cream cheese-frosted carrot bread pudding is fragrant from autumn spices, layered with a golden raisin purée and nutmeg crunch.

The Franklin Room

XX

C2

675 N. Franklin St. (bet. Erie & Huron Sts.)

Phone:	312-445-4686	Lunch Mon – Fri
Web:	www.franklinroom.com	Dinner nightly
Prices:	$$	🚇 Chicago (Brown)

With a motto like "Ladies and Gentlemen Welcome," it's no surprise that the subterranean space housing this modern-day tavern and whiskey bar is as inviting as they come. Surrounded by backlit bottles of top-notch spirits under wrought-iron latticework light panels, guests gather for convivial conversation and great drinks.

Fans of Bourbon will delight in the Derby Day Mule, which swaps out vodka for Buffalo Trace. Pair your libation with rib-sticking dishes like a sandwich of garlic- and balsamic vinegar-roasted portobello mushroom caps layered with a runny egg, grilled tomato, and blue cheese; or a steaming bowl of braised duck soup complete with thick and silky pappardelle. End on a high note—think Bourbon-infused milkshake with house-made ice cream, natch.

Frontera Grill

XX

D3

445 N. Clark St. (bet. Hubbard & Illinois Sts.)

Phone:	312-661-1434	Lunch & dinner Tue – Sat
Web:	www.fronterakitchens.com	
Prices:	$$	🚇 Grand (Red)

The linchpin in Rick Bayless' empire, Frontera Grill is decidedly unique in its homage to regional Mexican cuisine and displays a near cult-like devotion to local product. The service at this dining room, psychedelic in its color scheme, can verge on vapid, but find a seat on the bar side for a warmer (and worthier) experience.

The ever-changing menu is cohesive with a mix of classics and specialties like *sopa azteca*, a nourishing *pasilla chile* broth poured atop crisp tortilla strips, cool avocado, grilled chicken, and jack cheese. A version of the classic from Morelia, *enchiladas a la plaza* are first flash-fried, then folded over seasoned cabbage, potatoes, and carrots. Pair this plate with a side of spinach in green chile and you won't be unhappy. Ever.

BYO

Gene & Georgetti

C3

Steakhouse ✗✗

500 N. Franklin St. (at Illinois St.)

Phone: 312-527-3718
Web: www.geneandgeorgetti.com
Prices: $$$$

Lunch & dinner Mon – Sat

🏛 Merchandise Mart

No, it's not a Hollywood set. This Italian-American steak joint is the real thing, and those wiseguys at the bar have been clinking their ice cubes in this wood-paneled room for decades. The historic spot, founded in 1941, is boisterous downstairs with the aforementioned regulars and guys grabbing a bite; upstairs is more refined for local politico lunches and a bit of old-school romance at dinner.

Gene & Georgetti is a steakhouse with an Italian bloodline, prominently displayed in the heaping helping of fried *peperoncini* and bell peppers with the signature "chicken alla Joe." The cottage fries (oversized potato planks that come with most entrées) might necessitate a doggie bag, but all the better to leave room for a slice of classic carrot cake.

Gilt Bar 😊

C4

Gastropub ✗✗

230 W. Kinzie St. (at Franklin St.)

Phone: 312-464-9544
Web: www.giltbarchicago.com
Prices: $$

Dinner nightly

🏛 Merchandise Mart

In the shadow of Merchandise Mart, it's not easy to miss the revolving door entrance to Gilt Bar, a moody and imposing River North favorite. The bar up front mixes cocktails to a metronomic rhythm, while the back is more intimate with brick walls, studded leather banquettes, and nostalgic lighting.

However make no mistake: this is no Bugsy Malone speakeasy, but a grown-up version for bar-flies with astute palates. Snack on creamy burrata and shaved ham finished with a swig of extra virgin olive oil before savoring tender, flavorful pork meatballs on a bed of wilted kale with romesco and almond *gremolata*. In the end, gorge on an unctuous brown butter-apple cake with salted caramel and vanilla ice cream—perhaps to the dulcet tunes of Bob Dylan. Bliss.

Giordano's

Pizza ✗

F1

730 N. Rush St. (at Superior St.)

Phone: 312-951-0747
Web: www.giordanos.com
Prices:

Lunch & dinner daily

Chicago (Red)

Value, friendly service, and delicious deep-dish pizza make Giordano's a crowd sweetheart. With several locations dotting the city and suburbs, this restaurant has been gratifying locals with comforting Italian-American fare for years. Come during the week—service picks up especially at dinner—to avoid the cacophony.

Giordano's menu includes your typical salads, pastas, et al., but you'd do well to save room for the real star: the deep-dish. Bring backup because this pie could feed a small country. The spinach version arrives on a buttery pastry crust, filled with spreads of sautéed (or steamed) spinach with tomato sauce, and topped with mozzarella and parmesan. For those cold, windy nights, opt for delivery—their website sketches a detailed menu.

GT Fish & Oyster ⑬

Seafood ✗✗

C3

531 N. Wells St. (at Grand Ave.)

Phone: 312-929-3501
Web: www.gtoyster.com
Prices: $$

Lunch & dinner daily

Grand (Red)

Quaint seaside shacks have nothing on this urban spot that exudes nautical chic. A boomerang-shaped communal table by the raw bar makes a perfect oyster-slurping perch. Lead fishing weights keep napkins in place on nautically styled, brass-edged tables, lined up under an enormous chalkboard-style mural of a jaunty swordfish skeleton.

Pescatarians savor the numerous seafood dishes meant for sharing, but those who forego fish are limited to three meat options. Rectangular crab cakes, stuffed to the gills with sweet meat, get a crunchy sear on all sides. *Salade* Niçoise spotlights pristine slices of fresh tuna and snappy green beans in a cider-mustard dressing. Key lime pie, a traditional meal-ender, is transformed into light layers of curd and cake in a glass jar.

Hubbard Inn

Mediterranean ✕✕

D3

110 W. Hubbard St. (bet. Clark & LaSalle Sts.)

Phone: 312-222-1331   Lunch & dinner daily
Web: www.hubbardinn.com
Prices: $$ Grand (Red)

Handsome from head-to-toe, the Hubbard Inn takes the idea of a classic tavern and dresses it to the nines. Brass-clad globe lights glow above lacquered plank tables in the front bar room, leading to tufted leather couches and fireplaces in the book-lined and Hogwarts-worthy library. The second floor is low-slung and loungy. A wall-sized chalkboard behind the marble bar whets whistles with descriptions of house cocktails.

Shareable farm-to-table dishes appeal to nearly every appetite. Kale salad, that ubiquitous menu staple, gets a new twist when tossed with pickled blackberries, candied walnuts, and grated *ricotta salata*. And, a quartet of juicy, beautifully cooked lamb chops over rustic chickpea purée is brightened by a handful of chopped olives and mint.

Joe's

American ✕✕✕

F3

60 E. Grand Ave. (at Rush St.)

Phone: 312-379-5637   Lunch & dinner daily
Web: www.joes.net
Prices: $$$$ Grand (Red)

Despite the ample neighborhood competition, this outpost of the original Miami seafood, steak, and stone crab palace does just fine up north. Clubby, masculine décor fashions a classic scene, while business diners and lively martini-toasting groups keep the leather booths full from lunch through dinner.

Stone crab claws accompanied by signature mustard sauce are shared by nearly every table, followed by decadent dishes like a bone-in filet with their simple yet delicious coriander-spiked seasoning. Americana sides like Jennie's fontina and asiago mashed potatoes, or grilled tomatoes topped with cheesy spinach pesto, are ample enough to share. Joe's Key lime pie is rightly famous, but other retro sweets like coconut cream pie are worth a forkful.

The Kitchen

D4

316 N. Clark St. (bet. Kinzie St. & the Chicago River)

Phone: 312-836-1300   Lunch & dinner daily
Web: www.thekitchen.com
Prices: $$ 🖥 Merchandise Mart

Panoramic views and eye-popping spaces are par for the course at most of the lofty spots abutting the Chicago River, but The Kitchen's farm-to-table food manages to steer the focus back to the plate. The restaurant's approachable, community-minded take on straightforward seasonal food—along with its impressive drinks program—makes it easy to please.

Even if you're not attending a Monday "Community Night" dinner alongside many of the purveyors whose ingredients appear on the plate, you'll find a fresh, flavorful mix of dishes. Crushed white bean bruschetta is topped with a sprightly herb and frisée salad, which is in turn dressed with a blood orange vinaigrette. And wild Bristol Bay salmon is poached with care, its silkiness punctuated by garlic-chive aïoli.

The Lobby

F1

108 E. Superior St. (at Michigan Ave.)

Phone: 312-573-6760   Lunch & dinner daily
Web: www.peninsula.com
Prices: $$$ 🖥 Chicago (Red)

You can't say you weren't warned. The Peninsula people sensibly realized that honesty was best when naming this vast space which looks remarkably like…a lobby. At least the friendly staff manages to wrestle back some control, and you know your conversation won't be overheard—because there aren't any tables near you.

So why the recommendation? Because the food is very good. The lunch menu doesn't really get past lobster rolls and chicken legs, but at night the kitchen's innate skill is very much in evidence. Dishes are good-looking, but also have depth and ingredients are of irreproachable quality. Flavors marry well and there are intriguing touches of originality but never at the expense of the overall balance of the dish.

Mastro's

Steakhouse ✗✗✗

E3

520 N. Dearborn St. (at Grand Ave.)

Phone: 312-521-5100
Web: www.mastrosrestaurants.com
Prices: $$$$

Dinner nightly

Grand (Red)

Mastro's may be relatively young on the Windy City's steakhouse scene, but it shows up with the swagger of an old pro. Black SUVs unload VIPs in front of the revolving door, which leads to a gleaming wall of bottles at the gilded bar. Live lounge music may take the level of conversation up a notch, but sip on a shaken martini to blank out the surrounding din.

Steaks on screaming hot platters come unadorned unless otherwise listed, and servers will happily rattle off recommendations for toppings, sauces, and crusts. Salads like Mastro's house version, a local favorite stocked with chopped jumbo shrimp and a giant steamed prawn, are hearty (read: oversized), but smaller portions are on offer so you can leave room for the renowned butter cake.

Oak + Char

American ✗✗

C2

217 W. Huron St. (bet. Franklin & Wells Sts.)

Phone: 312-643-2427
Web: www.oakandchar.com
Prices: $$

Lunch & dinner daily

Chicago (Brown)

Despite its panoply of high-profile neighbors, this convivial haunt manages to maintain a relaxed, mellow vibe. Whether lounging over drinks and a bite from the innovative cocktail list and bar snacks menu, grabbing a quick soup-and-sandwich lunch, or going all out for dinner, guests are welcomed to sip, nibble, and chat as long as they like.

The self-described "modern Midwestern" menu pulls influences and ingredients from around the globe, yet maintains a distinctly American feel in dishes like cotton cake—an airy Japanese-style cheesecake kept light with streaks of persimmon jam and basil streusel. Smoky wood-grilled eggplant pairs with red pepper jam on a hearty ciabatta sandwich, with irresistibly salty homemade potato chips straight from the fryer.

NAHA ✿

American

D3

500 N. Clark St. (at Illinois St.)

Phone: 312-321-6242
Web: www.naha-chicago.com
Prices: $$$

Lunch Mon – Fri
Dinner Mon – Sat
🚇 Grand (Red)

There's a quiet elegance to Chef Carrie Nahabedian's dining room, a sleek, window-wrapped space with contemporary accents of concrete, wood, and greenery. Here, patrons aren't groupies checking off the latest table on their do list, but rather connoisseurs experiencing a magnificent meal with exceptional service.

If your idea of relaxation starts with pre-dinner drinks, the sizable bar and smattering of tables in the front lounge are an open invitation to begin. Despite its understated environs, NAHA's sweeping carte of seasonally driven Mediterranean cuisine is anything but. Shining starters include succulent lamb *boereg*, a delicate phyllo-wrapped parcel of ground meat plated with strained yogurt, juicy red pomegranate arils, and refreshing watercress salad. Perfectly toothsome and loaded with seasonal produce, the risotto is always a hit, while entrées like pan-seared Arctic char dressed with beluga lentils, mustard seeds, and savory apple-celery broth are a breath of fresh air.

Dessert highlights include the house sundae—a perennial favorite that's reimagined each season—and the gâteau Basque, a warm vanilla custard cake served with brown butter ice cream, corn pudding, and cubed pears.

Paris Club

French XX

D4

59 W. Hubbard St. (bet. Clark & Dearborn Sts.)

Phone: 312-595-0800 — Dinner nightly
Web: www.parisclubbistroandbar.com
Prices: $$ — Grand (Red)

Some of Paris Club was commandeered to create a ramen spot next door, but in return for this munificence, it got a first-rate makeover. Dressed in red leather seats, wood panelling and globe lighting, it perfectly captures the look of a traditional Parisian brasserie. The only thing missing is insouciant service and someone with a dog on their lap. The menu is unapologetically Gallic, "Le Prime Steakburger" notwithstanding, and all the classics are present: from *fruits de mer* to steak frites and *baba au rhum*. The pommes purée is so wonderfully buttery you'll need a defibrillator on standby. The wine list is all French too.
On the second floor find Studio Paris, a proper nightclub with bottle service and celebrity DJ appearances.

Prosecco

Italian XXX

C2

710 N. Wells St. (bet. Huron & Superior Sts.)

Phone: 312-951-9500 — Lunch Mon – Fri
Web: www.prosecco.us.com — Dinner Mon – Sat
Prices: $$ — Chicago (Brown)

No matter the hour, it's always time for bubbly at Prosecco, where a complimentary flute of the namesake Italian sparkler starts each meal. This fizzy wine inspires the restaurant's elegant décor, from creamy pale walls and damask drapes to travertine floors. Sit at the long wooden bar or in one of the well-appointed dining rooms for a second glass chosen from the long list of *frizzante* and *spumante* wines.
Hearty dishes spanning the many regions of Italy cut through the heady bubbles. Carpaccio selections include the classic air-dried *bresaola* as well as whisper-thin seared rare duck breast. *Saltimbocca di vitello* marries tender veal medallions with crispy Prosciutto di Parma and creamy mozzarella, with hints of sage in the tomato-brandy sauce.

Ramen-san

59 W. Hubbard St. (bet. Clark & Dearborn Sts.)

Phone: 312-377-9950   Lunch & dinner daily
Web: www.ramensan.com
Prices: 🍜   Grand (Red)

Lettuce Entertain You brings you bowlfuls of ingredient-driven noodle soups served up right next door to the restaurant group's Paris Club. The menu at this Asian concept revolves around a handful of tastefully crafted broths dancing with thin, wavy noodles produced by Sun Noodle. The *tonkotsu* ramen is a traditional pleasure afloat with sweet slices of *chashu*, *wakame*, and molten egg. Meanwhile, the smoked brisket ramen is a novel departure defined by a black garlic-enriched chicken broth and slices of Bub City's 18-hour brisket.

Ramen-san's loyal following is comprised of hipsters and suits alike, and they all seem to dig the salvaged look and booming playlist. Night owls take note: Japanese whiskies rule the bar and fried rice is served late into the night.

RL

115 E. Chicago Ave. (bet. Michigan Ave. & Rush St.)

Phone: 312-475-1100   Lunch & dinner daily
Web: www.rlrestaurant.com
Prices: $$$ Chicago (Red)

If you swoon for tartan and pine for the posh life Ralph Lauren represents, head for the boîte attached to the flagship Michigan Avenue store. Like a stylish private club but without the centuries of stuffiness, RL offers options for a quick solo lunch, cocktail at the mahogany bar, or full dinner. The odd Blackhawks jersey here and there doesn't detract from the overall aura.

The menu is as classically American as the name, featuring bistro favorites like Waldorf salad and raw bar offerings alongside well-prepared dishes like sweet and plump pan-seared scallops with white balsamic-crème fraîche. The thin, flaky crust of a goat cheese- and caramelized onion-tart nearly steals the show from the rich atmosphere of the wood-paneled dining room.

Roka Akor

Asian ✗✗

D3

456 N. Clark St. (at Illinois St.)

Phone: 312-477-7652
Web: www.rokaakor.com
Prices: $$$

Lunch Mon – Fri
Dinner nightly
Grand (Red)

There's no shortage of flash at Roka Akor, the local offshoot of a London-based-via-Scottsdale Japanese steakhouse and sushi temple. The massive LED-illuminated glass hood of the showstopping *robata* station grabs attention in the center of the vast space, with a brigade of black-clad line cooks working the flames. For a front row seat of the action, sit at the surrounding counter topped with charred *shou-sugi-ban* wood.

With such a prominent display, guests would be remiss not to try choices from the *robata*. Lightly blackened lamb chops in a sweet-and-spicy glaze are tender, smoky, and ready for dipping in crimson Korean chili sauce. A starter of plump Wagyu and kimchi dumplings nearly bursting with spicy, rich beef expertly toe the line between crispy and moist.

RPM

Italian ✗✗✗

E3

52 W. Illinois St. (at Dearborn St.)

Phone: 312-222-1888
Web: www.rpmitalian.com
Prices: $$

Lun Sun
Dinner nightly
Grand (Red)

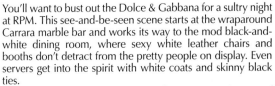

You'll want to bust out the Dolce & Gabbana for a sultry night at RPM. This see-and-be-seen scene starts at the wraparound Carrara marble bar and works its way to the mod black-and-white dining room, where sexy white leather chairs and booths don't detract from the pretty people on display. Even servers get into the spirit with white coats and skinny black ties.

If you can tune out the diversions, the poster-sized menu of modern Italian antipasti, snacks, and family-style plates won't disappoint. Classically prepared peppered beef carpaccio and shaved parmesan is garnished with crispy mushrooms, while a hearty entrée of gnocchi is tossed with mild Italian sausage and rapini. Save room to share a plate of freshly fried *bomboloni* oozing with Nutella.

RPM Steak

D4

🍴🍴🍴

66 W. Kinzie St. (bet. Clark & Dearborn Sts.)

Phone: 312-284-4990
Web: www.rpmsteak.com
Prices: $$$$

Lunch Mon – Fri
Dinner nightly
🚇 Grand (Red)

RPM Steak shares the same sleek, moneyed vibe as still-happening RPM Italian, its sister restaurant located just around the corner. Polished black, white, and wood décor speaks to the finer things in life, with a menu of succulent steaks, raw bar offerings, and sides to back it up. For the best people-watching, score one of the semicircular booths edging the room.

A massive single tiger prawn, served simply on ice with lemon, is a tasty, visually stunning starter. Steaks range from petite filets to dry-aged 24-ounce cowboy cuts with a list of big reds to match. Highlights include the classic, deeply satisfying steak frites, tender and pink inside, charred outside, and complemented by truffle béarnaise for the meat and Caesar dip for the fries.

Sable Kitchen & Bar

E3

🍴🍴

505 N. State St. (at Illinois St.)

Phone: 312-755-9704
Web: www.sablechicago.com
Prices: $$

Lunch Sat – Sun
Dinner nightly
🚇 Grand (Red)

Tucked into the spacious and beautiful Hotel Palomar, Sable Kitchen & Bar is a sleek, sultry, and sophisticated number, fitted out with different dining areas. There's the stunning 40-foot bar, tricked out in gorgeous dark paneling, soft leather seats, and unique light fixtures. The expansive dining room is equally elegant and urbane, attracting dates looking for more intimacy or friends catching up over dinner.

The chef manning the ship here is Lawrence Letrero, and an evening in his very capable hands might entail a decadently spicy and wonderfully complex starter of shrimp and roasted squash curry. Then diners may graduate to crispy, juicy adobo pork belly, served with sticky rice, and a pickled green papaya salad topped with a fried farm egg.

Side Door

F2

Gastropub ✗✗

100 E. Ontario St. (at Rush St.)

Phone: 312-787-6768   Lunch & dinner daily
Web: www.sidedoorchicago.com
Prices: $$ Grand (Red)

In a city with no shortage of steakhouses, Side Door dares to be different. It's the casual arm of Lawry's in the historic McCormick Mansion, offering the same quality and service without the power lunch vibe. Comfy leather banquettes and wide wooden tables are well spaced throughout the bi-level restaurant, offering a respite for shoppers to relax with a cheese plate and craft beer flight.

Share an order of prime rib poutine among friends—it's drenched in beef gravy and pepper jack cheese—or go whole hog with the prime rib sandwich, which is hand-carved to order and presented tableside with horseradish cream and *au jus*. For something lighter but just as pleasurable, try the kale Caesar, with white anchovies and a delicately creamy garlic dressing.

Siena Tavern

E4

Italian ✗✗

51 W. Kinzie St. (at Dearborn Pkwy.)

Phone: 312-595-1322   Lunch & dinner daily
Web: www.sienatavern.com
Prices: $$ Merchandise Mart

Chef Fabio Viviani's TV-ready Italian charisma extends to every corner of this huge, lively restaurant. A mixture of funky décor elements—like cascading plants "growing" from filing cabinets on walls—somehow manage to work in incongruous harmony with sexy black marble and stainless steel throughout the multilevel space.

Various bars offer pizza, crudo, fresh mozzarella, and house-made pasta, though even globally influenced dishes have a Mediterranean touch. The Tavern burger accompanied by parmesan-dusted fries is stacked with melted Taleggio, crispy speck, and garlic aïoli. Order the lush, creamy tiramisù for dessert, which gets a crunch from chopped nuts and crisp homemade meringues, and you'll be tempted to lick the bottom of the zinc tin.

Sixteen ✿ ✿

Contemporary 𝗫𝗫𝗫𝗫

E4

401 N. Wabash Ave. (bet. Hubbard St. & the Chicago River)

Phone:	312-588-8030
Web:	www.trumpchicagohotel.com
Prices:	$$$$

Lunch & dinner daily

🚇 State/Lake

This bold setting puts the Chicago River, Tribune and Wrigley buildings at your fingertips from the sixteenth floor of the Trump Hotel. The lobby entrance is as unremarkable as the dining room is dramatic, centered around an enormous Swarovski chandelier that hangs like an inverted wedding cake over a curving wall of African rosewood.

Beyond this lies a kitchen that takes itself very seriously, but that's ok.

Chef Thomas Lents' cuisine is extraordinary, accomplished, and even more of a draw than the décor. Meals here are very conceptual and include head-spinning affairs that articulate a theme, like the "Faces of Sixteen" as an homage to inspirations and employees. This may translate as a tribute to Joël Robuchon through a pot of wonderfully smooth, raw and seasoned langoustine artfully topped with gelée and sea buckthorn. Another theme "Food in Progress, Modern Fine Dining: Moving Forward with Respect to the Past" ponders the emergence of the Nordic through a gently smoked oyster, flavorful potato gelée, horseradish, and caraway. Grilled lobster with uni, coffee, and rice is downright unforgettable. Desserts like lemon tart with diplomat cream and fennel are as innovative as they are delicious.

Slurping Turtle

Chicago ▶ River North

Japanese 🍴

D3

116 W. Hubbard St. (bet. Clark & LaSalle Sts.)

Phone: 312-464-0466

Web: www.slurpingturtle.com

Prices: $$

Lunch & dinner daily

🏬 Merchandise Mart

Both turtles and noodles symbolize longevity, so a meal at Slurping Turtle should add a few years to your life (and warmth to your belly). Inside the minimalist bento box of a space, diners sit elbow-to-elbow at sleek white communal tables. Boutique Japanese beverages like Hitachino Nest beer and Ramuné bubble-gum soda bring smiles to patrons in the know.

Along with deep, steaming bowls of ramen and udon, the lengthy menu serves small plates, sushi, and other Japanese comfort food for snacking and sharing. Tender ribeye and chicken skewers arrive moist and glistening, straight from the *binchotan* charcoal grill. Deep-fried Brussels sprouts are crispy outside and tender inside without a hint of grease, topped with sliced scallions and fried shallots.

Sumi Robata Bar

Japanese 🍢

C2

702 N. Wells St. (at Huron St.)

Phone: 312-988-7864

Web: www.sumirobatabar.com

Prices: $$

Lunch Sun – Fri

Dinner nightly

🏬 Chicago (Brown)

There's a degree of authenticity to this traditional *robata* bar and that includes the discreet entrance, although a spacious patio ultimately lets you know you're not in downtown Tokyo. Sit at the counter to best appreciate their specialty— the Japanese art of grilling. For a good value lunch look no further than the bento boxes, but come at night and you'll be able to try a variety of grilled items where the natural flavors shine through, whether that's Wagyu beef or crab. You can also try more unusual cuts that you may hitherto have avoided, such as chicken heart or tail.

The service is smiley, helpful, and sincere. The guys behind the counter have a more serious countenance—well, good grilling is serious business.

Sunda

D3

Fusion

110 W. Illinois St. (bet. Clark & LaSalle Sts.)

Phone: 312-644-0500
Web: www.sundachicago.com
Prices: $$

Lunch & dinner daily

Grand (Red)

The Sunda shelf, an underwater outcropping that stretches along the coastline of Southeast Asia, connects the countries that provide culinary inspiration for this enormous River North lounge and restaurant. The beautiful people are naturally attracted to the clubby vibe Sunda radiates, complete with thumping music and a wide range of cocktail and sake selections.

The seafood is as fresh as the vibe is sultry, with numerous raw and cooked options like tempura rock shrimp tossed with candied walnuts in a creamy honey aïoli; or maki like the "tail of two tunas" pairing yellowfin and super white tuna with pickled jalapeños and fried shallots. Meat-eaters won't go hungry with creative plates like lemongrass beef lollipops and oxtail potstickers.

Tortoise Club

E4

American

350 N. State St. (bet. Kinzie St. & the Chicago River)

Phone: 312-755-1700
Web: www.tortoiseclub.com
Prices: $$$

Lunch Mon – Fri
Dinner nightly
State/Lake

Every city needs a restaurant with the word "club" in the title—somewhere reassuringly old-school where you'd take your future father-in-law if you want to marry his daughter. Tortoise Club fits the bill perfectly. If it was just a few years older, it would be called an institution because it also harks back to more dissolute times; order a Negroni at lunchtime here and no one will bat an eyelid.

The place has an unapologetically masculine look thanks to the mahogany paneling and dark leather seating. It has a lounge bar with nightly live jazz and a familiar menu of American classics, from big plates of seafood to great steaks. Where it differs from many similar spots is that here the service is sprightly and sincere and the welcome is warm.

Topolobampo ✿

Mexican ✕✕

D3

445 N. Clark St. (bet. Hubbard & Illinois Sts.)

Phone: 312-661-1434
Web: www.rickbayless.com
Prices: $$$$

Lunch Tue – Fri
Dinner Tue – Sat
Grand (Red)

This jewel in Bayless' culinary crown welcomes a rush of serious eaters and canoodlers for original south-of-the-border fare—with an upscale twist. While it may share an entrance and bar with sibling, Frontera Grill, that is where the likeness ends. Walk past a sliding door to enter this elegant, terra cotta-lined dining room, which feels worlds away from the fiesta upfront.

Lunch is notably laid-back, but chatty, over-eager servers turn dinner into a more exhaustive experience. Enduring their descriptive chalk talk may feel a bit like sitting through a college lecture for some, but be patient as you will be rewarded with exceptional food boasting a panoply of flavors, colors, and textures. A trio of ceviches highlighting albacore, tomato, and olive; Yucatecan shrimp and calamari; and tuna coctel make for divine starters. And, the *sopa seca de fideos*, tossed in a saucy tomato-*morita* broth and fortified with chorizo, *crema*, and Brussels sprouts, is perhaps the best in the country.

Desserts are flagrantly inventive and the strongest element of this epicurean show. A *torta de elote* or warm corn cake with golden corn ice cream, cherry preserves, and salty caramel corn is absolutey fantastic.

Travelle

E4

Mediterranean ✗✗✗

330 N. Wabash Ave. (bet. Kinzie St. & the Chicago River)

Phone: 312-923-7705
Web: www.travellechicago.com
Prices: $$$

Lunch & dinner daily

Grand (Red)

This contemporary Mediterranean dining room shares its home—a landmark Mies van der Rohe tower completed in 1972—with The Langham hotel. Floor-to-ceiling windows on the second floor space offer views of Marina City, but with its stunning kitchen displayed behind gradient glass panels, the scene inside is equally dramatic.

Creative add-ins bring flair and flavor to flawlessly executed and gorgeously composed dishes. A perfect, toothsome champagne risotto is enlivened by juicy, barely pickled grapes and toasted Marcona almonds, while a thick, creamy tranche of seared salmon rests on "healthy" fried green farro, finished with a tangy drizzle of spicy soy-mustard. Raspberry coulis and meringue shards are an ideal garnish for a fresh and zesty citrus tart.

Union Sushi + Barbeque Bar

C2

Japanese ✗✗

230 W. Erie St. (at Franklin St.)

Phone: 312-662-4888
Web: www.eatatunion.com
Prices: $$

Lunch Mon – Fri
Dinner nightly
Chicago (Brown)

The slogan of this big, bustling restaurant is "Uniting Japanese culinary tradition with a distinctly American persona," which roughly translates to "Japanese food with a party hat on." The cocktails are good, the noise levels are high, and there are more tattoos in the room than a Yakuza convention.

The menu will take forever to read so just go directly to their two specialties—the assorted sushi rolls, some of which use black rice, and meats and fish expertly cooked over an open flame on the seriously hot *robata*. The ingredients are good and the flavor combinations don't get silly. Just remember that sharing is the key to keeping that final check in check, especially as the T-shirted staff are masters of upselling with an iPad.

Untitled Supper Club 😊

Contemporary ✗✗

D4

111 W. Kinzie St. (bet. Clark & LaSalle Sts.)

Phone: 312-880-1511
Web: www.untitledchicago.com
Prices: $$

Dinner Mon – Sat

🚇 Merchandise Mart

An unmarked entrance leads the way to this sultry subterranean lair, its various rooms pumping out music and serving up handcrafted cocktails to a young, sexy clientele lounging in tufted leather banquettes. Lights are nice and sultry; tables are low-slung and casual; and there are no less than 507 whiskeys to choose from.

A charcuterie board may offer up silky duck rillettes, shot through with foie gras; textured and spreadable liverwurst; as well as thin slices of prosciutto and *coppa* accompanied by a house-made *mostarda*. Overstuffed squash blossom *rellenos* are filled with creamy ricotta and served over Agave-spiked corn relish and chili-lime *crema*. Don't miss the scrumptious meatloaf sandwich, slathered with Korean-style ketchup, and laced with rosemary-infused aïoli.

Vermilion

Indian ✗✗

E3

10 W. Hubbard St. (bet. Dearborn & State Sts.)

Phone: 312-527-4060
Web: www.thevermilionrestaurant.com
Prices: $$

Lunch Mon – Fri
Dinner nightly

🚇 Grand (Red)

Andy Warhol would feel right at home among these silver-painted brick walls, high-fashion black-and-white photographs, metallic chairs, and curtains. The cool lounge atmosphere is best for dressed-up evenings or a celebratory Latin-tinged cocktail at the bar.

Two expansive menus—one vegetarian, the other carnivorous—encompass Indian-inspired tapas and street foods. If feeling overwhelmed by the choices, stick to the chef's specialties or go for the prix-fixe and let the kitchen decide. Meaty delicacies include spice-rubbed Mysore lamb chops with pink pickled onions. *Gobi* Portuguese lets tart tomatillo chutney and crunchy eggplant offset sweet coconut gravy and tender cauliflower. *Shahi tukra* pleases the palate with crisp fried semolina cakes drenched in caramel sauce.

Streeterville

Bounded by the strategically set Chicago River, swanky Magnificent Mile, and sparkling Lake Michigan, Streeterville is a precious quarter in the Windy City, housing hotels and high-rise residences alongside offices, universities, and museums. If that doesn't bespeak cultural diversity, the sights and smells at Water Tower Place's **foodlife** offer indisputable proof. Located on the mezzanine floor of the shopping mall, this simple food court has been elevated to an art form. A veritable "United Nations of food courts," foodlife draws a devoted following to its 14 different kitchens that whip up everything from Chinese potstickers and deep-dish pizza, to crispy fried chicken. Unlike

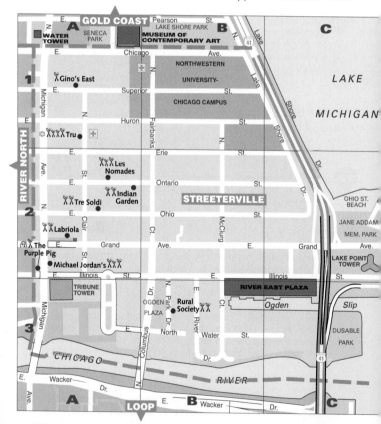

other food courts, you're given a card that can be swiped at as many stalls as you choose. Once you've had your fill, bring the card to the cash registers to receive your balance, and *voila*—a single bill to pay! Another notable tenant of Water Tower Place is **Wow Bao**, a spot known to dole out some of the best steamed veggie- and meat-filled buns in town. In fact, they were so popular that four locations sprouted downtown.

Hopping skyscrapers, the **John Hancock Center** is another iconic tower known to many as a "food lover's paradise." Lucky locals can

choose to dine with fine wine at **Volare Ristorante Italiano**; while bachelors in business suits may shop for groceries with sky-high prices to match the staggering view at **Potash Brothers** (open to residents only). For those whose tastes run more toward champagne and cocktails than cheeseburgers and crinkle-cut fries, there's always the **Signature Lounge**, located on the 96th floor of the John Hancock Center. A sensational setting for delicious nightcaps, this sleek spot also proffers an incredible brunch, lunch, dinner, and dessert menu that employs some of the finest ingredients around town. While their creative cocktails may result in sticker shock, one peek at the sparkling cityscape will have you...at hello.

ART & CULTURE

The Museum of Contemporary Art is located next to Lake Shore Park, the city's outdoor recreational extravaganza. Well-renowned for housing the world's leading collection of

contemporary art, patrons here know to balance the gravitas of the setting with fresh nourishment at cute and casual **Puck's** (Wolfgang, naturally) **Café**. But, it's also the peppers and potatoes that lure foodies to the farmer's market, held at the museum every Tuesday from June through October. Choose to bookend a home-cooked meal with some dark chocolate decadence at **Godiva Chocolatier**—a beautiful boutique carrying it all from chocolate-covered strawberries and truffles, to gourmet biscuits, chocolate bars, and snacks.

The world convenes at Chicago's lakefront **Navy Pier** for a day of exploration and eats. Showcasing lush gardens and parks in conjunction with shops and dining stalls, families usually flock to **Bubba Gump Shrimp Co.** for its convivial vibe and shrimp specials. But, locals looking for live music with their carnitas and margaritas may head to **Jimmy Buffett's Margaritaville Bar & Grill** (named after the rockstar himself). For stellar snacking in between meals, venture towards **Garrett Popcorn Shops**, which promises to have you hooked on sweet-and-salty flavors like CheeseCorn and Macadamia CaramelCrisp. The choices are plenty and you can even create your own tin here. Afterward, move on to more substantial chow like an all-natural Chicago-style dog (slathered with mustard, onion, relish, sport peppers, tomatoes, and celery salt) from **America's Dog**. This classic destination showcases an impressive range of city-style creations from Houston, New York, and Philadelphia, to Detroit, Kansas City, and San Francisco. Meat-lovers who mean business never miss **M Burger**, always buzzing with business lunchers, tourists, and shoppers alike. In fact, it should be renamed "mmm" burger simply for its juicy parcels of bacon, cheese, and secret sauce. Even calorie counters may rest easy as the all-veggie "Nurse Betty" is nothing short of crave-worthy. For a bit more intimacy and a lot more fantasy, **Sayat**

Nova is superb. Highlighting a range of *kibbee* alongside more exotic signatures like *sarma* or meat- and veggie-filled grape leaves bobbing in a light garlic sauce, this Middle Eastern marvel keeps its options limited but fan-base infinite.

Residents know that Chicago is big on breakfast—so big that they can even have it for dinner at Michigan Avenue's **West Egg**. This convivial café-cum-coffee corridor serves three meals a day, but it is their breakfast specials (choose between pancakes, waffles, or other "eggcellent" dishes) that keep the joint jumping at all times. Finally, the Northwestern Memorial Hospital complex is another esteemed establishment that dominates the local scene. Besides its top medical services, a parade of dining gems (think coffee shops, lounges, and ethnic canteens) catering to their staff, students, and visitors looms large over this neighborhood—and lake.

Gino's East

A1

Pizza ✗

162 E. Superior St. (bet. Michigan Ave. & St. Clair St.)

Phone: 312-266-3337
Web: www.ginoseast.com
Prices: $$

Lunch & dinner daily

Chicago (Red)

Pizza pilgrims continue to make the trek to the original location of this renowned local deep-dish chain, where a 45 minute wait is the norm. However, solo diners may rest assured as they can order personal pies from a walk-up counter. The walls, scribbled with years of graffiti, are nearly as iconic as the high-walled pies themselves, whose crusts get their signature crunch from cornmeal and searing-hot metal pans rife with two inch-high sides.

Filled with heaps of mozzarella and toppings like the "Meaty Legend" lineup of spicy pepperoni, Italian sausage, and both Canadian and regular bacon before getting sauced, it's hard to eat more than two wedges here. Nonconformists can of course opt for thin-crust pies, gussied-up by add-ons like roasted red peppers.

Indian Garden

A2

Indian ✗✗

247 E. Ontario St. (bet. Fairbanks Ct. & St. Clair St.)

Phone: 312-280-4910
Web: www.indiangardenchicago.com
Prices: $$

Lunch & dinner daily

Grand (Red)

Frequent diners know it as "The IG," but first-timers will appreciate the copious lunch buffet as much as the doctors, med students, and locals. These faithful droves routinely make the trip up a few flights of stairs to get their *pakora* and tandoori fix on, among kitschy but ornate touches like richly colored fabrics and wafting incense.

Though the à la carte menu offers Northern Indian dishes brought to the table in shiny copper vessels, the lunch buffet covers all bases with vegetarian, chicken, and lamb items. Staples like *saag*, *dal*, naan, and basmati rice are freshly made. *Bhuna gosht* mixes succulent lamb with tomatoes, onions, and spices; while *lassi* or masala tea provide refreshment along with a decent selection of wine, beer, and cocktails.

Labriola

Italian ✗✗

A2

535 N. Michigan Ave. (at Grand Ave.)

Lunch & dinner daily

Phone: 312-955-3100
Web: www.labriolacafe.com
Prices: $$

Grand (Red)

Supersizing his popular Oak Brook café, baker Rich Labriola expands his eponymous empire just off Michigan Avenue. The hangar-sized space is three operations in one: a café for pastries and casual bites; a bar; and a full-scale restaurant. Though the décor takes cues from French brasseries, the menus have a decidedly Italian focus.

No matter where you're seated, you can sample the quality imported *salumi* and *formaggio* selections like Parma ham and Granduca pecorino, accompanied by charred bread and sharp chutney. Neapolitan pizzas, *fritto misto*, and house-made pastas like *bucatini all'Amatriciana* don't disappoint, and tiramisù gets a new twist in a mélange of velvety smooth chocolate mousse, espresso-infused mascarpone, and coffee-soaked cake cubes.

Les Nomades

French ✗✗✗

A2

222 E. Ontario St. (bet. Fairbanks Ct. & St. Clair St.)

Dinner Tue – Sat

Phone: 312-649-9010
Web: www.lesnomades.net
Prices: $$$$

Grand (Red)

A giddy excitement bubbles through the air at Les Nomades, and with good reason: this intimate, charming restaurant feels like a secret hideaway within a gated Streeterville brownstone. Owner Mary Beth Liccioni welcomes all as if they were old friends, seating guests among the graciously arranged fresh flowers, framed artwork, and linen-topped tables.

Though the fragrant herb-loaded lavash presented at each table is good enough to make an entire meal out of, save room for entrées like grilled Scottish salmon, served medium-rare with a colorful, flavorful mélange of beets, cucumber, and black olive tapenade. A single translucent langoustine *raviolo* duets on a plate with tempura soft shell crab, both enhanced by harissa- and saffron-spiked rouille.

Michael Jordan's

A2

Steakhouse XXX

505 N. Michigan Ave. (bet. Grand Ave. & Illinois St.)

Phone: 312-321-8823
Web: www.mjshchicago.com
Prices: $$$

Lunch & dinner daily

Grand (Red)

Leave your dated 1993 Bulls jersey in the closet for a meal at this swanky steakhouse, tucked just off the lobby of the InterContinental Hotel. Leather and velvet accents telegraph an upscale vibe, and references to His Airness are subtle— from oversized sepia photographs of basketball netting to a 23-layer chocolate cake for dessert.

A glass of Amarone with a dry-aged Porterhouse is always a slam-dunk, but the kitchen also turns out pleasing modern twists on steakhouse classics. Chicago's famous Italian beef gets an upgrade with smoked ribeye and aged provolone. Similarly, the traditional wedge salad is presented as a halved small head of baby romaine, layered here with creamy Wisconsin blue cheese and thick slabs of crispy bacon.

The Purple Pig 🐷

A2

Mediterranean X

500 N. Michigan Ave. (at Illinois St.)

Phone: 312-464-1744
Web: www.thepurplepigchicago.com
Prices: $$

Lunch & dinner daily

Grand (Red)

This Windy City haunt is so popular that the patio provides valuable real estate all year long by way of screens and heat lamps. If you are able to score a seat inside, where tightly packed tables bolster the accommodations, you'll enjoy a view of the kitchen from the Carrara marble bar.

The extensive small plates menu is primed for pairing with the wine list, and unusual cuts of meat—like a panini with pork heart—take precedence. Inspired by a Chicago beef, this ciabatta roll is moistened with jus, stuffed full of pork, and dressed with sweet peppers and spicy-tangy giardiniera. A plethora of charcuterie, fried bites, and spreads like whipped feta with cucumbers guarantees all who sip and sup here leave with a full belly and wine-stained mouth.

Riva

Seafood ✗✗

D2

700 E. Grand Ave. (on Navy Pier)

Phone: 312-644-7482
Web: www.rivanavypier.com
Prices: $$

Lunch & dinner daily

If a stroll along Navy Pier works up an appetite, follow your nose (and stomach) past the Ferris wheel to Riva, a nautically themed escape from the carnival atmosphere. The upstairs dining room is a visual feast, with colorful murals above the open kitchen and sweeping lakeshore views; while a casual café downstairs serves drinks and light bites.

Though the menu swims with seafood, Prime steaks and Italian-inspired dishes like pear-and-cheese agnolotti offer variety. Caper-studded Louis sauce augments a single plump cake of jumbo lump crab with a crisp side of Asian slaw. A fillet of Atlantic salmon is placed atop a vibrant plate and paired with cherry tomato fondue, a handful of quartered Brussels sprouts, and bite-sized potato *gnocchetti*.

Rural Society

Steakhouse ✗✗

B3

455 N. Park Dr. (bet. Illinois & North Water Sts.)

Phone: 312-840-6605
Web: www.ruralsocietyrestaurant.com
Prices: $$$

Lunch & dinner daily

🚇 Grand (Red)

This buzzy Argentinean steakhouse from prolific Chef Jose Garces brings a touch of international flair to Chicago's already meat-heavy roster. The ranch-inspired space is smart and upscale, with oversized iron chandeliers, framed photos of show cattle, and a painted wood kitchen from which a wood-fired oven and grill fill the air with a smoky aroma.

In addition to excellent cuts of beef, Rural Society grills up stellar Maine lobster, chicken, and chops, while the oven produces mouthwatering Argentinean pizzas and homemade-spiced sausages. Be sure to try the *plana di hierro* and *fritas*, a South American version of traditional steak frites that boasts a subtly smoky flavor and a creamy, chili-spiced butter dip for those crispy chips.

Tru ✿

A1

Contemporary XXXX

676 N. St. Clair St. (bet. Erie & Huron Sts.)

Phone:	312-202-0001	Dinner Tue – Sat
Web:	www.trurestaurant.com	
Prices:	**$$$$**	📖 Chicago (Red)

Fine dining at Tru has a strong air of formality that extends from the service team to the moneyed, well-dressed clientele. Beyond the discreet exterior, find an intimate lounge with a spotlit and vivid blue sculpture. Decorative branches and net curtains divide the cavernous space; while white walls adorned with Warhol lithographs lend a luxe-gallery feel. Leather and velvet banquettes surrounding well-spaced tables are popular for quiet gatherings or romantic interludes.

The variety of dining options begins with an excellent prix-fixe, extending all the way up to a deep-pocketed caviar selection. However, the menu fulfills its literal promise of exploring Chef Anthony Martin's very modern kitchen. Superlative talent is abundantly clear in the smooth and silky foie gras covered in a thin shell of sugar and counterbalanced by segments of blood orange. Succulent and pearly white halibut is seared to perfection and seasoned with a warm, chive-infused cream sauce, while Berkshire pork is the center of an impeccable presentation of "petit vegetables" including brilliantly crisp and tender peas. Solid desserts include an apple strudel filled with golden currants and flanked by an icy scoop of pear sorbet.

Splurge on the extraordinary wine pairings.

Tre Soldi

A2

Italian

212 E. Ohio St. (bet. Fairbanks Ct. & St. Clair St.)

Phone: 312-664-0212
Web: www.tresoldichicago.com
Prices: $$

Lunch & dinner daily

Grand (Red)

Set a few steps above street level, Tre Soldi's tomato-red awning and floor-to-ceiling windows beckon Michigan Avenue shoppers and business lunchers. Inside, splashes of red-and-white allude subtly to those classic red-sauce joints complete with checkered tablecloths, but glossy ceramic-tiled columns and Italian stone floors up the ante.

Rome and its surroundings inspire the menu and all-Italian wine list. Local Slagel Family Farm's beef becomes carpaccio, shingled on the plate and drizzled with tangy mustard aïoli, fresh parsley, and celery leaves. Thin-crust pizzas strewn with quality ingredients like *cavolo nero*, featuring caramelized onions and pecorino, are large enough to share. Finish with dark chocolate-hazelnut tarts, perfectly balanced by apricot jam.

Look for our symbol 🍇,
spotlighting restaurants
with a notable wine list.

West Loop

GREEKTOWN · MARKET DISTRICT

Once home to warehouses and smoke-spewing factories, the West Loop is arguably the most booming part of Chi-town, whirring with art galleries, lofts, nightclubs, and cool, cutting-edge restaurants. Young residents may have replaced the struggling immigrants of yore; nevertheless,

traces of ethnic flavor can still be found here. They certainly aren't as dominant as before—what a difference a century or two can make—but nearby Taylor Street continues to charm passersby and residents alike with that timeless, slightly kitschy feel. It is delis, groceries, and food galore!

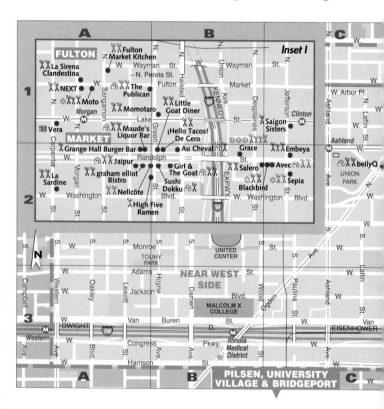

A MEDITERRANEAN MARVEL

For tasty, Mediterranean-inspired munching, make your way to Greektown where everybody's Greek, even if it's just for the day. Shout "opa" at the **Taste of Greece** festival held each August, or while away an afternoon at the always-packed **Parthenon**. Its moniker may not signal ingenuity, but the menu is groaning with gyros, signature lamb dishes, and even flaming *saganaki*, displaying serious showmanship. Sound all too Greek to you? Venture beyond the Mediterranean and into "Restaurant Row" along Randolph Street, where culinary treasures hide among beautiful, fine dining establishments. Whet your appetite with everything from sushi to subs—this mile-long sandwich breed is a best seller bursting with salty meats at **J.P. Graziano's**. Don't let their long lines deter you; instead, take your smoky temptation to **West Loop Salumi** and let their platters of glistening cured treats do the trick. If all else fails, round-up say 1,000 of your closest friends for Middle-Eastern meze at one of the Moroccan spots nearby.

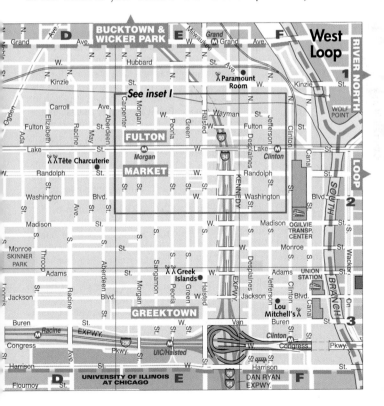

Wash down West Randolph's exquisite eats with intricately crafted sips at **The Aviary**. This bar in West Fulton Market is the brainchild of Chef Grant Achatz, and boy is it a charmer. Noted as much for its expert bartenders and their spherical concoctions as for its tedious reservation process (this is a Kokonas business, after all!), The Aviary is also highly devoted to product freshness and flavor. For even more of a scene, head downstairs to **The Office**, a super secret and super exclusive bar, before settling in for an intimate dinner at Next's private dining space, **The Room**. Some carousers may choose to continue the party at **CH Distillery**, which is known to cull the finest spirits in-house and couple them with such simple small plates as potato pancakes, to more lavish bites like red caviar atop pumpernickel blinis. Nerd alert: the name CH is a double-entendre indicating the molecular formula for ethanol as well as Chicago's abbreviation. Rather whip it up than wolf it down? Beef up your kitchen skills at the **Calphalon Culinary Center**, where groups can arrange for private hands-on instruction. After mastering the bœuf Bourguignon, get in line at **Olympic Meat Packers** (also known as Olympia Meats), or stroll into **Peoria Packing**, a veritable meat cooler where butchers slice and dice the best cuts to order. Aspiring cooks also make the rounds to Paul Kahan's **Publican Quality Meats**, another carnivorous mecca, filled with a mind-boggling array of specialty eats that are matched only by the spectacular setting. Think: intimate cocktail gathering-meets-extravagant dinner party.

For artisan food paradise savvy gourmands gather at **Dose Market**, a pop-up bazaar featuring the finest in food and chefs (as well as their own secret ingredients). Meanwhile, treasure hunters troll the stalls at **Chicago French Market**, an epicurean hub and multi-use arena catering to a variety of palates. Red meat fiends love **Fumaré Meats and Deli** for traditionally smoked cuts; Creole food fans stop by **Lafayette** for Louisiana bayou favorites like crawfish pie or shrimp étouffée; and health-nuts can't get enough of **Raw**, a grab-n-go vegan gem committed to providing the healthiest food money can buy. Moving beyond the market, even the most die-hard dieters need a lil' sugar and nearby **Glazed and Infused**, an early member of the current donut craze, is sublime. Then, spice things up at the flagrantly sexy **RM Champagne Salon**.

BEER & THE BALLGAME

Hoops fans whoop it up at Bulls games at the United Center, also home to the Blackhawks. Depending on the score, the most exciting part of the night is post-game, binging with buddies over beer and bar food. **The Aberdeen Tap**, for instance, is a neighborhood hangout where everybody knows your name as well as the exceptional selection of beers on tap—they boast over 65 brews. But, be sure to also take your more finicky pals to **Rhine Hall**, a boutique brandy distillery run by father-and-daughter duo. Finally, those who prefer a little brawl with their beer will fall for **Twisted Spoke**, a proverbial biker bar with tattoos and 'tudes to match. The music is loud and drinks are plentiful, but it's all in good testosterone- and alcohol-fueled fun.

Au Cheval 😊

B2

800 W. Randolph St. (at Halsted St.)

Phone: 312-929-4580   Lunch & dinner daily
Web: www.auchevalchicago.com
Prices: $$ 🔲 Morgan

This corner bar on Randolph Street's restaurant row may be dim, but it's got a few glittering edges. The reel-to-reel in the doorway lends a retro feel, but the rest is decidedly cushy. Late-night revelers prefer to sit at tufted leather booths or savor beers at the zinc-topped bar, rather than endure a wait for a table in the raucous space. Bartenders work just as hard as line cooks until the wee hours.

The kitchen puts a highfalutin spin on simple bar eats. In-house butchers craft 32-ounce pork Porterhouses for sharing; foie gras for folding into fluffy scrambled eggs; and house-made sausages for bologna sandwiches that go well beyond a kid's wildest dreams. Thin griddled cheeseburger patties are perked up by maple syrup-glazed peppered bacon.

Avec 😊

C2

615 W. Randolph St. (bet. Desplaines & Jefferson Sts.)

Phone: 312-377-2002   Lunch Sun – Fri
Web: www.avecrestaurant.com   Dinner nightly
Prices: $$ 🔲 Clinton (Green/Pink)

Fans have been clamoring for the dinner plates at this West Randolph mainstay for more than a decade—and now that lunch is on the menu, it's official: Avec is a non-stop hangout. It's a fun vibe, as diners are tightly packed at a long counter and communal seating in the chic wood plank encased room, and servers do a good job attending to the crowd.

Mediterranean flavors factor prominently in the kitchen's stimulating creations, like a kale and carrot salad dressed with delightfully herbaceous and spicy green harissa as well as sunflower seeds for crunch. A thick slice of excellent whole grain bread spread with walnut-beet *muhamarra* is the foundation of an open-faced roasted salmon sandwich, and other delights—there are many—come and go with the seasons.

bellyQ

C2

Asian 🍴🍴

1400 W. Randolph St. (at Ogden Ave.)

Phone: 312-563-1010
Web: www.bellyqchicago.com
Prices: $$

Lunch Sun
Dinner nightly
🚇 Ashland (Green/Pink)

This end of West Randolph Street might be quiet, but it's always a party inside bellyQ. The volume and energy are high throughout the lofty, concrete-heavy space with tabletop hibachi booths and industrial metal seating. A wall-length horse-themed screen separates the restaurant from casual sister spot Urban Belly, which shares the open kitchen. As imagined by prolific Chef/owner Bill Kim, the Asian barbecue experience at BellyQ takes its form in a number of genre-melding shareable plates. A side of *bibimbap*-style sticky rice is crunchy and tender, tossed with glistening slices of Chinese sausage and generously sprinkled with *togarashi*. Chewy chunks of brownie in vanilla soft-serve are drizzled with caramel-balsamic-soy "Seoul sauce" for a savory twist.

Embeya

C2

Fusion 🍴🍴🍴

564 W. Randolph St. (at Jefferson St.)

Phone: 312-612-5640
Web: www.embeya.com
Prices: $$

Lunch Mon – Fri
Dinner Mon – Sat
🚇 Clinton (Green/Pink)

Floor-to-ceiling windows put Embeya's industrial interior on display, letting passersby soak up its intriguing sculptural elements and Asian-inspired decor. Inside, blown-glass bouquets of light fixtures hang above communal tables, and wooden screens in intricate cutout patterns divide the lofty, airy dining room and open kitchen, where Chef Mike Sheerin and his team whip up enticing Pan-Asian fare.

The affordable lunch menu features dishes like carrot salad with shaved country ham, an assertively spicy *togarashi* dressing, and a swipe of yuzu curd; or udon in a thickened broth with diced tofu and seasonal vegetables. Dinner entrées display more ambition, as in poached halibut with coconut, hearts of palm, and mint fumet.

Blackbird ❀

Contemporary ✗✗

619 W. Randolph St. (bet. Desplaines & Jefferson Sts.)

Phone: 312-715-0708	Lunch Mon – Fri
Web: www.blackbirdrestaurant.com	Dinner nightly
Prices: $$$$	▣ Clinton (Green/Pink)

The bright, very contemporary boxy white façade is a brilliant contrast to its somewhat missable street—just as it has been since its 1997 opening. Inside the white and steel space, find clean lines and a modern aesthetic that moves from the black-and-white artwork to the bare tables and vases that seem to pop with colorful flowers. Service can be brusque, but that never seems to deter the crowds from packing in. Expect a wait.

A strong sense of style extends to the cuisine; this is a serious kitchen with an eye on artistic detail and elegance. The à la carte menu may offer dishes like duck rillettes spread on a sunflower seed cracker studded with poppy, raw sesame, and pumpkin seeds as well as compressed apple for a tart counterpoint to the rich duck. Meaty abalone mushroom confit is served with tiny and delicate sweet potato tortellini, braised mustard greens, and green apple in a soy-kissed broth.

Finish on a sweet note with the Bourbon gooey butter cake, inventively deconstructed and served with crushed and shatter-thin sheets of caramelized strudel, toasted pecans, and a delectable whoosh of wonderfully seasonal pumpkin pie filling, all topped with whipped goat cheese.

Fulton Market Kitchen

A1

Contemporary ✕✕

311 N. Sangamon St. (at Wayman St.)

Phone: 312-733-6900
Web: www.fultonmarketkitchen.com
Prices: $$$

Dinner Mon – Sat

🚇 Morgan

Fulton Market Kitchen practically epitomizes the term "feast for the eyes." The interior nearly explodes with color, featuring a series of contemporary art pieces that might include graffiti murals or quirky wood-and-steel assemblages. Fixtures like paint-dripped tables repurposed from bowling alleys and old barn doors complement the eye-catching display.

A cocktail list with sections like "Renaissance" and "Pop Art" and a menu divided into "canvases" carries the art theme further, with ingredients sourced from both global and local markets. A small canvas of ravioli is an intense starter with a melt-in-your-mouth foie gras and duxelles filling, and tender lamb hints at the flavors of North Africa with crisp marinated cucumber, creamy feta, and fresh mint.

Girl & The Goat

B2

Contemporary ✕✕

809 W. Randolph St. (bet. Green & Halsted Sts.)

Phone: 312-492-6262
Web: www.girlandthegoat.com
Prices: $$

Dinner nightly

🚇 Morgan

The revolving door never stops turning as Girl & The Goat's party keeps going. Even on a Monday night, guests linger for hours, shouting over the din at this sceney but always friendly stunner. Appropriately rustic wooden pillars and beams connect a warren of seating areas, from elevated platforms to banquettes to dim private corner nooks.

A pick-your-own-protein adventure, the menu is organized by ingredient with a dedicated section for goat. Paper-thin goat carpaccio is dusted with fried capers, beads of smoked trout roe, and an olive-maple vinaigrette. Red currants brighten the luxe meatiness of wood-fired scallops with subtly smoked uni cream. The kitchen will even send out mini portions of menu items for solo diners—a truly thoughtful touch.

graham elliot Bistro

A2

841 W. Randolph St. (bet. Green & Peoria Sts.)

Phone: 312-888-2258   Dinner Tue – Sat
Web: www.gebistro.com
Prices: $$ 🚇 Morgan

It's not likely you'll see peripatetic MasterChef Graham Elliot working the line at this bistro any time soon, but his namesake retains the pizzazz it brought years ago as a newcomer to the West Loop. Dramatic backlighting, colorful mosaics, and modern stained glass brighten the narrow, high-ceilinged space. The kitchen hums along in time to music bouncing off polished concrete floors.

Simple comfort food goes upscale with the kitchen's cleverly deconstructed dishes. A breakfast-for-dinner twist on salmon becomes a perfectly seared fillet atop a dilled cream cheese "schmear;" an everything bagel tuile and onion jam drive the point home. Chicken noodle soup becomes pillowy mousseline-filled agnolotti on a bed of sunchoke purée and roasted carrots.

Grange Hall Burger Bar

A2

844 W. Randolph St. (bet. Green & Peoria Sts.)

Phone: 312-491-0844   Lunch & dinner Tue – Sat
Web: www.grangehallburgerbar.com
Prices: ⊜⊝   🚇 Morgan

American Gothic accents (think Grant Wood) invade the big city at Grange Hall, where a down-on-the-farm vibe is telegraphed loud and clear through swinging barn doors, quilted panels hanging above the lunch counter, and mismatched knit napkins set atop tables with wooden chairs and stools. The glassed-in pie kitchen in the back hints dessert won't be an afterthought.

Choose your own adventure when building a burger, starting with a six- or nine-ounce grass-fed beef patty and adding toppings like Midwestern cheeses, smoked bacon, jalapeños, or homemade pickles. If a wedge of strawberry rhubarb pie or Bourbon-spiked milkshake is calling your name (especially when freshly churned ice cream is involved), go easy on those hand-cut farmhouse chili fries.

Grace ❀ ❀ ❀

Contemporary ✕✕✕✕

B2

652 W. Randolph St. (bet. Desplaines & Halsted Sts.)

Phone: 312-234-9494
Web: www.grace-restaurant.com
Prices: $$$$

Dinner Tue – Sat

🚇 Clinton (Green/Pink)

Ask a passing foodie to name one of Chicago's most elegant and sophisticated restaurants and they'll probably say Grace. This room is as handsome as it is urbane and provides a supremely comfortable environment for those spending an evening discovering the culinary wizardry of Curtis Duffy.

You'll be presented with a choice between two seasonally changing menus: "Fauna" or, for vegetarians, "Flora." Opt for the wine pairings and you're done on the decision making for the night. Trying to keep track of the ingredients of each dish will nullify the benefit of the wine, so instead just marvel at the clever presentation and dig in—because taste is what this food is all about. The dishes are intricate and elaborately constructed, with herbs playing an integral part rather than merely being a garnish. Occasionally your taste buds will get a little slap, perhaps with the odd Thai or Vietnamese flavor, and the courses will fly by.

This style of cooking is very labor-intensive and if you want to learn more, then take advantage of their offer of a post-prandial kitchen tour.

Greek Islands

Greek ✗✗

E3

200 S. Halsted St. (at Adams St.)

Phone: 312-782-9855
Web: www.greekislands.net
Prices: ⊖⊖

Lunch & dinner daily

🚇 UIC-Halsted

This Greektown retreat sports multiple dining areas as well as a perpetually bustling bar. Diners sup among a Disney-fied décor of faux-terraces and balconies, overhangs topped by terra-cotta tiles, and a trellised ceiling entwined with artificial greenery. The chance of a courteous someone whose name ends in "os" attending to you is good, but it's the food that has kept the joint hopping for more than 40 years.

Salads are crisp and refreshing, pan-seared cheese is flambéed tableside, and the fresh seafood doesn't disappoint: fish are grilled whole, filleted, and dressed simply with herbs, a few glugs of olive oil, and squeeze of lemon. Specialties include *spetsofai*, house-made sausage sautéed with onions and peppers in a red wine- and tomato-sauce.

¡Hello Tacos! De Cero

Mexican ✗✗

B2

816 W. Randolph St. (at Halsted St.)

Phone: 312-455-8114
Web: www.hellotacos.com
Prices: $$

Lunch & dinner Tue – Sat

🚇 Morgan

As a *muy* popular member of restaurant row, this spot takes the traditional taqueria and turns it on its head…with spice! Lively music keeps the energy level high, though low lighting lends a cozy vibe to the sleek wood-dominated space. Two rooms, each equipped with a bar, make it easy to get started with a strawberry-mint margarita or Mexican beer.

Don't let the name change fool you; ¡Hello Tacos! is still everything you've come to love about De Cero over the years. Tacos are made with hand-pressed corn tortillas and ordered individually, letting diners sample a range of fillings including rich duck confit and spicy corn salsa. Ample chunks of carnitas with habanero salsa and julienned radish is another fave, while jalapeño-marinated skirt steak tortas are pressed to order and ooze with melting *Chihuahua*.

High Five Ramen

Japanese ✗

A2

112 N. Green St. (bet. Randolph St. & Washington Blvd.)

Phone: N/A   Dinner Tue – Sat
Web: www.highfiveramen.com
Prices: 😊   🖳 Morgan

This re-purposed industrial setting is a hipster dining hall serving two hot foodie trends under one roof. The bulk of the sprawling space is devoted to Green Street Smoked Meats, a barbecue joint where crowds of cool kids sit side-by-side downing beers and heaps of pulled pork, brisket, and Frito pie.

More worthy of attention, however, is High Five Ramen, a downstairs nook where the queue for one of its 16-seats starts early. Once inside, slurp a bowl of the signature, crazy-spicy broth. Loaded with thin alkaline noodles, a slow-cooked egg, roasted pork belly, locally grown sprouts, and black garlic oil, this unique rendition is worth the burn. For sweet, icy relief, sip on a slushy tiki cocktail—then wipe your brow and dig back in.

Jaipur 😊

Indian ✗✗

A2

847 W. Randolph St. (bet. Green & Peoria Sts.)

Phone: 312-526-3655   Lunch & dinner daily
Web: www.jaipurchicago.com
Prices: $$ 🖳 Morgan

Business execs expecting the ubiquitous lunch buffet will be sorely disappointed by Jaipur—that is until they realize this popular weekday spot serves an affordable full-service lunch special that brings the buffet to your table in a parade of hammered copper *katoris*. In the evening, locals fill every sleek, nail-studded chair in the refined dining room as they await plates of boldly flavored Indian cooking.

The broad menu features a lengthy selection of fresh and authentically treated favorites, most of which are available as part of the bountiful lunch special. Staples on the vast à la carte menu may include *aloo papdi chaat;* a rich and creamy chicken korma; spiced carrot soup; and scarlet-red tandoori chicken, served with garlic naan.

La Sardine

A2

111 N. Carpenter St. (bet. Randolph St. & Washington Blvd.)

Phone: 312-421-2800

Web: www.lasardine.com

Prices: $$

Lunch Mon – Fri

Dinner Mon – Sat

🚇 Morgan

In a neighborhood packed to the gills with gastronomic innovation, La Sardine may be the most daring option of all, flaunting hearty French bistro food in a warm and rustic setting. The time-tested combination of wheezing accordion music, white linens, tile floors, and pastoral murals makes it all the rage among diners craving the familiar—and a $30 lunch prix-fixe doesn't hurt either.

From escargots and steak tartare to bouillabaisse and steak frites, Chef/owner Jean-Claude Poilevey nails the classic bistro dishes. Don't miss the steak haché, a patty of excellent ground beef seared to perfection, then topped with smoked goat cheese and plated with truffle-laced Bibb lettuce, a thick slice of maple bacon, and crunchy fried onion rings.

La Sirena Clandestina

A1

954 W. Fulton Market (at Morgan St.)

Phone: 312-226-5300

Web: www.lasirenachicago.com

Prices: $$

Lunch Sun – Fri

Dinner nightly

🚇 Morgan

A relaxing Caribbean vibe breezes its way northward to Fulton Market and settles within La Sirena Clandestina's aquamarine walls. Languidly spinning fans, light filtered through antique etched glass panels, and an international selection of sippable rum and mezcal all conspire to bring guests' blood pressure down a notch or two.

Baked empanadas rotate through a series of fillings, but these popular pockets never leave the menu. Whether stuffed with venison ragù or ricotta, hazelnut, and butternut squash, they're all exceptional. Handfuls of Manchego add decadence to plump bomba rice studded with fiery pickled jalapeño rings, toasted pepitas, and buttery white corn. Classic *alfajore* shortbreads filled with dulce de leche and sea salt are a memorable send-off.

Little Goat Diner

B2

American ✕✕

820 W. Randolph St. (at Green St.)

Phone: 312-888-3455 Lunch & dinner daily
Web: www.littlegoatchicago.com
Prices: $$ Morgan

Every Chicago neighborhood needs a good diner and in the booming West Loop, this enthusiastic homage to the reliable road trip stopover fits in perfectly. The décor gives a wink and a nod to classic design with retro booths, spinning chrome barstools, and blue-rimmed plates, but the top-quality materials keep it on the modern side.

A morning-to-night menu of amped-up diner favorites can be had no matter the hour: craving a shrimp cocktail at 7:00 A.M.? Five jumbo fried shrimp wrapped in *somen* noodles are ready to go. The Goat Almighty burger lives up to its name with fatty beef brisket, saucy pulled pork, and a ground goat patty. Before hitting the road, grab a cup of Stumptown—and maybe a s'mores cookie—from LG Bread, the next-door bakery and coffee bar.

Lou Mitchell's

F3

American ✕

565 W. Jackson Blvd. (bet. Clinton & Jefferson Sts.)

Phone: 312-939-3111 Lunch daily
Web: www.loumitchellsrestaurant.com Dinner Tue – Sat
Prices: ⓢⓢ   Clinton (Blue)

At the top of Chicago's list of beloved names is Lou Mitchell. This eponymous diner is by no means an elegant affair, but thanks to its delicious omelets and iconic crowd, it has been on the Windy City's must-eat list since 1923. Don't panic at the length of the lines: they are long but move fast, and free doughnut holes (one of the restaurant's signature baked goods) make the wait go faster.

Back to those omelets: they may be made with mere eggs, like everyone else's, but somehow these are lighter and fluffier, almost like a soufflé, stuffed with feta, spinach, onions, or any other ingredients of your choice. They arrive in skillets with an Idaho-sized helping of potatoes. The best part? Everyone gets a swirl of soft-serve at the meal's end.

Maude's Liquor Bar 😊

French 🗶🗶

A2

840 W. Randolph St. (bet. Green & Peoria Sts.)

Phone: 312-243-9712
Web: www.maudesliquorbar.com
Prices: $$

Dinner nightly

🚇 Morgan

Don't be fooled by the aged patina of this sexy boîte: though a few items like the overstuffed curio cabinet and salvaged French metal chairs are true antiques, this chicly disheveled hang has been hiding out on West Randolph for only a few years. Contemporary and classic cocktails like a violet-tinged Aviator are served in champagne coupes, adding to the vintage atmosphere.

Head to the second-floor bar to snack on oysters and frites, or fill up on Francophile comfort food under the glow of mismatched crystal chandeliers. Juicy, garlicky Toulouse-style pork sausage is served whole over bacon-stewed lentils, and smashed potatoes are rich with chicken jus. Sugar fiends will delight in the crème brûlée, which sports the perfect crackling sugar veneer.

Momotaro

Japanese 🗶🗶

B1

820 W. Lake St. (at Green St.)

Phone: 312-733-4818
Web: www.momotarochicago.com
Prices: $$

Dinner nightly

🚇 Morgan

Boka Restaurant Group's stunning West Loop canteen embraces a fantastical view of Japanese dining. An impressive selection of imported whiskies is listed on a retro-style departure board; a private dining room upstairs is styled to resemble a mid-century corporate boardroom; and a traditional *izakaya* beckons diners downstairs. Consistently packed, the AvroKO-designed space boasts numerous kitchens churning out a wide range of dishes.

Creative bites abound in the chef's omakase featuring torched baby squid wrapped in nori. Then a Hawaiian seaweed salad with diced nopales may be tailed by *robata*-grilled Wagyu skirt steak with foie gras, shisito pepper, and *yuzu kosho*. The steamed yuzu pudding cake is just one example of the surprisingly strong dessert roster.

Moto ⌘

American XXX

A1

945 W. Fulton Market (bet. Morgan & Sangamon Sts.)

Phone: 312-491-0058
Dinner Tue – Sat

Web: www.motorestaurant.com

Prices: $$$$

🚇 Morgan

Tucked into an unassuming block of warehouses in Chicago's trendy meatpacking district, Moto's well-dressed maître d' greets you at the door with a smile, then politely escorts you to one of its sexy high-backed booths or tables. From there, you're presented with the restaurant's newest tasting menu, courtesy of the talented Executive Chef Chris Anderson. It's a glamorous operation from the start—and the delicious food only ups the game.

The North Carolina-born chef brings a distinct Southern spirit to Moto's two nine-course tasting menus, available in "Hunt" or "Gather" (vegetarian) style. There is also a longer $170 Chef's Tour, combining items from both menus.

Dinner might include dishes like the wonderful smoked pork belly, paired with tart collard greens kimchi and raspberry and red pepper purée; or tender chicken roulade with crispy mascarpone and buttermilk dumplings. Then a beautifully seared duck breast features squash, zucchini, and fava bean succotash, a sprinkle of corn shoots and duck fat-infused black tea; while a side of Carolina beets laced in vinegar-soaked barbecue sauce is plated with seared Wagyu short ribs and a vibrant carrot purée.

It is with fond sentiment that we find Moto has persevered following the loss of Homaro Cantu.

235

Nellcôte

A2

833 W. Randolph St. (at Green St.)

Phone: 312-432-0500
Web: www.nellcoterestaurant.com
Prices: $$

Lunch Sat – Sun
Dinner nightly
🚇 Morgan

The orange canopy above Nellcôte's entrance and stylish plaque would not look out of place on the Côte d'Azur. Named after the villa where the Rolling Stones recorded their iconic *Exile on Main Street*, this West Loop rock star—decked out with a lacquered ivory bar, marble staircase, and antique chandeliers—feels like a playground for the glam.

Vases of dried lavender evoke scents of the Mediterranean, as do the kitchen's creations, which feature homemade ravioli filled with favas, a poached egg, and parmesan broth. A hearty and succulent Berkshire pork chop with sweet roasted yams and spicy grated horseradish needs no sides; whereas black pepper semifreddo between chocolate shortbread is particularly memorable when paired with red wine-poached pears.

NEXT

A1

953 W. Fulton Market (at Morgan St.)

Phone: N/A
Web: www.nextrestaurant.com
Prices: $$$$

Dinner Wed – Sun
🚇 Morgan

Welcome to dinner as theater, where the only thing more radical than each new theme is the success (or failure) of the cuisine. Next's conceit is reinvention. It may begin the year as, say, a culinary homage to French "Bistro" cooking with hit-or-miss fare that does little to underscore the kitchen's strengths. The long, dark, windowless room reflects that theme with a smattering of typical trappings, like chalkboard specials on the wall and little ceramic roosters on the table.

Some concepts may be rooted in regional innovation, offering an array of Spanish "Tapas." Months later, the chefs may craft small plates with an eye on wine and global "Terrior." This is a very unique place with an adept and dexterous kitchen, but the experience just isn't for everyone.

Paramount Room

Gastropub ✗

415 N. Milwaukee Ave. (bet. Hubbard & Kinzie Sts.)

Phone: 312-829-6300
Web: www.paramountroom.com
Prices: $$

Lunch Thu – Sun
Dinner nightly
🚇 Grand (Blue)

Though a few blocks north of the hot-and-heavy Fulton Market food scene, this edgy joint, equal parts gastropub and dive bar, more than holds its own. To start, make like the cool kids and order something from the well-stocked bar: Moscow Mules are presented properly in frosty copper mugs, killer Bloody Marys are fortified by skewers of huge olives and blocks of dill Havarti, and the beer list boasts there's "no crap on tap".

Paramount's menu features dishes that make the most of top-quality ingredients, like a plump burger crafted from 100 percent Wagyu beef on a toasted brioche bun. Daily specials have featured a trio of sweet and zesty pulled pork sliders sided by a heap of crisp and crunchy tempura-style green beans.

The Publican 😋

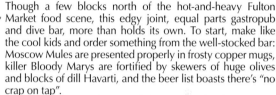

Gastropub ✗✗

837 W. Fulton Market (at Green St.)

Phone: 312-733-9555
Web: www.thepublicanrestaurant.com
Prices: $$

Lunch Sat – Sun
Dinner nightly
🚇 Morgan

The phrase "meat market" has many connotations at The Publican: everything about this bustling Fulton Market spot is communal, from the sprawling U-shaped table that dominates the space and the penned-in booths lining the perimeter to the sink outside the washrooms. That said, the ubiquitous pig-centric décor gives a more straightforward idea of what you'll find on the menu.

As expected, pork takes precedence here with rillettes, platters of paper-thin aged ham slices, and house-made blood sausage to pair with one of the superlative beer selections. Weekend brunch gets in on the game with thickly sliced Publican bacon basted with Burton's maple syrup, or savory mushroom-and-chard French toast topped with roasted tomato and a fried egg.

Saigon Sisters

C1

Vietnamese ✗

567 W. Lake St. (bet. Clinton & Jefferson Sts.)

Phone: 312-496-0090
Web: www.saigonsisters.com
Prices: 💰

Lunch Mon – Fri
Dinner Tue – Sat
🚇 Clinton (Green/Pink)

The sign of a great restaurant is when the owner is on-site, and such is the case at this local hot spot, where Mary Nguyen Aregoni is as gregarious and welcoming as her staff. Named after Mary and sister, Theresa Nguyen, the lofty space belies its compact size with huge glass windows and high ceilings. Simple banquettes and wood tables are a perfect canvas for the vibrant Vietnamese cuisine that comes speeding out of the kitchen.

Lunch is busy with business types ordering the likes of a fragrant, satisfying, and clear *pho* floating with soft noodles, bean sprouts, jalapeños, and cilantro. Meanwhile, noodles stir-fried with thinly sliced hoisin-glazed pork, char-grilled red pepper, and sliced avocado are a dream team of flavor and texture.

Salero

B2

Spanish ✗✗

621 W. Randolph St. (bet. Desplaines St. & Jefferson St.)

Phone: 312-466-1000
Web: www.salerochicago.com
Prices: $$

Lunch Mon – Fri
Dinner nightly
🚇 Clinton (Green/Pink)

Nestled in among neighboring Randolph Street hangouts, this upscale newbie holds its own. Accented by wood details set aglow with pillar candles and a turquoise wall hung with steer horns, the space boasts a chic front bar area for cocktails and a dining room that welcomes guests in for a meal .

A contemporary vision of Spanish cuisine turns out *pintxos* to start—try the Gilda, a single bite skewer featuring a brown anchovy, pickled guindilla pepper, and a manzanilla olive. Follow this up with a slick risotto-paella hybrid; or boneless roasted quail stuffed with chorizo and set over wilted spinach with toasted pine nuts. For dessert, order the *manzana* to receive a miniature apple cake dressed with rosemary crumble, cider reduction, and goat cheese ice cream.

238

Sepia ✿

American 🍴🍴

C2

123 N. Jefferson (bet. Randolph St. & Washington Blvd.)

Phone: 312-441-1920
Web: www.sepiachicago.com
Prices: $$$

Lunch Mon – Fri
Dinner nightly
🚇 Clinton (Green/Pink)

When a restaurant's excellence is this consistent, it should come as no surprise that the First Lady names it as one of her favorites. Set inside a 19th century print shop, the historic dining room does a fine job mixing original details with modern touches. Muted tones in the exposed brick walls and custom tile flooring complement newer elements like floor-to-ceiling wine storage and dramatic smoke-shaded chandeliers that drip with crystals. Though the décor may tip its hat to yesteryear, Chef Andrew Zimmerman's cuisine is firmly grounded in the 21st century.

Whether you visit for lunch or dinner, meals here always seem to reflect the amalgam of American cuisine, with hints of Southeast Asian, Korean, and Mediterranean tastes. Potato gnocchi may seem commonplace, but this version is memorable thanks to the flawless components and rich, profound flavors of lamb sugo with crunchy bits of ciabatta breadcrumbs. Chicken here is downright exciting, served tender and crisp-skinned with a supremely buttery Albufera sauce, crumbly chestnuts, caramelized fennel, and sausage.

Simple-sounding desserts keep the bar high, with offerings like toffee-coconut cake with chocolate ganache and burnt caramel.

Sushi Dokku

J a p a n e s e ✗

823 W. Randolph St. (at Green St.)

Phone: 312-455-8238
Web: www.sushidokku.com
Prices: $$

Lunch Fri – Sat
Dinner Tue – Sat
Morgan

Creatively adorned nigiri is the featured attraction at this hip sushi-ya that's all wood planks, stainless steel, chunky tables, and hefty benches.

Just one piece of Sushi Dokku's supple cuts showcasing quality and technique is not enough—thankfully each nigiri order is served as pairs. Among the terrific selection, enjoy the likes of hamachi sporting a spicy mix of shredded Napa cabbage, daikon, and red chili; or salmon dressed with a sweet ginger-soy sauce and fried ginger chips. South Pacific sea bream is deliciously embellished with a drizzle of smoky tomato and black sea salt. Those who wish to branch out from sushi should go for *tako yaki* (crispy fried octopus croquettes), grilled hamachi collar, or a brownie-crusted green tea-cheesecake.

Tête Charcuterie

F r e n c h ✗✗

1114 W. Randolph St. (bet. Aberdeen & May Sts.)

Phone: 312-733-1178
Web: www.tetechicago.com
Prices: $$

Lunch Mon – Fri
Dinner Tue – Sat
Morgan

No greater respect can be shown to a former meatpacking warehouse than by converting it into a restaurant specialising in charcuterie. This most ancient of culinary arts is joyfully celebrated here in all its forms—there are cured meats, wonderful glistening terrines, rich pâtés, and plump homemade sausages. This is roll-your-sleeves-up food that will put hair on your chest.

The enthusiasm of the on-view kitchen team is palpable. Curing is done in-house and there's a separate Sausage Room where they create their own varieties, which range from a French *boudin blanc* to Moroccan inspired merguez. But don't think they can't show a light touch when required: the "spring garden" served *en cocotte* is one of the prettiest things you'll see.

Vera

Spanish

A1

1023 W. Lake St. (at Carpenter St.)

Phone: 312-243-9770
Web: www.verachicago.com
Prices: $$

Dinner Mon – Sat

🚇 Morgan

Pimentón de la Vera, one of the most powerful spices in Spanish cuisine, also provides partial inspiration for this first-come, first-served wine bar in the West Loop dining corridor. (The other homage? Chef/owner Mark Mendez's grandmother.) Exposed brick walls and walnut floors are typically lovely, but do little to soften the din of a happy hour crowd after a few glasses of sherry.

Classic tapas as well as ham-and-cheese flights comprise the menu, along with larger plates like a piled-high paella with rabbit, duck, and chorizo. Shell out a few extra dollars for crusty bread to sop up the garlicky, lemony olive oil that bathes their plump head-on shrimp. Grilled rounds of octopus are sweet and smoky thanks to a liberal dose of good old pimentón.

Your opinions are important to us. Please write to us directly at:
michelin.guides@
us.michelin.com

Where to **Eat**

Alphabetical List of Restaurants

Indexes ▲ Alphabetical List of Restaurants

Restaurants by Cuisine

American

ampersand wine bar		✗✗	20
Aquitaine		✗✗	139
Au Cheval	🍸	✗	224
Bakin' & Eggs		✗	120
Bavette's Bar & Boeuf		✗✗	184
Birchwood Kitchen		✗	47
Bristol (The)		✗✗	48
DMK Burger Bar		✗	123
Dove's Luncheonette	🍸	✗	52
Franklin Room (The)		✗✗	192
Frontier		✗	54
gather		✗✗	26
Gemini Bistro		✗✗	144
Grange Hall Burger Bar		✗	228
Home Bistro		✗✗	125
Hugo's Frog Bar & Fish House		✗✗	87
Jam	🍸	✗✗	102
Joe's		✗✗✗	195
Kanela		✗✗	125
Kitchen (The)		✗✗	196
Kuma's Corner		✗	103
Little Goat Diner		✗✗	233
Lou Mitchell's		✗	233
Lula Cafe	🍸	✗✗	106
Magnolia Cafe		✗✗	31
mk		✗✗✗	88
Moto	❀	✗✗✗	235
NAHA	❀	✗✗✗	198
Nana	🍸	✗✗	174
NoMI Kitchen		✗✗✗	89
Oak + Char		✗✗	197
Parson's Chicken & Fish		✗	109
Perennial Virant		✗✗	148
Piggery (The)		✗	127
Promontory (The)		✗✗	79
Pump Room	🍸	✗✗	91
Remington's		✗✗	161
RL		✗✗✗	200
Ruxbin		✗✗	62
Sable Kitchen & Bar		✗✗	202
Sepia	❀	✗✗	239
Smoke Daddy		✗	64
Southport Grocery		✗	128
Stax Café		✗	176
Summer House Santa Monica		✗✗	150
Tortoise Club		✗✗✗	206
TWO	🍸	✗	67
White Oak Tavern & Inn		✗✗	151

Asian

bellyQ	🍸	✗✗	225
Han 202	🍸	✗✗	170
Oiistar		✗	60
Ramen-san		✗	200
Roka Akor		✗✗	201
Vora		✗✗	93

Austrian

Table, Donkey and Stick	🍸	✗✗	112

Barbecue

Bub City		✗	188
Chicago q		✗✗	86
County	🍸	✗	169
Fat Willy's		✗	100
Honky Tonk BBQ		✗	173
Lillie's Q		✗✗	57

Fusion

Belly Shack	⊛	✗	46
de Quay		✗✗	142
Embeya		✗ₓ✗	225
Mott St.	⊛	✗	59
Parachute	✿	✗	108
Sunda		✗✗	206

Gastropub

Bangers & Lace		✗	45
Dawson (The)	⊛	✗✗	51
Duck Inn (The)	⊛	✗✗	170
Dusek's (Board & Beer)	✿	✗	171
Farmhouse		✗	191
Gage (The)		✗✗	159
Gilt Bar	⊛	✗✗	193
Hopleaf	⊛	✗	28
Longman & Eagle	✿	✗	105
Owen & Engine		✗✗	61
Paramount Room		✗	237
Pl-zeň		✗	175
Publican (The)	⊛	✗✗	237
Side Door		✗✗	203
Three Aces		✗	177

German

Radler (The)		✗	109

Greek

Greek Islands		✗✗	230
Taxim		✗✗	65

Indian

Arya Bhavan		✗	21
Chicago Curry House		✗✗	75
Cumin	⊛	✗	51
Indian Garden		✗✗	214
Jaipur	⊛	✗✗	231
Paprika		✗	32
Sabri Nihari	⊛	✗✗	35
Vermilion		✗✗	209
Viceroy of India		✗✗	37

Indonesian

Rickshaw Republic		✗	149

International

Bar Pastoral		🍶	121
Beatrix	⊛	✗✗	185
Boarding House (The)		✗✗	186
Bread & Wine		✗	98
Red Door		🍶	62
Taus Authentic		✗✗	65

Italian

Acanto		✗✗	158
Anteprima		✗	21
A10	⊛	✗✗	73
Baffo		✗✗	184
Balena	⊛	✗✗	139
Briciola		✗✗	48
Cafe Spiaggia		✗✗	85
Ceres' Table	⊛	✗✗	121
Coco Pazzo		✗✗	190
Dolce		✗✗	191
Due Lire		✗✗	23
Frasca		✗✗	124
Labriola		✗✗	215
Merlo on Maple		✗✗	87
Nando Milano Trattoria		✗✗	60
Nellcôte		✗✗	236
Nico Osteria		✗✗	88
Ombra		✗✗	32
Osteria Langhe		✗✗	107
Pelago		✗ₓ✗	90
Piccolo Sogno		✗✗	61
Pizzeria da Nella		✗	148
Prosecco		✗ₓ✗	199
Riccardo Trattoria	⊛	✗✗	149

Moroccan

Shokran Moroccan Grill	✗	110

Persian

Noon-O-Kabab	✗✗	107

Peruvian

Taste of Peru	✗	36
Via Lima	🌁 ✗✗	130

Pizza

Coalfire Pizza	✗	50
Connie's Pizza	✗✗	75
Gino's East	✗	214
Giordano's	✗	194
Pequod's Pizza	✗	146
Pizano's	✗	90
Spacca Napoli	🌁 ✗	35

Polish

Staropolska	✗	112

Seafood

Angry Crab (The)	🌁 ✗	20
C Chicago	✗✗✗	188
Fish Bar	✗	124
GT Fish & Oyster	🌁 ✗✗	194
Riva	✗✗	217

Southern

Big Jones	✗✗	22
Carriage House	🌁 ✗✗	49
Luella's Southern Kitchen	🌁 ✗	30
Pearl's Southern Comfort	✗✗	33
Table Fifty-Two	✗✗✗	91

Southwestern

Flo	✗	53

Spanish

Black Bull	🍲	47
Mercat a la Planxa	✗✗	78
mfk.	🌁 ✗	145
Salero	✗✗	238
Vera	🍲	241

Steakhouse

Benny's Chop House	✗✗✗	185
Chicago Cut	✗✗✗	189
Community Tavern	✗✗	99
David Burke's Primehouse	✗✗	190
Gene & Georgetti	✗✗	193
Mastro's	✗✗✗	197
Michael Jordan's	✗✗✗	216
Prime & Provisions	✗✗✗	161
Rosebud Prime	✗✗✗	162
RPM Steak	✗✗✗	202
Rural Society	✗✗	217

Thai

Arun's	✗✗	98
ATK	✗	120
Herb	🌁 ✗✗	28
Jin Thai	🌁 ✗	30
P.S. Bangkok	✗✗	127
Royal Thai	✗	128
Sticky Rice	✗	129
TAC Quick	🌁 ✗	129
Taste of Thai Town	✗	113

Vegetarian

Chicago Diner	✗	122
Green Zebra	🌁 ✗✗	54
Mana Food Bar	🌁 ✗	57

Vietnamese

Pho 777	✗	33
Pho Xe Tang - Tank Noodle	✗	34
Saigon Sisters	✗	238

Cuisines by Neighborhood

Indexes ▲ Cuisines by Neighborhood

CHICAGO

Andersonville, Edgewater & Uptown

American
ampersand wine bar	✗✗	20
gather	✗✗	26
Magnolia Cafe	✗✗	31

Belgian
Vincent	✗✗	37

Contemporary
Elizabeth	❁	✗✗	24
42 Grams	❁❁	✗✗	25
Goosefoot	❁	✗✗	27

Ethiopian
Demera	✗	23
Ras Dashen	✗	34

Filipino
Isla	✗	29

French
Bistro Campagne	✗✗	22

Gastropub
Hopleaf	🍴 ✗	28

Indian
Arya Bhavan	✗	21
Paprika	✗	32
Sabri Nihari	🍴 ✗✗	35
Viceroy of India	✗✗	37

Italian
Anteprima	✗	21
Due Lire	✗✗	23
Ombra	✗✗	32

Japanese
Miku Sushi	✗✗	31
Taketei	✗	36

Korean
Gogi	✗✗	26
Jin Ju	✗	29

Peruvian
Taste of Peru	✗	36

Pizza
Spacca Napoli	🍴 ✗	35

Seafood
Angry Crab (The)	🍴 ✗	20

Southern
Big Jones	✗✗	22
Luella's Southern Kitchen	🍴 ✗	30
Pearl's Southern Comfort	✗✗	33

Thai
Herb	🍴 ✗✗	28
Jin Thai	🍴 ✗	30

Vietnamese
Pho 777	✗	33
Pho Xe Tang - Tank Noodle	✗	34

Bucktown & Wicker Park

American
Birchwood Kitchen	✗	47
Bristol (The)	✗✗	48
Dove's Luncheonette	🍴 ✗	52
Frontier	✗	54
Ruxbin	✗✗	62
Smoke Daddy	✗	64
TWO	🍴 ✗	67

Indexes ▲ Cuisines by Neighborhood

Indexes ▲ Cuisines by Neighborhood

258

Starred Restaurants

Within the selection we offer you, some restaurants deserve to be highlighted for their particularly good cuisine. When giving one, two, or three Michelin stars, there are a number of elements that we consider including the quality of the ingredients, the technical skill and flair that goes into their preparation, the blend and clarity of flavours, and the balance of the menu. Just as important is the ability to produce excellent cooking time and again. We make as many visits as we need, so that our readers may be assured of quality and consistency.

A two or three-star restaurant has to offer something very special in its cuisine; a real element of creativity, originality, or "personality" that sets it apart from the rest. Three stars – our highest award – are given to the choicest restaurants, where the whole dining experience is superb.

Cuisine in any style, modern or traditional, may be eligible for a star. Due to the fact we apply the same independent standards everywhere, the awards have become benchmarks of reliability and excellence in over 20 countries in Europe and Asia, particularly in France, where we have awarded stars for 100 years, and where the phrase "Now that's real three-star quality!" has entered into the language.

The awarding of a star is based solely on the quality of the cuisine.

❀❀❀

Exceptional cuisine, worth a special journey

One always eats here extremely well, sometimes superbly. Distinctive dishes are precisely executed, using superlative ingredients.

Alinea	XxxX	138
Grace	XxxX	229

❀❀

Excellent cuisine, worth a detour

Skillfully and carefully crafted dishes of outstanding quality.

Acadia	XxX	72
42 Grams	XX	25
Sixteen	XxxX	204

❀

A very good restaurant in its category

A place offering cuisine prepared to a consistently high standard.

Blackbird	XX	226
Boka	XxX	141
Dusek's (Board & Beer)	X	171
EL Ideas	XX	172
Elizabeth	XX	24
Everest	XxX	160
Goosefoot	XX	27
Longman & Eagle	X	105
Moto	XxX	235
NAHA	XxX	198
North Pond	XX	147
Parachute	X	108
Schwa	X	63
Sepia	XX	239
Spiaggia	XxX	92
Topolobampo	XX	207
Tru	XxxX	218

Bib Gourmand

This symbol indicates our inspectors' favorites for good value. For $40 or less, you can enjoy two courses and a glass of wine or a dessert (not including tax or gratuity).

Brunch

Credits

Notes

Notes

Michelin is committed to improving the mobility of travellers

ON EVERY ROAD AND BY EVERY MEANS

Since the company came into being – over a century ago – Michelin has had a single objective: to offer people a better way forward. A technological challenge first, to create increasingly efficient tires, but also an ongoing commitment to travelers, to help them travel in the best way. This is why Michelin is developing a whole collection of products and services: from maps, atlases, travel guides and auto accessories, to mobile apps, route planners and online assistance: Michelin is doing everything it can to make traveling more pleasurable!

→ Michelin Apps

Because the notions of comfort and security are essential, both for you and for us, Michelin has created a package of six free mobile applications—a comprehensive collection to make driving a pleasure!

→ *Michelin MyCar* • *To get the best from your tires; services and information for carefree travel preparation.*

→ *Michelin Navigation* • *A new approach to navigation: traffic in real time with a new connected guidance feature.*

→ *ViaMichelin* • *Calculates routes and map data: a must for traveling in the most efficient way.*

→ *Michelin Restaurants* • *Because driving should be enjoyable: find a wide choice of restaurants, in France and Germany, including the MICHELIN Guide's complete listings.*

→ *Michelin Hotels* • *To book hotel rooms at the best rates, all over the world!*

→ *Michelin Voyage* • *85 countries and 30, 000 tourist sites selected by the Michelin Green Guide, plus a tool for creating your own travel book.*

A tire...
→ what is it?

Round, black, supple yet solid, the tire is to the wheel what the shoe is to the foot. But what is it made of? First and foremost, rubber, but also various textile and/or metallic materials... and then it's filled with air! It is the skilful assembly of all these components that ensures tires have the qualities they should: grip to the road, shock absorption, in two words: 'comfort' and 'safety.'

1 TREAD
The tread ensures the tire performs correctly, by dispersing water, providing grip and increasing longevity.

2 CROWN PLIES
This reinforced double or triple belt combines vertical suppleness with transversal rigidity, enabling the tire to remain flat to the road.

3 SIDEWALLS
These link all the component parts and provide symmetry. They enable the tire to absorb shock, thus giving a smooth ride.

4 BEADS
The bead wires ensure that the tire is fixed securely to the wheel to ensure safety.

5 INNER LINER
The inner liner creates an airtight seal between the wheel rim and the tire.

Michelin
➔ *innovation in movement*

Created and patented by Michelin in 1946, the belted radial-ply tire revolutionized the world of tires. But Michelin did not stop there: over the years other new and original solutions came out, confirming Michelin's position as a leader in research and innovation.

➔ *the right pressure!*

One of Michelin's priorities is safer mobility. In short, innovating for a better way forward. This is the challenge for researchers, who are working to perfect tires capable of shorter braking distances and offering the best possible traction to the road. To support motorists, Michelin organizes road safety awareness campaigns all over the world: "Fill up with air" initiatives remind everyone that the right tire pressure is a crucial factor in safety and fuel economy.

The Michelin strategy:
→ *multi-performance tires*

Michelin is synonymous with safety, fuel saving and the capacity to cover thousands of miles. A MICHELIN tire is the embodiment of all these things – thanks to our engineers, who work with the very latest technology.

Their challenge: to equip every tire – whatever the vehicle (car, truck, tractor, bulldozer, plane, motorbike, bicycle or train!) – with the best possible combination of qualities, for optimal overall performance.

Slowing down wear, reducing energy expenditure (and therefore CO_2 emissions), improving safety through enhanced road handling and braking: there are so many qualities in just one tire – that's Michelin Total Performance.

MICHELIN
Total Performance

Every day, **Michelin** is working towards sustainable mobility

OVER TIME, WHILE RESPECTING THE PLANET

Sustainable mobility
→ *is clean mobility... and mobility for everyone*

Sustainable mobility means enabling people to get around in a way that is cleaner, safer, more economical and more accessible to everyone, wherever they might live. Every day, Michelin's 113,000 employees worldwide are innovating:

- by creating tires and services that meet society's new needs.
- by raising young people's awareness of road safety.
- by inventing new transport solutions that consume less energy and emit less CO_2.

→ *Michelin Challenge Bibendum*

Sustainable mobility means allowing the transport of goods and people to continue, while promoting responsible economic, social and societal development. Faced with the increasing scarcity of raw materials and global warming, Michelin is standing up for the environment and public health. Michelin regularly organizes 'Michelin Challenge Bibendum', the only event in the world which focuses on sustainable road travel.

Where to **Eat**

Classification

More pleasant if in red

✗	Comfortable
✗✗	Quite comfortable
✗✗✗	Very comfortable
✗✗✗✗	Top class comfortable
✗✗✗✗✗	Luxury in the traditional style
🎎	Small plates

Average Prices

🍝	Under $25
$$	$25 to $50
$$$	$50 to $75
$$$$	over $75

Awards

Stars

✿	High quality cooking, worth a stop
✿ ✿	Excellent cuisine, worth a detour
✿ ✿ ✿	Exceptional cuisine, worth a special journey

😋	**Bib Gourmand**
	Inspectors' favorites for good value

Facilities & Services

💵	Cash only	🍇	Notable wine list
♿	Wheelchair accessible	🍶	Notable sake list
🏖	Outdoor dining	🍸	Notable cocktail list
🍳	Breakfast	🍺	Notable beer list
🥞	Brunch	🗝	Valet parking
🥢	Dim sum	⎵	Private dining room

Map Legend

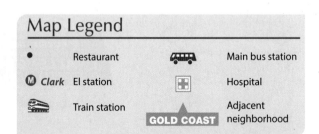

•	Restaurant	🚌	Main bus station
Ⓜ *Clark*	El station	✚	Hospital
🚆	Train station	**GOLD COAST**	Adjacent neighborhood